John McCaul

Britanno-Roman Inscriptions

John McCaul

Britanno-Roman Inscriptions

ISBN/EAN: 9783742829948

Manufactured in Europe, USA, Canada, Australia, Japa

Cover: Foto ©Thomas Meinert / pixelio.de

Manufactured and distributed by brebook publishing software
(www.brebook.com)

John McCaul

Britanno-Roman Inscriptions

BRITANNO-ROMAN INSCRIPTIONS,

WITH CRITICAL NOTES,

BY THE REV. JOHN MᶜCAUL, LL.D.,

PRESIDENT OF UNIVERSITY COLLEGE, TORONTO, &c.

TORONTO:
HENRY ROWSELL.

LONDON:
LONGMAN, GREEN, LONGMAN, ROBERTS, & GREEN.

MDCCCLXIII.

PREFACE.

During the last five years I occasionally contributed to the *Canadian Journal* some articles on Britanno-Roman Epigraphy, under the designation, "Notes on Latin Inscriptions found in Britain." The favour, with which these papers were received, has induced me to believe, that they might be more acceptable and more generally useful, if they were presented in the more convenient form of a separate volume. Acting on this belief, I have collected in the following pages all my published notes on the subject, and have added many more which have hitherto never appeared in print.

I have availed myself of the opportunity to revise the articles, and with a view to facility of reference have distributed the notes, according to the counties in which the stones were found, and have arranged the inscriptions themselves, according to their subjects. I have also added an index, and have found it necessary to subjoin additions and corrections. For the number of the items thus subjoined, and of others of the same class which may have escaped my observation, a sufficient excuse may, I trust, be found in the disadvantages, under which I have prosecuted the investigations and have prepared the work, for in this young country we are as yet without some of those aids and appliances, which are commonly found in older communities. I have especially felt the want of books for reference. Our University Library is a valuable collection, but the number of volumes is small; and although it is well supplied with works on Epigraphy, it is deficient in some of those adjuncts, that are required in the local researches which I have been pursuing, such as county histories and topographical descriptions. I have, consequently, been obliged in some cases, much against my will, to accept the quotations of others without verification.

As my object has been to discuss only those inscriptions, which seemed not to have been satisfactorily explained, I have necessarily called in question the readings or interpretations proposed by those who had previously examined them. In thus impugning the opinions or statements of Antiquaries of the highest authority in British Archæology, it is far from being my wish to detract from their well-earned reputation: I have simply felt it to be a duty both to them and to myself, not to reject their views without stating my objections to them. In this, as in all other such enquiries, whether scientific or literary, it is of comparatively little consequence who is right or who is wrong; the great objects are the advancement of knowledge and the attainment of truth.

Univ. Coll., Toronto,
    February 14th, 1863.

CONTENTS.

INSCRIPTIONS.

ALTARS, VOTIVE TABLETS, AND OFFERINGS.

*I.

```
  I·O·M·TANARO
  T·ELVPIVSGALER
  PRAESENS·GVNTIA
  PRI·LEG·XXVV
     COMMODO ET
  LATERANO COS
     VS·L·M
```
P. 3.

II.

```
  . . O·SALDOMIN
  . . . M·NNINVI
  . . . . SIMORVM
  AVGG·GENIOLOCI
  FLAVIVS·LONG . .
  TRIBMIL·LEG XX *
  * LONGINVS·FIL
  . VS·DOMO
     SAMOSATA
       V    S
```
P. 4, note.

III.

```
  * . . . .  ΗΡΣΙΝ
  . . ΕΡΜΕΝΕΣΙΝ
  ΕΡΜΟΓΕΝΙΙΣ·
  ΙΑΤΡΟΣ ΒΩΜΟΝ
  ΤΟΝΔΑΝΕΘΙΙΚΑ
```
P. 9.

IV.

```
  DEAEM
  NERVA
  FVRIV
  FORTV
  NATVS
  MAG
  V
```
P. 10.

---

* The authorities for the text of the inscriptions, and the emendations of it are stated in the notes. Where the number of missing letters seemed certain, full points are used to indicate it, and in other cases asterisks are employed to mark deficiencies; but this distinction has not always been observed in the text as given in the notes.

2

V.

DVICI BRIG
ET NVMM AVGG
T AVR AVRELIAN
VS DD PRO SE
ET SVIS SMAGS

P. 11.

VI.

* * *
ET·NVM * * * *
N·COII·II·TVN
GROR·GOR· ꝏ·EQ
. L·CVI·PRAE
EST * * * CLAV
D * * * * * PRA
EF·INSTANTE
AELMARTINO
PRINC·XKAL * * *
IMPDNG * * AVG·III PO
MPEIANO COS

P. 12.

VII.

I   O   M
COII·II·TVNGR
ꝏ EQ·C·L·CVI
PRAEEST·ALB
SEVERVS·PR
AEF·TVNG·IN
STA·VIC·SEVRO
PRINCIPI

P. 13.

VIII.

I   O   M
.OIIITVNG.
ILEC CLCV . . .
ARES.AVRE * *
OPTA.VSP * * *
FVII STAN . .
MESOPSP * * *
PI.INC * * *

P. 14.

IX.

I O M
COH·I·AELI
DAC·ANIO

P. 17.

X.

GENIO LOCI
FORTVNAE REDVCI
ROMAE AETERNAE
ET FATO BONO
G CORNELIVS
PEREGRINVS
TRIB COHOR
EX PROVLNCIA
MAVR CAESA
DOMOSE * *

P. 18.

XL

I·O M
COH
II·GAL EQ
T DOMTI
VS HERON
D NICOMEDIA
·PRAEF

P. 20, and Additions.

XII.

I O M
PRO SALVTE IMPERATORIS
M·ANTONI GORDIANI P·F·
INVICTI AVG ET SABINIAE FVR
IAE TRANQVILLE CONIVGI EIVS TO
TAQVE DOMV DIVIN·EORVM A
LA AVG GORDIA OB VIRTVTEM
APPELLATA POSVIT CVI PRAEEST
AEMILIVS CRISPINVS PRAEF
EQQ NATVS IN PRO AFRICA DE
TVSDRO SVB CVR NONNII PHI
LIPPI LEG·AVG·PROPRETO
ATTICO ET PRAETEXTATO
COSS.

P. 20, and Additions.

XIII.

I O M
ALA
AVG OB VIRTVTE
APELATACVI PRAE
EST IAE IVBISE.
GIA MAG.VS D
MVRSA EX PANON
INFERIOR PR
APRONINO ET BR

P. 20, and Additions.

XIV.

I O M
COHNRVAN
GERMANORVM
MIL   EQ
CVI PRAEEST
• PIVS CLCLND
AHNIANV
I R II V·

P. 21.

XV.

DEO
SANCTO
COCIDIO
PATERNVS
MATERNVS
TRIBVNVS C.H
I NERVANE
EX EVOCATO
PALATINO
V S L M

P. 22.

XVI.

FORTVNAE
COH·I
NERVANA
GERMANOR
∞·EQ

P. 21.

XVII.

I O M
COH·I·NERVANA
GERMANOR· ∞·EQ
CVI PRAEEST L FANI
VS FELIX TRIB

P. 22.

XVIII.

MATRIBVS
M>NAN
IONIVS
ORBITOAL
V S L M

P. 27, note.

XIX.

DEI·HERC . . . . . .
VICTI·COI • • • • •
TIBVS·PRO·S . . . . .
COMMILITON . .
BARBARORV .
  OB VIRTV . . .
P·SEXTANTIV . . . . .
TAT·TRAIA • • • •

P. 90.

XX.

GENIO PRAETORI
CL EPAPHRODITVS
CLAVDIANVS
TRIBVNVS CHO
I LING VLPM

P. 68.

XXI.

I · O M
L · CAMMI
VS MAXI
PREFEC
I · IIIS · EQ
V S L M

P. 59, note, and Additions.

XXII.

NVMINIB
AVGVSTOR
COII IIII GAL
EQ
FEC.

P. 50, note, and Additions.

XXIII.

DIS
MOVNTI
BVSIVL
FIRMIN
VSDECE.

P. 61.

XXIV.

SANCTO CO
CIDEO TAVRVNC
FELICISSI
MVS · TRIBVN
EX EVOCATO
V.S·L·M

P. 64.

XXV.

DEAE
SETLO
CENIAE
L · ABAR
EVSCE
V · S · L · M ·

P. 65, note.

XXVI.

. MANDVS
EX · C · FRIS ·
VINOVIE
V · S · L · M

P. 65.

XXVII.

D · M · NODONTI
FL · BLANDINVS
ARMATVRA
V · S · L · M

P. 66.

XXVIII.

PECTILLVS
VOTVMQVOD
PROMISSIT
DEO NVDENTE
M DEDIT

P. 67.

XXIX.

DIVO
NODENTI SILVIANVS
ANVLVM PERDEDIT
DEMEDIAM PARTEM
DONAVIT NODENTI
INTER QVIDVS NOMEN
SENICIANI NVLLIS
PERMITTAS SANITA
TEM DONEC PERF.RA..
VSQVE TEMPLVM NO
DENTIS

P. 67.

XXX.

SEOESAM
ROLNASON
OSALVEDN
AL·Q·Q·SAR
BREVENM
BEDIANIS
ANTONI
VS MEG·VI
IC DOMV
ELITER

P. 78.

XXXI.

PRO SALVTE
AVGG N·N·
SEVERI ET ANTONI
NI ET GETÆ CÆS
P·SALTIENVS P·F·MAE
CIA THALAMVS HADRI·
PRAEF·LEG·II·AVG
C·VAMPEIANO ET
LVCILIAN * * *

P. 101.

XXXII.

SALVTI RE
GINAE·P·SAL
LIENIVS·P·F·
MAECIA ET . . .
MVS HAD * *
PRAEF·LEG·$\overline{II}$ . . .
CVM FILIIS SVIS
AMPEIANO ET LV
CILIANO D·D·

P. 101.

XXXIII.

* NCTO
. . . IIRAE
* * * SFVSTVS
. . . IIAVG
M·F

P. 106.

XXXIV.

. . . TVNE ETBONºEVE
NTOCORNELᴵ·CASTVSETIVLᴵ
BELISIM.VS CONIVGES
POS · · R

P. 107.

XXXV.

DEO SOLINVIC
TIBCLDECMVS
CORNELANTO
NIVS·PRAEF
TEMPL·RESTIT

P. 111.

XXXVI.

NN
AVGG
GENIO
LEG
II AVG
IN II°N°
RENMI°T
M VA
FII
IV
LE
SC
PP
DD

P. 125.

XXXVII.

VICTORIAE
· ·GG AIFE
NSSENECIO
N COS FELIX
ALALAST°
· · M   PRA

P. 133.

XXXVII. a

DEO
ANTENOCITICO
ET NVMINIB·
AVGVSTOR·
AEL·VIBIVS
>LEG·XX·V·V·
V·S·L·M·

Additions to p. 134.

XXXVII. B

DEO ANOCITICO
IVDICIIS OPTIMO
RVM MAXIMORVM
QVE IMPP·N·SVBVIB·
MARCELLO COS·TINE
IVS LONGVS IN PRAE
FECTVRA EQVITV.
LATO CLAVO EXORN.
TVS ET Q·D·

Additions to p. 184.

XXXVIII.

M·MARI
VS VELLI
A LONG
VS·AQVI
S IIANC
POSVIT
V·S·L·M

P. 185.

XXXIX.

* * * * * * *
MILC . .
PRAEEST·M
PEREGRINIV
SVPER·TRIB

P. 187.

XL.

D R S
DVPL·N·EXPLOR
BREMENARAM
INSTITVERVNT
N·EIVS C·CAEP
CIIARITINO TRIB
V S L M

P. 187.

XLI.

G D N ET
SIGNORVM
COIIIVARDVL
ETNEXPLORA
TORBREMCOR
EGNATLVCILI
ANVSLEGAVGPRPR
CVRANTECASSIO
SABINIANOTRIB

P. 189.

XLII.

SILVANO
PANTIIEO
PRO·SAL
RVFIN·TRIB·ET
LVCILLAE·EIVS
EVTYCIIVS
LIB·COS
V·S·L·M·

P. 140.

3

XLIII.

LEG·A * * *
Q·CALPVRNIVS
CONCESSINI
VS·PRAEF·EQ
CAESA·CORI
ONOTOTAR
VM·MANVPR
AESENTISSIMI
NVMINIS DEI VS

P. 142.

XLIV.

* * PVMCVMBAS
ET TEMPLVM
FECIT CIV
MAXIMINVS
LEG VI VI
EX VOTO

P. 144.

XLV.

MOGONT CAD
ET·N·D·N AVG
M·G·SECVNDINVS
DF·COS·HABITA
NCI PRIMASTA
PRO SE ET SVIS POS

P. 147.

XLVI.

DIISDEABVSQVESE
CVNDVMINTERPRE
TATIONEMORACV
LICLARIAPOLLINIS
COH·I·TVNGRORVM

P. 154.

XLVII.

SOLI
APOLLINI
ANICERO

P. 100.

XLVIII.

ΑΣΤΑΡΤΗΣ
ΒΩΜΟΝ Μ'
ΕΞΟΡΑΣ
ΠΟΤΑΧΕΡ Μ'
ΑΝΕΘΗΚΕΝ

P. 155.

XLIX.

ΗΡΑΚΛΕΙ
ΤΙΡΡΙΩ
ΔΙΟΔΩΡΑ
ΑΡΧΙΕΡΕΙΑ

P. 165.

L.

PEREGRINVS
SECVNDI FIL
CIVIS·TREVER
IOVCETIO
MARTI·ET·
NEMETONA
V·S·L·M

P. 184.

LL

BVLEVIS
SVLINVS
SCVLTOR
BRVCETI·F
SACRVM·F·L·M

P. 190.

LII.

DEAE
SVLIMI
NERVAE
SVLINVS
MATV
RIFIL
VSLM

P. 191.

LIIL

RVM CAES
AVG.
ANTONINI
ET VERI
IOVI DILECTI
CAECILIVS
LVCAN . S
PRAEF COH

P. 212.

LIV.

DEAE
FORTVNAE
SOSIA
IVNCINA
Q·ANTONII
ISAVRICI
LEG·AVG

P. 216.

LV.

. . . .
OMNIVM
GENTIVM
TEMPLVM
OLIMVETVS
TATECONIAD
SVMG·IVL·
PITANVS
P·P·RESTITVIT

P. 219.

LVI.

MAT·A ? ? IA·? A
M ? I ? ? ? ? DE
MIL·LEG·VIVIC
GVBER·LEG·VI
V·S·L·LM

P. 221.

LVII.

MATRIB
ITALIS GER
MANIS·
GAL . . . BRIT
.NTONIVS
. . CRETIANVS
.F·COS·REST

P. 223.

LVIII.

BRIGANTIE·S·AMANDVS
ARCITECTVS EX IMPERIO·IMP·I·

P. 237.

LIX.

DEAE
HARIMEL
LAE·SACGA
MIDIAHVS·
ARCXVSL*

P. 239.

LX.

DEAE VIRADES
THI PAGVS CON
DRVSTIS MILI
IN COH II TVN
GR·SVB SIVO
DAVSPICE PR
AEFE

P. 240.

*LXI.

DEAE RICAG^M
BEDAE PAGV^S
VELLAVS MILIT
COH II TVNG
V S L M

P. 240.

*LXII.

MARTI ET VICT°
RIAE·AVG·C·R^{AS}
TIMILIT·IN·COII
II TVNGR·CVI·
PRAEEST SILVIVS
AVSPEX·PRÆF·
V·S·L.M

P. 244.

LXIII.

DEAE
MINERVAE
COII II TVN
GRORVM
MIL EQ CL
CVI PRAEEST CS.L
AVSPEX PRAEF

P. 245.

LXIV.

FORTVNAE R * * *
SALVTE P CAM * *
ITALICI PRAEF CO * *
TVNCELER LIBER
LLM

P. 246.

LXV.

MATRIBALA
TERVIS·ET
MATRIBCAM
PESTRIBCOIII
TVNGRIŃS
VERSCARM
OI^{S·} SXXVV

P. 251.

LXVI.

VICTORIAE
COII VI NER
VIORVM . . .
A·BELIO>IEG.
XX VV
V·S·LL·M

P. 252.

---

* Here, and in a few other instances, I have indicated the different class of the letters as they appear in the originals. It is impossible, however, with ordinary type to give an exact representation of the ligatures or shapes and sizes of the letters.

LXVII.

APOLLINI
GRANNO
Q LVSIVS
SABINIA
NVS
PROC
AVG
V·SS·L·V·M

P. 253.

LXVIII.

CAMPESTR
SACRVM AEL
MARCVS
DEC·ALAE AVG
VOCONTIO
V·S·L·L·M

P. 258.

LXIX.

DEO SILVA
NO PROSA
LVTE·SVA·ET
SVORVM CAR
RIVS DOMITI
ANVS C LEGXX
VV·VS·LL·M

P. 258.

LXX.

DEAE SVRI
AESVBCALP
VRNIO AGR
ICOLALEG·AVG
PR·PR·A·LICINIVS
CLEMENS PRAEF
III·A·IOR

P. 259.

LXXI.

FORTVNAE·AVG·
PRO·SALVTE·L·AELI
CAESARIS·EX·VISV
T·FLA·SECVNDVS
PRAEF·COII·I·IIAM
IORVM·SAGITTAR
V·S·L·M

P. 260.

LXXII.

MARTI
MINERVAE
CAMPESTRI
BVS IIERO * *
EPONA
VICTORIAE
M·COCCEI
FIRMVS
OLEG·II·AVG

P. 261.

COMMEMORATIVE TABLETS.

<table>
<tr><td>LXXIII.</td><td>LXXIV.</td></tr>
<tr><td>IV ••••••••••••••</td><td>SVB·MODIOIV</td></tr>
<tr><td>M•••••••••••••••</td><td>LIOLEGAVGPR</td></tr>
<tr><td>CVPA L•••••••••••</td><td>PRCOIIIAELDC</td></tr>
<tr><td>LEG : AVG : PP : COII : I:</td><td>CVIPRAEESTM</td></tr>
<tr><td>TVNG POSVIT</td><td>CLMENANDER</td></tr>
<tr><td>P. 17.</td><td>TRID·</td></tr>
<tr><td></td><td>P. 20.</td></tr>
</table>

LXXV.

IMP·CÆS·M·ANT·GORDIA
NVS·P·F·AVG·BALNEVM·CVM
BASILICA A SOLO INSTRVXIT
PREGNLVCILIANVM·LEG AVG
PR·PR CVRANTE M·AVR
QVIRINO PRE COHILGOR

P. 56.

LXXVI.

IMP·CÆSAR·M·ANTONIVS
GORDIANVS·P·F·AVG
PRINCIPIA ET ARMAMEN
TARIA CONLAPSA RESTITV
IT PER MAECILIVM FVSCVM LEG
AVG·PR·PR·CVRANTE·M·AVR
QVIRINO PR·COII I·L·GOR.

P. 56.

LXXVII.

IMP·CAES·T·AELIO
HAD·ANTONINO·AVG·PIO PP
SVB·Q LOLVRDICO
LEG·AVG·PRO·PRAE
COH T LING
E Q F

P. 58.

LXXVIII.

D. A ... FLAVIVS·SENILIS·PR·REL·EX·STEPIDVS·
POSSVIT O....ANTE·VICTORINO·INTER...ATE.

P. 78.

LXXIX.

IMPP·VALERIANVS ET GALLIENVS
AVGG·ET VALERIANVS NODILISSIMVS
CAES·COHORTI VII·CENTVRIAS·A SO
LO RESTITVERVNT·PER·DESTICIVM IVBAM
VC·LEGATVM AVGG·PR·PR·ET
VITVLASIVM LAETINIANVM LEG. LEG
II·AVG·CVRANTE·DOMIT·POTENTINO
PRAEF·LEG EIVSDEM

P. 104.

LXXX.	LXXXI.
LEG	LII AVG
II	CHO VIII
AVG	FEC
FEC	P. 116.
P. 116.	

LXXXII.

COII·I·BAT
AVORVM F

P. 116.

LXXXIII.

IM*p*
M AV*relio*
ANTO*nino*
AVG
SEVER Lu*cii*
FILIO
LEG II Aug *p.*

P. 128.

LXXXIV.

DEDICATV
VRF
OG   ES
VE   NIO
MAXIMOIE
FVRPAN°
COS

P. 124.

LXXXV.

DD
VIIII
OCCB
PRCR
EIML
COS
CVR
VRSO
AGT*æ*
EI : IVS.

P. 124.

LXXXVI.

CAESARES·L·SEPTI
VG . . . SEPTIMIVS
ORRVPTVM

P. 129.

4

LXXXVII.

```
· · · · · · · · · · GALLOR
· · · · · · · · · · VOTANV
..NIEIVS POP · · · · IRRIBVS · · ·
FVNDAMEN.. · · · ....ERVNT SVB
CL·XENEPHO... · · · .EG AV PR
CVRANTE · · · · · · · · · ·
```

P. 186.

LXXXVIII.

```
B.NOGENERIS
HVMAN·IMPE
RANTE·C · · ·
· · · · · · · · · · ·
AVG·PR·PR·POSVIT
AC·DEDICAVIT
· C·A·ACIL · · ·
```

P. 140.

LXXXIX.

```
· · · · · · · ICOMAXI
COSIII ET M AVRELANTONINOPIO
COS II AVG · · · · · · · ·
PORTAMCVMMVRISVETVSTATE DI
LAPSISIVSSVALFENSENECINIS VO
COSCVRANTE COLANITI ADVENTO PRO
AVGG NN C.I·I·VANGON O PF S
CVMAEMI SALVIANO TRIB
SVOASOLO RESTI.
```

P. 147.

XC.

IMP·CÆSMAVR SEVE
RVSALEXANDERPIE
AVG IIORREVMVETV
STATECONIABSVMM
COII IIASTVRVM S·A
ASOLORESTITVERVNT
PROVINCIA REG * * *
MAXIMO LEG * * * *
* AIMARTI * * * *

P. 154.

XCL

IMP·CAES·M AVRELIO
SEVERO·ANTONINO
PIO·FELICI AVG·PARTHIC
MAX·BRIT·MAX·GERM
MAX·PONTIFICI MAXIM
TRIB·POTEST XVIIII IMP·II
COS IIII PROCOS PP COIII
FIDA VARDVL CREQ ∞ ANTO
NINIANAFECIT SVBCVRA *
* * * * * * LEGAVGPRP

P. 157.

XCIL

IMP CAE * * * * * * * * * *
* * * * * * P·F * * * * * * *
* * * * * * * CII·I·F·VARD
* * * * BALLIS A SOLO REST
SVB C·CLAP..LINI LEG AVG
INSTANTE AVR QVINTO TR

P. 160.

XCIII.

IMP·CAES·M·AV · · ·
· · · · · · PIO · F · · ·
TRIB·POT · · · COS · · ·
P · P · BALLIST · A SO ·
VARDVL · · · · · · · ·
TIB·CL·PAVL · · · · ·
PR·PR · FEC. · · · · ·
P·AEL · · · · · · · · ·

P. 101.

XCIV.

(1.)

.LAVDIVS·LIGVR
E·NIMIA·VETVST

(2.)

OLEGIO·LONGA·SERIA
VNIA·REFICI·ET·REPINGI·CVR

P. 180.

XCV.

PRO·SALVTE IMP·CES·M·AVR
ANTONINIPIIFELICISINVIC
TIAVG..NAEVIVS AVG
LIBADIVTPROCCPR...I
PIARVINAOPRESS·ASOLORES
TITVIT.

P. 183.

XCVI.

* *   .EPT·SEVERVS·PIVS·PER * * *
* * . .VREL·ANTONINV. *   *   =   *
.AQVAEDVCTIVM VETVS . . . . * * *
* * * * BS·COII·I·SVNC·RESIT . . . .
  * * * * * VIPF * *
  * * * * IVL *   *   *

P. 226.

XCVII.

IMP·C
T·AE·IIADRIA
NO·ANTONINO·AVG·PIO·P·P
VEX
LEG·XX
VV·FE
PPIIII   CDXI

P. 229.

XCVIII.

.MP·C·T·AE
.ADRIANO
.NTONINO
. . G·PIO·P·P·
.EG·XXVV
* * * DXI

P. 229.

XCIX.

IMP·C·T·AELIO
IIADRIANO·ANTO
NINO·AVG·P·P·
VEX·LEG·VI·VIC
P·F·OPVS·VALLI
P·∞∞∞∞CXLI

P. 230.

C.

LEG
ÎI
AVG·F·
PIIIICXI

P. 231.

CL

IMP   ANTON
AVG   PIO
P   P
     LEG
      II
     AVG
FPIIIICCLXX

P. 231.

CII.

IMP·C
T·AE·HADRIANO
ANTONINO
PIO·P·P·VEX LEG
XX VV·FEC
P.

P. 231.

CIII.

IMP·C·TAELIO·HADR
IANO ANTONINO·AVG
P·P·VEX·LEG·VI
VICTRICS·P·F·
OPVS·VALLI·P·
∞ ∞ ∞ CCXL·P

P. 231.

CIV.

IMP C
T AELIO
HADRIANO
ANTONINO
AVG·PIO P·P
VEX·LEG·XX·V
P·P   III

P. 231.

CV.

IMP CAES TITO AELIO
HADRIANO ANTONINO
AVG·PIO PP LEG II
AVG·PERMP IIIDC
LXVI·S

P. 231.

CVI.

IMP·CAESAR·T·AELIO
HADRIANO ANTONINO
AVG PIO PPVEXILLATIO
LEG VI·VICTR·P·F
PER·M·P IIIDCLXVIS

P. 232.

CVII.

IMP·CAES·T
AELIO HADRI
ANTONIN·AVG
PIO P·P VEXILLA
LEG·VI·VICPF
PER·M P IIIDCL ...

P. 282.

CVIII.

IMP CAES TITO AELIO
HADRIANO ANTONINO
AVG PIO·P·P·LEG II AVG
PERMPIIIDCLXVIS

P. 232.

CIX.

LEX XX
V V FEC
MPIIIP
IIICCCIV

P. 232

CX.

IMP·CAESARIT·
AELIO·HADRINO
ANTONINO·AVG
PIO·P·P·VEXILLA
LEG·VI·VIC·P·F·
PERM·

P. 232.

CXI.

IMP CAES
TAE HADRI
ANTONINO
AVG PIO PP
VEXILATIVS

P. 232.

CXII.

VEXILLATIONS
LEG·II·AVG·ET
LEGXXVVF

P. 282.

CXIII.

IMP·CAESARI
T·AELIO HADRI
ANO ANTONINO
AVG PIO PP
VEXILLATIO
LEGXXVALVICF
PER·MIL·P III

P. 232.

CXIV.

IMP·CAES·TÆLANT
AVG·PIO PP·
COH I TVNGRO
RVM FECIT ꝏ

P. 232.

CXV.

*.P·LEG·II A..
Q·LOLLIO VR....
LEG AVG·PR·PR

P. 201.

CXVI.

• • • .ILSER .
QVINANAT • •
GALATIA· DEC.
BVIT GALA • • •
XIT ANN • • • •
MORITV • • • • •
DESIDER • • • •
RIS · INT • • • •

P. 25.

CXVII.

D M S
NEMMONTANVS DEC
VIXITANN·XL·NEM
SANCTVSFR·ET·COHERR
EX TESTAMENTO FECERT

P. 60.

CXVIII.

RVFVS·SITA·EQVES·CHO VI
TRACVM· ANN· XL STIPXXII
HEREDES·EXS·TEST·F·CVRAVE
II S E

P. 76.

CXIX.

L·SEMPRONI·FLA
VINI·MILTIS·LEGVIIII
Q (?) ALAVDISEVERI
AERVIIANORXXX
ISPANICALERIA
CIVIMA

P. 88.

CXX.

D·M
FL·HELIVSNATI
ONEGRECVS VI
XITANNOSXXXX
FL·INGENVACO
NIVGIPOSVIT

P. 90.

CXXI.

DISMNIBVS
NOMINI SACRI
BRVSCI·FNI CIVIS
SENONI·IICARSS
NAE CONIVGIS
. . . .

P. 91.

CXXII.

I·VALERIVS·I·F
CLA·PVDENS·SAV·
MIL·LEG·II·A·P·F·
> ·DOSSENNI
PROCVLI·A·XXX
AERA • I D·SP
II·S·E·

P. 92.

CXXIII.

* * * * * AELIVS·
* * * VS·M·AVRE
* * * VM·ILIB
* * * CINO·
* * * * XXV·
* * * * ENIVS·VE
* * * EX·LEG·XIIII
* * * II E·TEST·P·

P. 93.

CXXIV.

DIIS·MANIB
C IVLI GAL
CALEN·F LVC
VET EX·LEG·VI
VIC·PF NASEMF

P. 94.

CXXV.

D·M·
IVL·VALIVS
MIL·LEG·XXVV
AN·XL·II·S·E·
C·A·FLAVIO
ATTIO·HER

P. 97.

CXXVI.

D·M
IVLIA VENERI
A·AN·XXII
I·ALESAN·CON
PIENTISSIMA
ET·I·BELICIANVS
F·MONIME
F_C

P. 99.

CXXVII.

D   M
Q·IVLI·SEVERI·
DINIA·VETERANI
LEG·II·AVG·CONIVX·F·C·

P. 111.

CXXVIII.

· · · · AIBERNAVX·S
TANNOSXVIMESSEXF
CFLAFLAVINAMATER
·   P. 122.

CXXIX.

· ·   AL ·
.EG·II·AVG
· E·RO·SE··IV
· ECIANVS
F·   C·

P. 122.

CXXX.

. M
ORVI
NISXVII
P. 123.

CXXXI.

D   M
TADIA·VALLAVNIVS·VIXIT
ANN·LXV·ET·TADIVS·EXVPERTVS
FILIVS·VIXIT·ANN·XXXVIII·DEFVN
TVS·EXPEDITIONEGERMANICA
TADIAEXVPERATA·FILIA
MATRI·ETFRATRI·PIISSIMA
SECVSTVMVLVM
PATRIS   POSVIT

P. 127.

CXXXII.

...IS NORICIAN
ESSORIVS·MAGNVS
RATEREIVSDVPLALVE
SABINIANAE

P. 134.

CXXXIII.

C·VALERIVS·C·VOL·
IVLLVS·VIAN·MIL
LEG·XX·V·V

P. 158.

CXXXIV.

. . . . .ALAE

II ASTVR[VM]

P. 164.

CXXXV.

D M
AEL·MERCV
RIALICORNICVL
VACIA·SOROR
FECIT

P. 164.

CXXXVI.

D·M PLACIDA AN·LV CVR·AG CONIA XXX	D·M DEVCCV S·ANXV CVR·G RATRE·	

P. 167.

CXXXVII.

C·MANNIVS·
C·F POL·SECV
NDVS·POLLEN
MILLEG·XX
ANORV·LII
STIP·XXXI
BEN·LEG·PR
II S E

P. 170.

CXXXVIII.

M PETRONIVS
L·F·MEN
VIC·ANN
XXXVIII
MIL·LEG
XIIII GEM
MILITAVIT
ANN·XVIII
SIGN·FVIT
II·S·E

P. 171.

CXXXIX.

    ....MINIVS T·POLIA
    ...ORVMXXXXVSTIPXXIIMIL·LEG
    *IIGEMMILITAVIAQNVNCIIICS..
    *LEGITEETFELICES·VITAIIVS·? IN??
    ??????????AQVAII ? IIII ??????
    ? ?????? ADITISVIVITED.MS ????
    ??????? AEDATEMPVS · IIONES..

P. 172.

CXL.	CXLI.
C·MVRRIVS	DIS MANIBVS
C·F·ARNIENSIS	M·VALERIVS·M
FORO·IVLI·MO	FILLATINVS (·EQ
DESTVS·MIL·	MILES LEQ·XX·AN
.EG·II·AD·P·F	XXXV STIPENXX.
IVLI·SECVNDI	II· S. E
ANNXXVSTI. *	P. 181.
H . .	
P. 180.	

CXLII.

        D   M
    SVCC·PETRONIAE VIX
    ANN·III·M·IIII·D·IX·V∃·O
    MVLVS·ET·VICTSAPINA
        FIL·KAR·FEC
          P. 182.

CXLIII.

L·VITELLIVS·MA
NIAI·F·TANCINVS
CIVES·HISP·CAVRIESIS
EQ·ALAE·VETTONVM·CR
ANN·XXXXVI·STIP·XXVI
II·S·E·

P. 182.

CXLIV.

IVLIVS VITA
LIS FABRICIES
IS·LEG·XX·V·V·
STIPENDIOR
VMIX ANNOR X̄X̄
IX·NATIONE DE
LGAEX·COLEGIO
FABRICE·ELATV
S·II S E

P. 187.

CXLV.

D · M
C.CALPVRNVS
[R]ECEPTVS SACER
DOS DEAE SV
LIS·VIXAN·LXXV
CA[LP]VRNIATRIFO
SA · · EPTE CONIVNX
F·C·

P. 101.

CXLVI.

DMS
CADIEDI
.IAE FO.
TVNA*
PIA·V·AX*

P. 209.

CXLVII.

MEI * * AL·THEODORI
ANI.OMEN·VIXIT·ANN·
XXX.V·M·VI·EMI·THEO
DO.A·MATER·E·C·

P. 213.

CXLVIIIL

D·M· FLAVIAE·AVGVSTINAE
VIXIT·AN·XXXVIII·M·VII·D·XI·FILIVS
• • NVS·AVGVSTINVS·VXT·AN·I·D·III
• • • AN·I·M·VIIII·D·V·CAERESIVS
• • • • •I·LEG·VI·VIC·CONIVGI·CARI
. . . . ET·SIBI·F·C·

P. 217.

CXLIX.

D M
CORNVICTOR·S·C
MIL·ANN·XXVICIV
PANN·FIL SATVRNI
NI·PP·VIX·AN·LV·D·XI
CONIVX·PROCVRAVI

P. 220.

CL.

DIS MANIBVS AFVTIANO BASSI ORDINATO *Tri-*
buno COIIortis *II*
TVNG*rorum* FLAVIA BAETICA CONIVNX FAC*ien-*
dum CVRAVIT

P. 247.

CLL	CLIL
DIS MANIBVS	D·M
AMMONIVS DA	C·IVLII
MIONIS • COII	MARCELLINI
I HISPANORVM	PRAEF
STIPENDIORVM	COII·I·ILAMIOR
XXVII HEREDES	P. 259.
F C	
P. 255.	

CENTURIAL STONES.

CLIII.

Ɔ C IVLII
CAECINIANI

P. 112.

CLIV.

CHOR·V̄I·ḤAST·PBI·
>ROESƆMODERA

P. 112.

CLV.

CΠO·V
>·PAETINI

P. 112.

CLVI.

COΠ·ĪI
>VALERI·FL
AVI

P. 112.

CLVII.

>MVN
.AXSV

P. 114.

CLVIII.

>VALERI
VERI

P. 115.

CLIX.

COΠVI
Ɔ STATII SOLONIS

P. 115.

CLX.

LEG·II·AVG
>IVLI·TE
RTVLLIA

P. 116.

CLXI.

LĪI AVG
Ɔ VOLVSIANA
P. 115.

CLXII.

>CASSI
PRIS
CI
COII·VI
P. 115, note.

CLXIII.

>COII VII
[MA]XI[M]IAN[A].
P. 115, note.

CLXIV.

COII·I·>OCRATI
MAXIMI ꜱL·M·P
P. 116.

CLXV.

Ɔ CANDIDI
FIDES·XX·
IIII
P. 117.

CLXVI.

COIIO·I·FRISIN
Ɔ MASAVONIS
P·XXIII
P. 117.

CLXVII.

>VALERI
CASSIA
N ? ? PXIX
P. 118.

CLXVIII.

Ɔ FLORINI
PXXII
P. 118.

CLXIX.

>CLAVDI
P·XXX·S
P. 117.

CLXX.

>ANTONR ? M
N CXX
P. 117.

CLXXI.

COII IIII PR·POS
>IVL·VITALIS
P. 120.

PIGS OF LEAD.

CLXXII.

BRITANNIC··AVG II

P. 82.

CLXXIII.

TI CLAVDIVS·CAESAR·AVG·P·M·TRIB·P·VIIII· IMP·XVI·DE·BRITAN

P. 32.

CLXXIV.

TI·CL·TR·LVT·DR·EX·ARG

P. 82.

CLXXV.

NERONIS AVG·EX·KIAN $\overline{IIII}$ COS BRIT

P. 32.

CLXXVI.

IMP·VESP·$\overline{V}$ :: T·IMP·III·COS

P. 82.

CLXXVII.

IMP·VESP·VII·T·IMP·$\overline{V}$·COS

P. 82.

CLXXVIII.

IMP·DOMIT·AVG·GER·DE CEANG

P. 82.

CLXXIX

IMP·CAES·DOMITIANO·AVG·COS·VII

P. 32.

CLXXX.

CAESAR ····· VADON

P. 32.

CLXXXI.

IMP·CAES·HADRIANI·AVG·MET·LVT

P. 33.

CLXXXII.

IMP·HADRIANI·AVG

P. 33.

CLXXXIII.

IMP·DVOR AVG ANTONINI
ET VERI ARMENIACORVM

P. 33

CLXXXIV.

L·ARVCONI·VERECVNDI·METAL·LVTVD

P. 33.

CLXXXV.

C·IVL·PROTI·BRIT·LVT·EX·ARG

P. 33.

CLXXXVI.

IMP·CAES·HADRIANI·AVG·T·M·LV

P. 33.

MISCELLANEOUS.

CLXXXVII.

[IMP·C]AESAR·DIVI·NERVAE·F·NERVA·TRAIANVS
[AVG]VSTVS·GERMANICVS·DACICVS·PONTIFEX·MAX
IMVS·TRIBVNIC·POTESTAT·VII·IMP·IIII·COS·V·P·P
[E]QVITIBVS·ET·PEDITIBVS·QVI·MILITANT·IN·ALIS
[Q]VATVOR·ET·COHORTIBVS·DECEM·ET·VNA·QVAE·AP
PELLANTVR·I·THRACVM·ET·I·PANNONIORVM·TAM
PIANA·ET·II·GALLORVM·SEBOSIANA·ET·HISPA
NORVM·VETTONVM·C·R·ET·I·HISPANORVM·ET·I
VALCIONVM·MILLIARIA·ET·I·ALPINORVM·ET·I·
MORINORVM·ET·I·CVGERNORVM·ET·I·BAETASI
ORVM·ET·I·TVNGRORVM·MILLIARIA·ET·II·THRA
CVM·ET·III·BRACAR·AVGVSTANORVM·ET·IIII·
LINGONVM·ET·IIII·DELMATARVM·ET·SVNT
IN·BRITANNIA·SVB·I·NERATIO·MARCELLO·
QVI·QVINA·ET·VICENA·PLVRAVE·STIPENDIA
MERVERVNT·QVORVM·NOMINA·SVBSCRIPTA
SVNT·IPSIS·LIBERIS·POSTERISQVE·EORVM·CIVITA
TEM·DEDIT·ET·CONVBIVM·CVM·VXORIBVS·QVAS·
TVNC·HABVISSENT·CVM·EST·CIVITAS·IIS·DATA
AVT·SI·QVI·COELIBES·ESSENT·CVM·IIS·QVAS
POSTEA·DVXISSENT·DVMTAXAT·SINGVLI·SIN
GVLAS·A·D·XIIII·K·   FEBR
M··LADERIO   MAXIMO·II
Q··GLITIO·ATILIO·AGRICOLA·II·COS·
ALAE·I·PANNONIORVM·TAMPIANAE·CVI·PRAEST
C·VALERIVS   CELSVS

                    DECVRIONI
REBVRRO·   SEVERI·F·   HISPAN

DESCRIPTVM·ET·RECOGNITVM·EX TABVLA·AENEA·
QVAE·FIXA·EST·ROMAE·IN MVRO·POST·TEMPLVM
[DIVI AVG]VSTI AD·MINERVAM·

Q·POMPEI	HOMERI
C·PAPI	EVSEBETIS
T·FLAVI	SECVNDI
P CAVLI	VITALIS
C VETTIENI	MODESTI
P·ATINI	HEDONICI
TI·CLAVDI	MENANDRI

P. 5.

CLXXXVIII.

SE | NI | CIA | NE | VI | VA | S | II | NDE

P. 70, note.

CLXXXIX.

IMP CAES
DIVITRAIANPARTIIFDIV.NER · ·
TRAIANHADRIANAVG · · ...B.
POTIV COSIIARATIS
II

P. 86.

CXC.

IX
NVMC · · · · · · ·
IMP CAESAR·M .....
AVREL·ANTONINVS
PIVS·TI.IX AVG·ARAB
IX

P. 227.

CXCI.

....NINO AVG.PIO
PP·COS III

∗ I·I·CVGERNOR
.M•III·MP

P. 233.

CXCII.

MÆMRVS

P. 106.

CXCIII.

IIAVGANT

P. 107.

CXCIV.

LEG·VI·
VIC·PF
G·P·R·F·

P. 116, note.

CXCV.

COIIVI
LOVS
SVAVI3

P. 118, note.

CXCVI.

CATTIVS
MANSINVS

P. 127.

CXCVII.

PRIMVSTES
ERA

P. 131.

CXCVIII.

T. IVNIANI IIOFSVMADρV
EC VMODELIOTA A MEDICIS

P. 177.

CXCIX.

Γ. 203.

CC.

SOCIO

ROMAE

Additions to p. 54.

NOTES.

ENGLAND.

CHESHIRE.

§ 1. Amongst the *Marmora Oxoniensia* is an altar, found at *Chester, bearing an inscription of the date A.D. 154, which has been frequently copied and explained.†

There can be but little doubt that the true reading of the inscription is as follows :

```
    I·O·M·TANARO
    T·ELVPIVS·GALER
    PRAESENS·GVNTIA
    PRI·LEG·XX·V·V
    COMMODO  ET
    LATERANO  COS
    V·S·L·M
```

Of the interpretations which have been proposed, the most extraordinary is that given by De Wal, in his *Mythologiæ Septentrionalis Monumenta, Utrecht*, 1847. He expands it thus:

> " Jovi Optimo Maximo Tanaro,
> Titus Elupius, Galeria *tribu*,
>   et Præsens, Guntia *tribu*,
> Primipilares legionis xx ‡Valeriæ Victricis,
>   Commodo et
>   Laterano consulibus,
> Votum solvunt lubenter merita."

---

* The *Deva* of the Itinerary of Antoninus.

† It is especially interesting on account of the epithet *Tanarus*, which is given to Jupiter; and the supposition is not improbable, that *Tanarus, Taran,* and *Taranucnus* denote the same deity, the *Thor* of the northern nations.

‡ I prefer this explanation (scil. VALERIA) of the first of the V·V commonly applied to this legion, to V[ALENS] adopted by Horsley, Orelli and Bruce, and V[ALERIANA]

[Q]VATVOR·ET·COHORTIBVS·DECEM·ET·VNA·QVAE·AP
PELLANTVR·I·THRACVM·ET·I·PANNONIORVM·TAM
PIANA·ET·II·GALLORVM·SEBOSIANA·ET·I·HISPA
NORVM·VETTONVM·C·R·ET·I·HISPANORVM·ET·I
VALCIONVM·MILLIARIA·ET·I·ALPINORVM·ET·I·
MORINORVM·ET·I·CVGERNORVM·ET·I·BAETASI
ORVM·ET·I·TVNGRORVM·MILLIARIA·ET·II·THRA
CVM·ET·III·BRACAR·AVGVSTANORVM·ET·IIII
LINGONVM·ET·IIII·DELMATARVM·ET·SVNT
IN·BRITANNIA·SVB·I·NERATIO·MARCELLO
QVI·QVINA·ET·VICENA·PLVRAVE·STIPENDIA
MERVERVNT·QVORVM·NOMINA·SVBSCRIPTA
SVNT·IPSIS·LIBERIS·POSTERISQVE·EORVM·CIVITA
TEM·DEDIT·ET·CONVBIVM·CVM·VXORIBVS·QVAS·
TVNC·HABVISSENT·CVM·EST·CIVITAS·IIS·DATA
AVT·SI·QVI·COELIBES·ESSENT·CVM·IIS·QVAS·
POSTEA·DVXISSENT·DVMTAXAT·SINGVLI·SIN
GVLAS·AD·XIIII·K   FEBR
M   LABERIO   MAXIMO·II
Q OLITIO ATILIO AGRICOLA·II·COS
ALAE·I·PANNONIORVM·TAMPIANAE·CVI·PRAEST
C·VALERIVS   CELSVS
              DECVRIONI
REBVRRO   SEVERI·F   HISPAN
DESCRIPTVM·ET·RECOGNITVM·EX·TABVLA·AENEA
QVAE·FIXA·EST·ROMAE·IN·MVRO·POST·TEMPLVM
[DIVI·AVG]VSTI·AD·MINERVAM·

Q·POMPEI	HOMERI
C·PAPI	EVSEBETIS
T·FLAVI	SECVNDI
P·CAVLI	VITALIS
C·VETTIENI	MODESTI
P·ATINI	HEDONICI
TI·CLAVDI	MENANDRI

The date of this record is fixed by its internal evidence to the 20th day of January, A. D. 103. The other similar monuments found in Britain are all of the same year. The example given above may be translated thus:—
The emperor Cæsar, deified Nerva's son, Nerva Trajanus Augustus, the German, the Dacian, Pontifex Maximus, invested with the tribunitian power the seventh time, emperor the fourth year [time], consul the fifth time, father of his country, to the cavalry and infantry who serve in the four alæ and eleven cohorts, which are called the first of the Thracians and the first of Pannonians, termed the Tampian, and the second of Gauls termed Sebosian, and the first of Spanish Vettones, Roman citizens, and the first of Valciones, a milliary one, and the first of Alpini, and the first of Morini, and

the first of Cugerni, and the first of Daciasi, and the first of Tangrians, a
milliary one, and the second of Thracians, and the third of Bracaso
Augustani, and the fourth of Lingones, and the fourth of Dalmatians,
and they [dele] are in Britain under Julius Neratius Marcellus, who
have served twenty-five or more years, whose names are written below, to
themselves, their children and posterity, has given civitas and connubium
(the rights of citizenship and marriage) with their wives, whom they might
then have when citizenship was given to them, or if any of them were
unmarried, with those whom they might afterwards take, that is to say,
each with each. On the 13th Kalends of February. To M. Laberius
Maximus twice, and Q. Glitius Atilius Agricola twice consuls, to the first
ala of the Pannonians, termed the Tampian, which is commanded by C.
Valerius Celsus, to the decurion Reburrus, son of Severus, the Spaniard.
Copied and revised from the tablet of brass which is fixed at Rome on the
wall behind the temple of divine Augustus near that of Minerva.

Quintus Pompeius Homerus, Caius Papius Euseles, Titus Flavius Secundus, Publius Caulus Vitalis, Caius Veitieaus Modestus, Publius Atluius
Hedonicus, and Titus Claudius Menander."

In this account there are some serious errors, which it seems
important to point out, as the work in which they are found is
justly regarded as a very useful and able compendium of British
Archæology. **The statement that " they are all decrees of the
emperor Trajan" is erroneous. Of the three tabulæ honestæ missionis, given in Monum. Hist. Brit., pp. cv., cvi., two are Trajan's
and one Hadrian's. Again, **the statement that "the date of
this record [the inscription found at Malpas] is fixed by its internal evidence to the "20th day of January, A.D. 103" is erroneous.
TRIB·POT·VII·IMP·IIII·COS·V correspond to A. D. 104.
**The statement is also erroneous that "the other similar monuments found in Britain are all of the same year." The dates of the
others are correctly given in Monum. Hist. Brit. as A.D. 105-6 and
124. Mr. Wright's text is, I believe, taken from that in Lysons's
Reliq., the same which is adopted in Monum. Hist. Brit., but it
requires emendation. **Instead of VALCIONVM in the 9th
line we should evidently read, with Henzen, VANGIONVM;

**The errors marked thus ** are here noticed by me for the first time, while those
marked †† were emended in my article published in the Chronicon Journal for May,
1852. Mr. Wright, in his 2nd edition, 1861, corrects the latter, but leaves the former as
they originally stood.

* Mr. Wright reads XIII·K·FEBR· which corresponds to Jan. 20, but in Monum. Hist.
Brit. we find XIIII·K·FEB· i.e. Jan. 19.

he also gives instead of I·NERATIO, L·NERATIO. This legate was the brother of the distinguished lawyer, *Lucius Neratius Priscus*, and had been *consul the year before, i. e. A. D. 103. See Borghesi, *Ann. Inst. Arch.*, 1852, p. 5. ††Again, the meaning of the words, *damnarnt singuli singulas*, is not expressed by "each with each." The sense is "provided they have but one each." Martini, *Diss. sopra Claud.*, explains this as prohibiting their having more than one wife at the same time; but Spangenberg, *Tab. Neg.*, p. 520, regards it as a limitation of the privilege of marriage; and, in confirmation of this view, refers to two *tabulæ*, in which *primæ* is expressed. The constructions, also, are in some cases incorrect. **Instead of "on the 13th kalends of February" as the translation of A·D·XIII·K·FEBR, it should be "on the thirteenth day before the kalends of February." Again, the words *M. Laberio Maximo* II. *Q. Glitio Agricola* II. *Cos.* should not have been translated as if they were in the dative case. The expression is the ordinary form in the ablative. ††Nor do I regard *alæ primæ Tampianæ* as being in the dative: they are in the genitive after *decurioni*. Finally, the name of the last witness is not ***"Titus Claudius Menander," but *Tiberius* Claudius Menander.

† Reburrus, the son of Severus, a Spaniard, a decurio of the first *ala* of Pannonians termed the Tampian, is specially named, as one of those to whom the privileges of *civitas* and *connubium* were given, either because this revised copy belonged to him, and was made for his use, or because he was the bearer of the *diploma* to the army in Britain. According to the first of these explanations, whilst the original at Rome gave the names of all those to whom the privileges had been ceded, in each copy made for an individual only his name was given, with occasionally the addition of the names of his wife and children. The seven names, with which the inscription ends, are those of the witnesses who attested the truth of the copy. On this subject, see Marini, *Atti de Frat. Arv.*, ii. p. 133; Platzmann, *Juris Romani Testimoniis, &c.*; Morcelli, *de Stil.*, ii. p. 309; Borghesi, *Att. Acad.*

* His pronomen is usually given as P.

† This name is on a stone found in Yorkshire. See Camden's *Brit. ed.*, Gough, iii. p. 272.

pont. *Archæol.* x. p. 131 ; Carliuali, *Diplomi Imperiali* ; Arneth, Zwölf Römische Militär-diplome ; and Henzen, *Rhein Jahrbb.* xiii. p. 98.

§ 3. Camden, *Gough's edit.*, iii. p. 45, notices the discovery of 20 pigs of lead on the coast of Cheshire. The inscription on some was—

IMP·VESP·$\overline{VII}$·T·IMP·$\overline{V}$·COS,

on others

IMP·DOMIT·AVG·GER·DE
CEANG

In 1838 a pig of lead was found about a mile from Chester, on the road to London, and very near the Roman road from Chester to Manchester. It bore the inscription

IMP·VESP·$\overline{V}$ :: T·IMP·$\overline{III}$·COS.

In 1859 another pig of lead was found near Common Street, Chester. It bore the imperfect inscription

CAESAR ***** VADON.

On these see my notes on inscriptions found in *Derbyshire.*

§ 4. In *The Journal of the Archæological Association* v. p. 223, Mr. C. Roach Smith figures a stone bearing the following inscription :

COH·I·> OCRATI
MAXIMI QL·M·P

On this see my notes on inscriptions found in *Monmouthshire.*

§ 5. In the year 1854 [?] an altar was found in Chester bearing the following imperfect Greek inscription :

................ΗΡΣΙΝ
**ΕΡΜΕΝΕΣΙΝ
ΕΡΜΟΓΕΝΗΣ
ΙΑΤΡΟΣ ΒΩΜΟΝ
ΤΟΝΔΑΝΕΘΗΚΑ

On this see my notes on inscriptions found in *Northumberland.*
B

§ 6. In *The Gentleman's Magazine* for March, 1862, there is a report of the proceedings of the Chester "Architectural, Archæological, and Historic Society," in which an account is given of an altar found in 1861, in Bridge St. Row.

"At some early period a piece had been chipped away from the proper left front of this altar, whereby the inscription had become somewhat diffi-cult to decipher; but what remained was easily discernible, and ran as follows :—

DEAEM
NERVA
FVRIV
FORTV
NATVS
MAG
V

This, on the supposition that MAG represented the word *Magister*, and that the initial S completed the inscription when perfect, Mr. Ffoulkes translated thus :—"To the goddess Minerva, Furius Fortunatus the magis-ter performs his vow." The *magister* was a personage of the highest rank, and there were but few of them met with in the whole history of the empire: the letters in question might therefore bear some other construc-tion, as it might fairly be doubted whether Furius Fortunatus of Chester would be likely to be a man of such an excellent position."

The argument adduced here against *mag.* standing for *magis-ter* is, in my judgment, inconclusive, as the statement that "the *magister* was a personage of the highest rank, and there were but few of them met with in the whole history of the empire" is erroneous. Besides the *magistri* of different kinds who held high positions under the emperors, there are many examples of the application of this term to presiding officers in towns and in colleges. See Henzen's *Index*, p. 163 and p. 177. The reading, however, of Mr. Hughes, who regarded "the sup-posed first three letters of the title *magister* as in reality initial letters of independent words," is to be preferred, especially as he was led to this reading "by distinctly seeing stops or contracting marks between each of those letters as well as the remains of a P farther on in the same line." "It is understood," the report proceeds, "that Mr. Ffoulkes has, since the meeting, examined the inscription more minutely, and has arrived at a similar opinion."

There can be no reasonable doubt as to the correctness of Mr. Hughes's reading. The same letters, MAG, are found in a similar position in Horsley's *Yorkshire*, n. xvii :

```
DVICI BRIG
ET NVMM AVGG
T AVR AVRELIAN
VS DD PRO SE
ET SVIS SMAGS
```

Dr. Musgrave read the last five letters of the last line—*snerum memori animo gratis solvens:* Horsley preferred—*susceptum merito animo grato solvit:* and Orelli, n. 1989, gives for the four last—*memor animo grato (or agens gratias) solvit.* Of these I prefer *memor animo grato solvit.* The phrase *animo grato* resembles A·L·, *animo libente,* so often found in the African inscriptions. In the same way, I think, the same letters, MAG, in *Monum. Hist. Brit.,* p. cix. n. 24 b, should be expanded, not MAGNAM, as suggested by Mr. Mathews, *Gentleman's Magazine,* 1842, p. 598. If Mr. Hughes be correct as to P following the MAG, the last two lines may be read :—

```
M[EMOR] A[NIMO] G[RATO] P[OSVIT]
    *V[OTO] [S[OLVTO] or [S]VSCEPTO.
```

§ 7. From a well known passage in the *Agricola* of Tacitus, c. 35, we learn that amongst the Roman auxiliaries serving in Britain in A D. 84 were two cohorts of Tungrians. The numbers of these cohorts are not stated, but the inscriptions which have been found warrant the belief that they were the 1st and 2nd. The continuance of the 1st in the island is attested by many memorials, and was long ago known to archæologists, but no traces of the 2nd were discovered until a comparatively late period. It is not mentioned in the *Notitia* nor in the *Tabulæ honestæ missionis;* no recognised records of it had been found in the times of Camden or Horsley; and even within the last few years, Böcking, in his elaborate edition of the *Notitia*, 1839–1853, makes no mention of any traces of it, whilst Roulez, in an article, *Mem. l'Acad. Royale de Belgique*, 1853, xxvi., p. 12, on "the contingent furnished to the Roman army by the peoples of Belgium," remarks:

" Nous ne savons pas ce que devint la seconde des cohortes (ce qui ne veut pas dire la cohorte II, car elle a pu avoir un autre numéro) qui avaient combattu sous les drapeaux d'Agricola: l'absence de tout vestige de son séjour dans la Bretagne doit faire croire qu'elle quitta ce pays long temps avant l'autre."

The inscriptions, which have been found at Castle Steads in this county, and at *Birrens in Scotland, prove that the 2nd cohort was quartered at both these places, and we can establish its presence at the first of them so late as A. D. 211. Mr. Thomas Hodgson, *Archæologia Æliana*, ii. p. 80, has discussed the inscriptions on the two altars erected by this corps, which have been found in this county since the publication of the *Britannia Romana*. The following are the inscriptions :

ET·NVM * * * *
N·COH·$\overline{\text{II}}$·TVN

---

* For my notes on inscriptions found in Dumfriesshire.

```
      GROR·GOR· ∞ ·EQ
    * L·CVI·PRAE
    EST * * * CLAV
    D * * * * * PRA
    EF·INSTANTE
    AEL·MARTINO
    PRINC·X·KAL * * *
    IMP·DNG * * AUG·III PO
       MPEIANO COS


      I    O    M
    COH·II·TVNGR
    ∞ EQ·C·L·CVI
    PRAEEST·ALB
    SEVERVS·PR
    AEF·TVNG·IN
    STA·VIC·SEVRO
    PRINCIPI
```

Mr. Hodgson expands them thus :

[Jovi optimo maximo] et Numinibus Augusti nostri cohors secunda Tungrorum Gordiana milliaria equitata civium Latinorum, cui praeest Sicilius Claudianus praefectus, instante Aelio Martino principe, decimo kalendarum J————, imperatore Domino nostro Gordiano Augusto tertium Pompeiano consulibus.

* *Jovi optimo maximo cohors secunda Tungrorum milliaria equitata civium Latinorum, cui praeest Albus Severus praefectus Tungrorum, instante Victore Sevro (or Severo) principi.*

The chief doubts which I have as to these expansions relate to the names of the praefect and *princeps* in the 2nd. I would substitute *Albius* for *Albus*, and *Victorius* for *Victor*. The difficulty about III in the last line but one of the 1st, marking the *third* consulate of Gordian, when it was really his *second*, I know not how to get over except on the supposition, suggested by Hodgson, "of some unrecorded or forgotten petty consulate." Henzen suggests, as a remedy, the reading II·ET. In this he was anti-

* Dr. Bruce, *Roman Wall*, 2nd ed., p. 294, adopts Mr. Hodgson's expansion.

cipated by Hodgson, who abandoned it, when he was informed by the lady, in whose possession the altar was, that "the I was too distinctly cut to be mistaken."

Let us now consider the "two imperfect inscriptions given by Camden," from which Horsley was led to believe that *Castle Steads was for a short time garrisoned by the *cohors prima Tungrorum.*

The first, as figured, pl. xxi, fig. 8, iii. p. 422, *ed. Gough,* may be thus represented :

I   O   M
OIIITVNG
ILEC CLCV
AEES AVRE
OPTA VSP
FVII STAN
MES OPSP
PI INC

The stone was broken on the left side (proper), and a crack extended from the top to the bottom, passing a little to the right of O in the first line, and of T in the second, between CC in the third, S and A in the fourth, through A in the fifth, between I and S in the sixth, S and O in the seventh, and I and I in the eighth. It may be restored thus :

I · O · M
COII · II · TVNG · M
IL · EQ · CL · CVI · PR
AEEST · AVREL
OPTATVS · PRAEF
TVN · INSTANTE
MESSOR · SP ......
PRINCIPI

i. e. Jovi optimo maximo, cohors secunda Tungrorum, miliaria, equitata, civium Latinorum, cui praeest Aurelius Optatus praefectus Tungrorum, instante Messorio Sp........ principi.

---

* Otherwise called *Cambeck fort.* It is regarded by Horsley and Bruce as the *Petriana* of the *Notitia.* MacLauchlan, *Memoir written during a survey of the Roman Wall,* p. 62, observes that "the garden at Walton House is placed within the station, which includes the flower garden, and extends about twenty yards beyond the north wall."

In the second line I read, with Hodgson, II instead of I, as the second I seems to have been lost by the fracture, and we have the II quite distinct on the other two altars also found here. In the third, I read *mil. eq. i. e. *milliaria equitata, as suggested by Hodgson. Mr. Carlisle, *Archæologia*, xi., correctly explained them, as they occur in the first inscription, by a reference to Hyginus *de castrametatione*, from whose statement it appears that a *cohors equitata milliaria* consisted of 760 foot soldiers and of 240 horsemen.† In the explanation of C·L·—i. e. *civium Latinorum*, I

: * Otherwise *milliaria*, which is at present preferred.

† It is strange that the author of an article, manifesting so much careful research as these observations by Mr. Hodgson evidently do, should be so little acquainted with the character of the auxiliary forces employed by the Romans as to remark relative to this cohort :

"The description here given of the *cohors milliaria*, may not at first sight, perhaps, appear applicable to the cohort now under consideration, from the circumstance of its being the *second*, and not the *first*, cohort of the *Tungri*; but it should be recollected that it is an auxiliary, and not a *legionary*, cohort; and, as is well observed by Mr. Cale, "though the second of the *Tungri*, it might yet be the first, or military, cohort of the auxiliary legion to which it belonged." No such body as an "auxiliary legion," composed of such "auxiliary cohorts," ever existed, and the term *miliary*, as applied to an auxiliary cohort, was in no way connected with its number, whether 1st or not. In this particular case, *vril.* of the Tungrians, both 1st and 2nd cohorts were *military*. But as this whole subject has received little attention from English scholars, and is not treated of in any of our works on Roman Antiquities, it may, perhaps, be useful for me to discuss it more particularly. There were three classes of auxiliary forces—cavalry, infantry, and mixed cavalry and infantry. To the first of these classes belong the *alæ*, to the second the *cohortes peditum*, or *peditatæ*, and to the third the *cohortes equestres*, or *equitatæ*. Both the *alæ* and cohorts were numbered, I, II, III, &c., probably according to the order in which they were formed, and were designated by the name of the people amongst whom they were raised. Thus ala I Tungrorum, cohors I·II Nerviorum, &c. They also bore titles similar to those conferred on the legions, such as ala Aug. Gordiana, ala Flavia pia fidelis mil., cohors I Ælia Dacorum Gordiana, &c. The alæ had also titles, probably derived from the names of the officers who first organised or commanded them, such as ala Frontoniana, ala Sulliana. Of each of those bodies there were two kinds, denominated according to their number of men quingenaria or milliaria, i. e. 500 or 1000 strong. In the ala quingenaria there were 16 turmæ or troops. In the ala milliaria 24. Each of the troops was commanded by a decurio, and the whole ala by a præfectus equitum. In the cohortes peditum or peditatæ, there were six or ten centuriæ or companies, according as they were respectively quingenaria or milliaria. Each century was commanded by a centurio, and the cohort by an officer styled præfectus or tribunus. In the cohortes equestres or equitatæ, there were six centuriæ of infantry and six turmæ of cavalry, or ten of infantry and ten of cavalry, according as the cohort was quingenaria or milliaria. The commanding officer was called præfectus. Such was the 2nd cohort of the Tungrians—milliaria equitata. The advantages of this mixed body of infantry and cavalry were first known to the Romans at the siege of Capua. See Livy xxvi. 4. Cæsar, Bell. Gall. I, 54, vii. 65, viii. 13, adopted this usage from the Germans, and under Vespasian cohorts of this description were in the Roman service. See Josephus, Bell. Jud. iii. 4. They then consisted of 600 infantry and 120 cavalry. From Trajan's time there were the two classes already noticed—quingenaria and milliaria. The first consisted of

have followed Mr. Hodgson, not that I am quite satisfied with it, as I know no authority for it, but because it is probable and I have myself nothing more likely to propose. The readings of the remaining lines are justified by reference to the second of the two altars explained by Mr. Hodgson; indeed the inscriptions are precisely similar, with the exceptions of the names of the individuals, who are mentioned, the use of the symbol $\overline{CO}$ for MIL·, and TVNG·, for TVN· which I propose in the 6th line, as there does not seem to be room for the G.

Relative to *instante*, Mr. Hodgson judiciously remarks :—

" *Instante*, say both Mr. Ward and Mr. Gale, is the same as *curante*, but this I take to be an opinion not exactly warranted by inscriptions. From these it appears to me that by *cura* or *curans*, is expressed one species of duty, and by *instans*, another and inferior duty. The former terms seem to have been applied to those who gave orders, or provided the necessary funds for the erection of any work; and the latter to those, on whom devolved the duty of carrying the others' directions into execution, and of superintending the progress of the work."

The gradations in rank of the persons engaged in the execution of a work are marked by the words, *jubente* or *imperante* (or *jussu* or *imperio*),—*curante*, (or *cura*, *sub cura*, *per curam*, or *per*) —and *instante* or *insistente*, (or *instantia*.) The first of these is applied to the emperor or the imperial legate, or the person supplying the funds, the second never to the emperor but to the legate or other officer or individual charged with the direction of the work, and the third never to the emperor or legate but to the

3rd infantry and 120 cavalry; the second of 760 infantry and 240 cavalry. I have mentioned that such cohorts were styled *equestres* or *equitatae*, but the latter word is the term used in inscriptions, and was, I suspect, a vulgarism. Pliny, *Ep.* x. 107, 108, uses *equestres*. The following are the varieties, which I have noticed, in the epigraphic designation of such cohorts:—MILLIAR·EQUIT·, MIL·EQ., œ EQ·—but I do not recollect having ever met with the two words together in evidence. The style of the 1st cohort of the Vardulli, which served in Britain, is peculiar, as these designations are inverted in order; and if the inscription given in Gough's Camden, iv. p. 65, be correct—

FORTVNAE·COH·I·NERV
M·GERMANORVM·EQ

we have an example of the *milliaria* and *equitata* separated by the name of the people. I suspect, however, that the M should have been read AN· or ANA· e. cohors prima Nervana Germanorum equitata. See § 10.

* Henzen, nn. 6700, 6781, suggests as an emendation C·R·, but the reading C·L· cannot be questioned.

officer or individual under whose immediate superintendence the work was executed. Mr. Hodgson also judiciously rejects the opinion that *Princeps* is a proper name. He correctly regards it as a designation of military rank, and cites in confirmation of his view, a passage from *Manutius*, in which it is stated that there were centurions called *primus princeps, secundus, et similiter.* He would have expressed the opinion, which he seems to have held, more clearly, if he had added that *princeps* alone stands for *primus princeps.* The first centurion of the *principes* was called *princeps*, and in military rank stood next to the first centurion of the *triarii*, who was called *primipilus.*

The other imperfect inscription which was found here, as noticed by Camden, is—

IV.................
M.................
CVPA L............
LEG : AVG : PP : COII : I :
TVNG POSVIT

Instead of CVPA read CVRA, taking L as the initial of the *prænomen* of the legate. The other lines are, of course, LEG[ATI] AVG[VSTI] P[RO]P[RAETORE] COH[ORS] PRIMA TVNG[RORVM] POSVIT. It must be confessed that this inscription seems to countenance the statement that the 1st cohort of the Tungrians at one time garrisoned the station at Castle Steads ; and yet, as no certain memorial of the 1st has been found here, it is not improbable, as Hodgson suggests, that in the injury which the stone has sustained by fracture, the second numeral may have been obliterated.

§ 8. On a fragment of an altar, found within the station of *Birdoswald, is the following inscription :

IOM
COH·I·AELI
DAC·ANIO

C

Horsley, *Brit. Rom.* p. 253, observes : "*Anio* must be the name, or part of the name, of some person who belonged to this cohort. The name *Anionius* is in Gruter, but I will not say that this has been the name here." The true reading is ANTO, the beginning of ANTONINIANA. The *cohors prima Ælia Dacorum* was also styled *Gordiana*, *Postumiana*, and *Tetriciana* or *Tetricianorum*. *P. S.*—Henzen, n. 6689., has anticipated me.

§ 9. One of the most highly ornamented altars discovered in England was found "in the camp at *Maryport*." It is figured in Dr. Bruce's *Roman Wall*, 2nd ed , p. 377. The inscription, which has been known since the time of Camden, is easily deciphered and interpreted, with the exception of the last two lines. In Dr. Bruce's copy it stands thus :

GENIO LOCI
FORTVNAE †REDVCI
ROMAE AETERNAE
ET FATO BONO
G CORNELIVS
PEREGRINVS
TRIB COHOR
EX PROVINCIA
MAVR CAESA
DOMOSE

It is accompanied by the following translation and remarks :

"To the Genius of the place,
To ‡returning Fortune,
To eternal Rome,
And to propitious fate
Gaius Cornelius
Peregrinus

---

* This station, otherwise known as *Ellenborough* or *Eleabod*, is regarded by Horsley as either *Virosidum* or *Olenacum*. Camden believed it to be the la ter.

† In Horsley's plate the line is complete without VCI.

‡ This does not express the meaning of *reduci* as applied to *Fortuna*. It means " running the course," " bringing back."

Tribune of a cohort,
From the province of
Mauritania Cæsariensis

....
....

The lower lines of the inscription of this altar are much injured ; they probably refer to the restoration of some buildings."

Orelli, n. 1776, following Gruter, MIVII. 7, gives the last two lines thus :

DOMO SETEDES
DECVR·

Gruter, cvii, 5, has a different reading of the last line but one, scil., DOMOS·AEDES ; whilst Horsley, *Cumberland*, lxviii., gives DOMOS ⁻EÆD.

Camden, *ed. Gough*, iii , 423, remarks :—" Every thing is perfectly plain on this inscription, except that in the last line but one ET and ÆDES are expressed in abbreviations. The end is imperfect. Perhaps we are to restore it thus, DECVRIONVM ORDINEM RESTITVIT, &c. The Decuriones were in the *municipia* the same as the senatores at Rome and in the colonies." Horsley justly remarks that he is at a loss to understand Camden's meaning, but suggests no explanation of the difficulty. Gough, p. 438, adds : " Peregrinus was a tribune of a cohort from Mauritania Cæsariensia, and repaired the houses and apartments of the decuriones." ⁴ Gale, M. S. n., supplies it *Decuria rest.*"

These observations are evidently most unsatisfactory. What has the restoration of the order of *decuriones* or the repairing of their houses to do with the erection of such an altar as this ? Wright, *Celt. Roman, and Saxon*, p. 275 (p. 279, 2nd ed), remarks : "The last line of the inscription, probably the usual formula, V S L L M, has been entirely erased, and we have only two letters of the name of the town from which Peregrinus came ; perhaps it was on the river Serbes." To this is subjoined the note : " The last remaining letters of the inscription have usually

been explained *domos e[versus]* [sic], and supposed to refer to some
buildings which the tribune Peregrinus had restored, but the
interpretation given above is the only one authorised by a comparison of other similar inscriptions."

There can, I think, be but little doubt that Mr. Wright's is the
true explanation; but the conjecture noticed by Orelli, n. 1776,
scil. *Sitifi*, is much more probable than "the river *Serbes*."
According to this view SETE may be regarded as a misreading
of SITIF., *i. e.*, *Sitifi*, the well known colony on the borders
of Numidia. But the chief difficulty, the interpretation of
DES DECVR, remains for consideration. On the supposition
that *these letters have been correctly read, (which I regard
as very doubtful), the only feasible explanation, which I can suggest, is DE S[VO] D[EDIT] ET CVR [AVIT]. The letter
read as E may be ligulate ET, an abbreviation which is not
uncommon.

The use of *domo* in the sense "birth-place," or as Mr. Wright
expresses it, "native of," is very common: thus Virgil, *Æn.* viii.,
114, *unde domo?* Dr. Bruce's translation " of a house," *Roman
Wall*, 2nd edit., pp. 375, 410, fails to convey the meaning
in English, as *house* may be regarded as signifying *family*.
Sometimes instead of DOMO we have only D·, as in the
inscription last cited; whence I would expand D NICOMEDIA,
in Horsley's *Cumberland*, n. lii., *domo Nicomedia*, not *de Nicomedia* as he has read it; also in n. lvii. of the same county
D MVRSA, *domo Mursa*, not *de Mursa*; and yet, it must be
remembered, in favour of his explanation, that in n. lv. we have
†DE TVSDRO *in extenso.*

Camden's conjecture, from the words on the back of the altar—
VOLANTI VIVAS—that the place was called *Volantium*, is
unquestionably erroneous. Horsley correctly explains them as a

---

* On the first view the reading DEC DECVR· *i. e. decreto decurionum* at once presents
itself, but this seems scarcely appropriate to the circumstances.

† The use of the *de* here may, perhaps, be accounted for by referring it to *native*, which
is found in this inscription, but not in the others. *Domo*, or *domu*, are used with the
ablative or genitive of the place, *e. gr. domo Brixia, domo Florentia, domo Philippis,
domo Bononia*; sometimes with the ethnic adjective, *e. gr. domo Histria*.

good wish for some person named *Volantius*—scil.—"O Volantius may you live"—"long life to you Volantius." Altars and sepulchral monuments were often profaned by such *graffiti*.

§ 10. In the *Archaeologia Æliana*, ii., p. 420, we have the following inscription, copied from a stone "found about two miles from the station on the Roman wall at *Burgh-upon-Sands*" :—

I O M

COHNRVAN

GERMANORVM

MIL   EQ

CVI PRAEEST

PIVS CLCLND

AIINIANV

I R II V·

Mr. C. Hodgson, who communicated a paper on the subject, mentions the opinion of his brother, "that it had been an altar erected to Jupiter, the best and greatest of the Gods, by a miliaria equitata cohort of German soldiers, called Vangiones, which was commanded by a Prefect, whose first name was Pius, and the second, perhaps, Secundus. The last line but one seems to have contained his agnomen, and the last, in sigla or notes, the reason for dedicating the altar. The sigla N·R· in the second line, may be synonymous to C·R· in several inscriptions in Gruter and Horsley, and C·L· in those above at p. 91, and in English may mean—"by nation Romane."

It is plain that the proposed reading must be at once rejected; nor can there be any doubt, that the cohort mentioned here is the same as that named in the following inscriptions, the first found at †Netherby in this county, the others at Birrens in Scotland :

---

* Either the *Congavata* or *Aximobanum* or *Gabrosentis* of the *Notitia*, but which is uncertain.

† Supposed to be the *castra exploratorum* of the Itinerary of Antoninus.

(1)

DEO
SANCTO
COCIDIO
PATERNVS
MATERNVS
TRIBVNVS C.II
I NERVANE
EX EVOCATO
PALATINO
V·S·L·M·

*(2)

FORTVNAE
COH·I
NERVANA
GERMANOR
∞· EQ

†(3)

I   O   M
COH·I·NERVANA
GERMANOR· ∞ ·EQ.
CVI PRAEEST L FANI
VS FELIX TRIB.

‡Henzen, n. 5888, gives the first of these inscriptions, and proposes for NERVANE, which he can scarcely accept as standing for NERVIANE, the reading NERV·[IORVM] AVG. He states, however, §an objection to this conjecture, which I regard as decisive against it, that when AVG· (i. e. AVGVSTA) is thus applied, the usage is that it precedes the name of the nation.

---

* This seems to be the inscription, which is incorrectly given by Pennant, *Append.* p. 408. Gough. *Camden's Britannia.* iv., p 12. Hodgson iii., pt ii., p. 253, Newton, *Monum Vet. Brit.* 71 n, and Prof. D. Wilson, *Prehistoric Annals*, p. 399.

† First published by Prof. D. Wilson, *Preh. Ann.*, p. 400.

‡ Henzen notices the unique designation of a military officer which is found in this inscription—viz. EX EVOCATO PALATINO. I have never met with another example of it. The signification of its is plainly that *Paternus* [?] *Maternus* had been promoted to the rank of *tribunus* of this cohort, from the position of *evocatus Palatinus*, by which expression we may understand a soldier who, after the expiration of his time of service, had been called on to discharge some extraordinary duty as a Palatine soldier, i. e., as one of the household guards. See *Suetonius, Galba*, c 10. Or it may be that he had been a Palatine soldier, and from that position was called out for foreign service, in which he received his promotion. It is worthy of remark that the *Nervii* supplied one of the Palatine legions, mentioned in the *Notitia.* See p 19, ed. Böcking.

§ Independently of this the reading cannot be questioned.

Mr. Roach Smith, *Collect. Antiq.*, iii., p. 202, figures the altar, which bears inscription (2), and in his observations on it, p. 204, remarks:

"Hodgson, though he corrects the mistake of Lysons [who traced the epithet NERVANA to the emperor NERVA] by referring to the rescripts of Trajan and Hadrian, did not perceive the full force of the association of the words *Nervana* and *Germanorum* and *Nerviorum Germanorum*. The solution is afforded by Tacitus, who informs us that the Nervii and Treviri were proud of their descent from the Germans: *circa affectionem Germanicæ originis ultro ambitiosi sunt.*"

This is a very ingenious, but not certain application of the passage in the *Germania*. According to Mr. Smith's view, we must regard NERVANA, either itself or as standing for NERVIANA, as an ethnic adjective from NERVII. Now this is liable to the objection that there are examples of the adjective NER-VIVS, NERVIA, (see Orelli, nn., 2075, 5968), but none of either NERVANVS or NERVIANVS. It is strange, also, if this explanation be correct, that neither the *3rd nor the *6th cohort of the *Nervii*, of both of which memorials have been found in Britain, adopted the style. Mr. Smith, indeed, suggests *Germanorum* as an explanation of GR, applied to the 3rd, in Horsley's *Northumberland*, cxiii., but the letters are much more probably a misreading of C·R, *civium Romanorum*. The opinion of Mr. Lysons was that the term was derived from the name of the emperor Nerva. *i. e.*, as I understand, his view was that the first cohort of the Germans was styled *Nervana Germanorum*, as the first cohort of the Dacians was styled *Ælia Dacorum*, or of the Spaniards, *Flavia Hispanorum*. It is not easy to understand how "a reference to the rescripts of Trajan and Hadrian" could prove that this opinion was erroneous. I have no opportunity of referring to Hodgson's statements on the subject, but suppose that his objection to Lysons's opinion is that there is no notice of a cohort of Germans in any of the *tabulæ* found in Britain. If this was his objection, it is not conclusive, for on this principle we should have to reject some *e. gr. cohors prima Hamio-rum*, of which there is unquestionable evidence. And yet it must

* The *tabula honesta missionis* prove that the 1st and 2nd also served in the blood, but no traces of the 2nd have been found, nor indeed of the 1st, unless we accept COH·I·NERVANA as representing it.

be admitted that his view is not without its difficulties. When an auxiliary body received a title formed from the name of an emperor, it was the usage, (at least in later times), that that taken from his *nomen gentilitium* was placed before the name of the people—*e. gr., cohors* I *Ælia Dacorum, ala* I *Flavia Gætulorum,* whilst that taken from his *cognomen* was placed after the name of the people—*e. gr., cohors* II *Tungrorum Gordiana, ala* I *Tungrorum Antoniniana,* &c. It is possible, however, that this may be an exception, as *ala* I *Vespasiana Dardanorum,* Henzen, 6857. Nor are we without difficulty as to the formation of the adjective, if we trace it to NERVA. In Henzen's n. 5335 we have NER-VANA applied to *Sitifis,* a colony called after the emperor, but in Renier's edition of the inscriptions found at that place, including that given by Henzen, he always reads the adjective with the *i.* And yet it seems not improbable to me that both forms, scil. *Nervanus* and *Nervianus* derived from *Nerva,* were in use ; certainly the adjective *Nervanus* is more reasonably traced to *Nerva* than to *Nervii.* It is difficult to decide which opinion should be preferred, as there are objections to both : on the whole I incline to Mr. Smith's, but I am not satisfied that it is correct.

As to the inscription, on which Mr. Hodgson comments in the *Archao'ogia Æliana,* I would read it thus :

```
        I[OVI] O[PTIMO] M[AXIMO]
        COH[ORS NERVAN[A]
          GERMANORVM
        MIL[IARIA] EQ[VITATA]
          CVI·PRAEEST
 [AP]PIVS CL[AVDIVS] CLAVD[IA] [TRIBV]
         ATINIANV[S]
      PR[A]EF[ECTVS] V[OTVM] [SOLVIT]
```

i e., Jovi optimo maximo, cohors Nervana Germanorum, miliaria, equitata, cui, praeest Appius Claudius, Claudia *tribu,* Atinianus, praefectus, votum solvit.

§ 11. A remarkable example of the danger of attempting to restore an inscription without sufficient data is to be found in Mr. Roach Smith's remarks on a lettered stone, found, I believe, at the station at Maryport.

It is figured in the *Collectanea Antiqua*, ii. pl. 48, fig. 7, and the following (p. 202) are Mr. Smith's observations on it :—

```
. . . . ILSER .
QVINANAT . .
GALATIA · DEC
BVIT GALA. . . .
XIT ANN . . . . .
MORITV . . . . .
DESIDER . . . .
RIS·INT . . . .
```

" This inscription is incorrectly given by Gordon, and Hodgson does not attempt to restore it. Two lines seem wanting at the beginning and one at the end. What is left may probably be read thus :—*fILius* SERVii QVI NATus GALATIA DECeBVIT GALATIA viXIT ANNOS ·· MORITVrus DESIDERavit patRIS IN *Tumulo sepeliri ?*"

Mr. Wright, *Celt, Roman, and Saxon*, p. 320 (p. 325, 2nd ed.), gives the translation according to this reading :—

" ......IL SER	......son of Servius,
QVI NANAT	who born
GALATIA DEC	in Galatia
BVIT GALA ...	died in Galatia ;
XIT ANN	He lived......years;
MORITV	On his death-bed
DESIDER.........	he desired
RIS INT	in his father's tomb to be buried."

To this is subjoined the following note :—

" The translation of this inscription is made after the ingenious restoration of Mr. Roach Smith, who (*Collectanea*, ii p. 202) explains it, I believe, correctly, as follows :—*fILius* SERVii QVI NATus GALATIA DECeBVIT GALATIA viXIT ANNOS...MORITVrus DESIDERavit patRIS IN *Tumulo sepeliri*. In the second line, NANAT appears to be an error of the stone-cutter for NAT."

In p. 319, Mr. Wright refers to this inscription in the following terms :—

" A broken inscription in one of the stations along the wall of Hadrian

D

commemorates a native of Galatia, whose father having, as it appears, died
in Britain, the son, who died in his native country, wished on his death-bed
to be carried into Britain to be laid in his father's grave."

This simple statement of the story, as it is told in the restored
inscription, manifests its improbability.   It is not common, even
now, with our increased facilities of transportation, for the bodies
of the dead to be removed such a distance as Galatia was from
Britain; and when these cases do recur, they are usually of
members of families of distinction or in affluent circumstances,
and with the object of having the remains deposited near those of
relatives of the deceased in their native lands.   Here the case
seems to be of a son, whose remains, in accordance with his desire
on his death-bed, were removed from his birth-place Galatia,
being the place also of his death, to the grave of his father in
Britain, whose presence there and whose death there are equally
unexplained; and indeed inexplicable, unless on the supposition
that he had gone there with the corps in which he was serving,
probably as a private soldier.   But besides this, at the time of
the inscription (to whatever date during the Roman occupation
of the island it should be referred) this power of removal seems
not to have been at the pleasure of individuals.   We know that
the Romans did not allow a body, even temporarily interred, to
be removed to any other place without the permission of the
pontifices or other proper authorities.   Of this we have an example in Gruter, p. DCVII. n. 1, where we find a copy of the memorial addressed by *Velius Fidius* for permission to remove the
bodies of his wife and son from an *obruendarium*, or sarcophagus of
clay, to a monument of marble, with the object—*ut quando ego
essedeviero, pariter cum iis ponar.*   See p. 14 of *Roman Sepulchral Inscriptions*, a scholarly and very interesting little work,
by the Rev. J. Kenrick, of York, England; and Orelli, nn. 794,
2439.   I do not mean to say that there is no authority for the
removal of human remains, without a statement of permission,
for there are examples, but I think that the absence of the notice
in this case of both removal and permission throws additional
doubt on a reading previously highly improbable.   It must also
be admitted, that the improbability of the removal of the bones,
which in those times would, perhaps, be the only remains, is less
than that of the transportation of the body.

But if we examine the restoration in detail, we shall, I think, find the degree of improbability considerably increased.

Mr. Smith reads the fragment of the first line thus: [F]IL· SER[VII]. Now the obvious objection to this reading is that the order is contrary to usage: the name of the father should precede, and FIL· or F·follow. There can, I think, be but little doubt, that the name of the father was in the mutilated portion of the line before FIL· and that SER· stands for SER [GIA] *tribe*, which is thus in its proper place. In the second line—QVINANAT— NANA is treated as "a blunder of the stone-cutter, who inadvertently doubled the NA, i.e., the reading

---

* That the ancient stone-cutters, like their brethren in our day, sometimes disfigured their work by gross errors, there can be no doubt. Sidonius Apollinaris, III., 12, refers to this in his request—*vide et vitium non foriat in marmore lapicidis*; and there are unquestionable examples still extant. Nor can it be doubted that the provincial workmen were inferior in knowledge and skill to the Roman and Italian. Yet I cannot but think that more errors are attributed to them than those for which they are justly responsible, and that modern critics sometimes impute to the blundering of the mason what might more properly be charged to the ignorance of his employer, or to the peculiarities of the language at the time in which the inscription was cut, or not unfrequently to the mistakes of the critics themselves. The most remarkable example, which I have noticed, of Smith's assumption of " the ignorance or neglect of the mason," is in Mr. Beach Smith's *Collectanea Antiqua*, iv., 45, where he proposes to get over the difficulties of a perplexing inscription on an altar found at Doncaster by transposing a whole line, making that which is fourth stand second. Even if the effort of this novel mode of " rectification" were wholly satisfactory, so that such a change could not fail to be received with suspicion or even aversion, but what shall we think of it when, even after this, we have to read the transposed line—ORBITOAL— ORBIS·TOTALIA, in the sense—" *of the whole world.*" and receive no additional light on the obscurity of the line, which has been thus displaced from second to third. The whole inscription may be represented thus:

MAT·IBVS
M·NAN
TONIVS
ORBITOAL
V·L·M

In the 4th line the R is placed within the O, the I is a prolongation of the upright of the R, and the perpendicular of the T bisects the upper semicircle of the O.

By Mr. Smith's process the inscription assumes the following form:

MATRIBVS
ORBITOAL
M·NAN
TONIVS
V·S·L·M

Now even if we make the concession (for which we have no warrant) that ORBITOAL stands for ORBIS·T·JAL· and that for ORBIS·TOTALIS. what authority have we for the word TOTALIS? Again, what is the interpretation of M·N preceding ANTONIVS? Mr. Hunter, p. 45, takes no notice of the centurial mark, which appears very plainly in the

QVI·NAT[VS] is given instead of QVINANAT[VS]. Sooner
than resort to this uncritical expedient, I prefer regarding
QVINA as the *cognomen*,* even though I can produce no example of it. The letters are certainly in the position where the
cognomen should be expected, scil. after the tribe. The translation of DECVBVIT—"died"—is liable to the objection, that
this is not the ordinary meaning of the word. *Decumbere* commonly means "to fall sick," although there are examples of its
gladiatorial application, "to fall in death." It is not impossible,
however, that it may be used here in the sense—"he took to his
bed and never left it alive." The last two lines of the inscription,† as given by Mr. Smith, scil. DESIDER* * * * RIS·INT
* * * * are restored thus: DESIDER[AVIT· PAT]RIS·IN·
T[VMVLO]; and to this is added, to complete the conjectural
sense, but without a trace of authority on the stone, the word
SEPELIRI.

The objection here is to the Latinity of the phrase *desideravit
sepeliri.* So far as I am aware, there is no authority for its use ;
and the appearance of it in an inscription would, in my judgment,
at once suggest doubts of the correctness of the reading or of the
genuineness of the inscription.

It is not my intention to suggest any conjectural reading of
the inscription which we have been examining ; it seems to be
too far gone to be within the reach of hopeful critical treatment.
I may be permitted, however, to observe, that the reading GALA
[TI],‡ the Κάλατον of Ptolemy, is more probable than GALA
[TIA] ; and that the fragmentary words MORITV **** DESI-
DER**** may be more plausibly explained as intimating that the

---

wood-cut. p. 54, but gives M·N· as names of ANTONIVS, whilst Mr. Smith passes over the
whole in silence. The only results of this assumption of "a blunder of the mason" are
the consequent transposition of the lines are the introduction of a word, known only in
sparkrae Latinity, and the shifting of an unexplained difficulty from the second line to the
third. The inscription, as it stands, certainly seems inexplicable, but a candid admission
of this is, in my judgment, much preferable to any attempt at explanation at variance
with the principles of sound criticism.

* It has occurred to me, that perhaps the true reading is QVINA, a name, of which the
first four letters are found in Mommsen, *Inscript. Neapol.* n. 6311.

† In Gruton's *Itinerary,* pl. 45, we find NON VA in a line under RIS INT.

‡ The mention of the place of death is so uncommon, that there was probably some special reason for noticing it here. Perhaps the resemblance of *Galatum* to *Galatia* was the
cause. It has been identified with *Galacum* of the Itinerary.

deceased pined and died from fretting for his distant or deceased father, mother, or brother, scil. *desiderio patris, matris,* or *fratris.* Thus we have in Henzen, n. 7378 :—

D·M·S
TELESINIAE·CRISPI
NILLAE·CONIVGI·SANCTIS
SIMAE·QVAE·OB·DESIDERIVM
P·LALI·GENTIANI·VICTORIS
FILI·SVI·PIISSIMI·VIVERE
ABOMINAVIT·ET·POST·DIES·XV
FATI·EIVS·ANIMO·DESPONDIT
&c. &c. &c.

and in Cicero, *Epist. ad. Attic.* i. 3. *Aviam tuam scito* desiderio tui mortuam esse.

§ 12. In the *Archæologia Æliana,* vol. iv., a broken slab, which was found in Birdoswald during the excavations which were made under the direction of Mr. Potter in 1852, is figured ; and that gentleman gives the following expansion of the inscription which it bore :

"SVBMODIOIV   Sub[li]mo Dio Ju-
LIOLEGAVGPR   -lio leg[ato Aug[ustali] Pro-
PRCOIIIAELDC   Prætori Coh[ors] i Æl[ia D[a]c[orum]
CVIPRAEESTM   cui præest M[arcus]
CLMENANDER   Cl[audius] Menander
TRIB   Trib[unus]."

Mr. Potter is of opinion that "if this reading be correct, there is reason to suppose that the Julius here mentioned was Julius Severus, who, in the time of Hadrian, was propraetor of Great Britain ;" and, after examination, rejects a different reading which had been suggested, viz. : *sub Medio Julio.*

I am unable to comprehend the grounds on which Mr. Potter adopted *Sublimo Dio,* a reading which is wholly unprecedented and scarcely intelligible. I concur with Mr. Smith, *Collectanea Antiqua,* iii., p. 20, in preferring *sub Medio Julio,* which (as Mr. Potter remarks) gives "the name of a propraetor of Britain not

hitherto known." I am not satisfied, however, as to the correctness of *Julio*. The fracture of the slab seems to have so materi-
ally injured the letters, in the second line, given as LI, that it
may reasonably be doubted (at least by one who has not seen the
stone) whether that be the right reading; especially as *Modius*
is a rare *nomen*, *Julius* a rare *cognomen*, and the combination of
the two, so far as I know, unprecedented. Under such circumstances, I am inclined to venture on the conjectures, that the injured
letters are ST, and that the *Modius Justus* named here is the
same, who, at a different time, was LEG·AVG·PR·PR of Numidia. He is mentioned in the following inscription given by
Renier, *Inscriptions de l'Algérie*, n. 44.

STAT·AGRIP	Stat[iæ] Agrip-
PINAE CON	pinæ, con-
IVGIS MO	jugis Mo-
DI IVSTI LEG	di[i] Justi, leg[ati]
AVG·PR·PR	Aug[usti], Pr[o] Pr[ætore],
CONSVLIS	Consulis,
SPECVLATO	Speculato-
RES ET	res et
BENEFICIARI	Beneficiari[i].

In Mommsen's *Inscript. Neapolit.* n. 5274, we also find the
names *Modius Justus*.

§ 13. In the *Journal of the Archæological Institute*, 1860,
p. 159, there is a report of a notice by Dr. Bruce of an inscribed
stone recently found at Carlisle.

" The portion of the inscription now remaining may be read as follows :—

```
        DEI·HERC · · · · ·
        VICTI COI  · · · · ·
        TIBVS·PRO S · · · ·
        COMMILITON · · · ·
        BARBARORV · · · ·
            OB VIRTV · · ·
        P· SEXTANTIV · · ·
        TAT·TRAIA · · · · ·
```

The letters are occasionally combined, or tied, but are here printed separately. The inscription (Dr. Bruce remarked) is difficult to interpret, as a

portion of each line is lost; it is also peculiar in several respects. The following reading may be conjecturally proposed:—"Dei Herculis Invicti comiti numini et Dis Penatibus pro salute commilitonum barbarorum, ob virtutem, Publius Sextantius" · · · · Of the concluding letters no satisfactory explanation has been proposed; it cannot be supposed that the Emperor Trajan is here referred to, none of his usual titles being given. The name Trajanus was by no means common; the epithet Trajana was sometimes applied to the second Legion, but there appears no ground for the conjecture that this inscription may have been connected with that legion."

TAT seem to me to be the last three letters of CIVITAT·, i. e., civitate and TRAIA the beginning of TRAIANENSIS, or, rather, TRAIANOPOLI. Thus we have in Orelli, n. 2003, CIVES·TRAIANENSES·, and in Museum Veronense, p. 221, n. 7, CIV[ITATE] POLLENT[IAE].

§ 14. Many centurial inscriptions have been found in this county. On these see my notes on inscriptions found in Monmouthshire.

§ 15. Horsley, n. xxxiv., gives the following found at Castle Steads :—

OMNIVM
GENTIVM
TEMPLVM
OLIMVETVS
TATECONIAB
SVMG·IVL·
PITANVS
P·P·RESTITVIT

On this see my notes on inscriptions found in Yorkshire.

DERBYSHIRE.

§ 16. Few Latin inscriptions have been found in Derbyshire, and of these the majority are on blocks of lead. As the types presented by the blocks of this county are of great importance in the examination of such remains, I propose discussing in this article the general subject of the relics in lead of Roman metallurgy in Britain.

Mr. Albert Way, *Journal of Archæological Institute*, 1859, n. 61, has carefully collected the scattered notices of all the objects of this class, which have at various times been found in Britain, and has thus produced a valuable *précis* of almost all that is known on the subject.

The blocks, or "pigs," according to the information given in that article, present the following varieties in inscription :

(1) BRITANNIC**AVG. (*a*)
(2) TI·CLAVDIVS·CAESAR·AVG·P·M·TRIB·P·VIIII·
     IMP·XVI·DE·BRITAN. (*b*)
(3) TI·CL·TR·LVT·BR·EX·ARG. (*c*)
(4) NERONIS AVG·EX KIAN IĪII COS BRIT. (*d*)
(5) IMP·VESP·V̄:·T·IMP·III·COS. (*e*)
(6) IMP·VESP·VĪĪ·T·IMP·V̄·COS. (*f*)
(7) IMP·DOMIT·AVG·GER·DE
        CEANG (*g*)
(8) IMP·CAES·DOMITIANO·AVG·COS·VII. (*h*)
(9) CAESAR ***** VADON. (*i*)

(*a*) Found on Blackdown Range, Mendip Hills, Somerset.
(*b*) Found near Wookey-hole, Somerset.
(*c*) Found at Matlock, Derbyshire; also in Pulborough, Sussex.
(*d*) Found near Stockbridge, Hants.
(*e*) Found about a mile from Chester, on the road to London.
(*f*) Found at Hints, Staffordshire; also on the coast of Cheshire.
(*g*) Found on the coast of Cheshire.
(*h*) Found about eight miles from Ripley, in Yorkshire.
(*i*) Found near Common Hall Street, Chester.

(10) IMP·CAES·HADRIANI·AVG·MET·LVT. (*k*)
(11) IMP·HADRIANI·AVG. (*l*)
(12) IMP·DVOR AVG ANTONINI
    ET VERI ARMENIACORVM. (*m*)
(13) L·ARVCONI·VERECVNDI·METAL·LVTVD. (*n*)
(14) C·IVL·PROTI·BRIT·LVT·EX·ARG. (*o*)

To these is to be added another of Hadrian's, communicated to me by Prof. D. Wilson:

(15) IMP·CAES·HADRIANI·AVG·T·M·LV. (*p*)

It is plain, on inspection, that the simplest of these are nn. (2), (5), (6), (8), (11), and (12). We shall therefore take these up first, and then proceed to the more obscure.

(2) Ti[berius] Claudius Cæsar Aug[ustus] P[ontifex] M[aximus] Trib[unitia] Po[testate] viiii. Imp[erator] xvi. de Britan[nis].

The date is A.D., 49.

Following Mr. Way, I have regarded the object of lead, bearing this inscription, as a pig. Leland, *Collect. Assert. Artur.*, v., p. 45, describes it as *trophæum ex oblonga plumbi tabula*. Similarly Camden, i., p. 82, *Gough's edit.*, but Gough, p. 104, applies the term "pig" to it. In the *Monum. Hist. Brit.* it is called *lamina*. The learned author of the *Historical Ethnology of Britain, Cran. Brit., Dec.* iii., *chap. V., p.* 101, speaks of it as "often described as a pig, but really an oblong plate, 'oblonga plumbi tabula,' and part, probably, of a trophy." It is plain from the context of the passage in which Leland mentions it that it was not a *lamina* or sheet, for just before noticing it he more than once mentions *laminæ plumbeæ*, but in describing it he substitutes, for *lamina, tabula*, the difference being, as I understand, that the latter was thicker.

(*k*) Found near Matlock, Derbyshire.
(*l*) Found about ten miles from Shrewsbury, Shropshire; also about seven miles north of Bishop's Castle, Salop; also about four and a half miles from Montgomery, Shropshire; also near Sydney Buildings, Bath.
(*m*) Found at Broton, Somerset.
(*n*) Found upon Matlock Moor, Derbyshire.
(*o*) Found about six miles from Mansfield, Nottinghamshire.
(*p*) Found on the bank of the river Carron, in Scotland. See the *Stirling Observer* of Sept. 19th, 1840.
E

Mr. Way, p. 23, speaks of these objects generally as "the *massæ plumbi*, Ελασμοὶ μολίβδινοι of Dion, in the medieval times termed *tabulæ*." The passage in Dion, referred to by Mr. W., is in lvii., 18, and there can, I think, be but little doubt that the ἐλασμοὶ mentioned there, were what the ancient Romans called *tabula*.

The idea of its being a trophy was, I conceive, suggested by the name being in the nominative, and by the use of the proposition *de*, which seems to denote that the object was not an article of commerce or of tribute, but of spoil; thus Virgil, *Æn*. iii., 288, *Æneas hæc de Danais victoribus arma*. This supposition derives support from the use of the same formula—*de Britannis* —on the coins of Claudius of the years 46 and 49, A.D., which also bear on the reverse a triumphal arch surmounted by an equestrian statue between two trophies. The first issue of these coins was most probably to commemorate the completion of the triumphal arch decreed for his triumph over the Britons in A.D., 44, and the second, which bears the same legend as this object of lead, was in honour of his enlargement of the pomœrium in A.D., 49. It seems no improbable supposition, that objects of lead were prepared in Britain to grace the triumphal procession on the first occasion and some pageant on the second. It is possible, too, that the word *tropæum* may correctly designate one of these objects, as a trophy won from conquered enemies, or as intended to form[*] part of a trophy. Even with these admissions, however, it may have been "a pig," for the block, as well as the plate, seems appropriate for the purpose. On the whole, I am inclined to think that it was of the same class of leaden objects as that bearing the inscription IMP·DOMIT·AVG·GER·DE CEANG. If this be "a pig," as seems to be universally admitted, then it is probable that the other of Claudius DE BRITAN· was the same. Leland appears to have applied the term *tabula* to one of these objects which others after his time called *massæ*.

---

[*] There is a passage in Statius, *Silv.* iv., 3, which at first sight seems to support this supposition, scil.:

> "*Hujus Janua, prosperumque litora*
> *Arena, belligeri Ducis trophæis*
> *Et totis Ligurum altron metallis.*"

Statius, however, both here and elsewhere, uses *metalla* in the sense of "slabs of marble."

(5) Imp[eratore] Vesp[asiano] v. T[ito] Imp[eratore] iii.
Co[n] s[ulibus].

The date is A.D. 74.*

(6) Imp[eratore] Vesp[asiano] vii. T[ito] Imp[eratore] v.
Co[n] s[ulibus].

The date is A.D. 76.†

(8) Imp[eratore] Cæs[are] Domitiano Aug[usto] Co[n] s[ule]
vii.

The date is A.D. 81, and refers to the last three months and a
half of the year, for Titus died on the 13th of September.

On the side of one of the blocks, bearing this inscription, the
letters BRIG· are found, which have been interpreted very
probably as referring to the *Brigantes*, in whose territories the
lead was produced.

(11) Imp[eratoris] Hadriani Aug[usti].

The date is A.D. 117—138.

(12) Imp[eratorum] duor[um] Aug[ustorum] Antonini et
Veri Armeniacorum.

The date is A.D. 161—169.‡

We shall now take up n. (7), as there is but one word in it
the interpretation of which is obscure. It may be read thus:
Imp[erator] Domit[ianus] Aug[ustus] Ger[manicus] de Ceang[is].

<hr>

* Mr. Way, in the heading of his notice of this pig, assigns it to the right date, but inadvertently gives "Vespasian, third Consulate," instead of "Vespasian, fifth Consulate, and
Titus, third Consulate."

† In the heading of Mr. Way's notice of this pig also, there is a similar slip. Instead of
"Vespasian," fifth Consulate, as given, he intended "Vespasian, seventh Consulate, and
Titus, fifth Consulate."

‡ Mr. Way, gives as the date 163—169. This is correct, as far as it relates to Verus; but
Antoninus did not take the title Armeniacus until 164, and here the epithet is applied to
both.

The date is A.D. 84—96.*

The *Ceangi* mentioned here, and also in the inscriptions on the sides of the blocks bearing nn. (5) and (6), seem to be the same as the *Cangi* of Tacitus, *Ann.* xii., 32 : *ductus in Cangos exercitus.* Different opinions have been formed relative to their position. Camden, *Gough's Edition*, i., 82, Gibson, Gough, and the author of the Index of the *Monum. Hist. Brit.* place them in Somersetshire. Camden subsequently, iii., 45, altered his opinion, and was inclined to place them in Cheshire. Thus also Latham (Smith's *Dic. Gr. and Rom. Geogr.*) regards "North Wales as a likelier locality" than Somerset. In this opinion I concur. The position suits better the description of Tacitus—*jam ventum haud procul mari quod Hiberniam insulam aspectat.* It accords also with the situation of *Cancanorum* (or *Ganganorum*) *Promontorium* of Ptolemy ; and Flint-shire, in which, and the adjoining counties of Cheshire and Denbighshire, I would place them, was probably even then noted for its lead-mines, at present the most productive in the island.

Horsley and the author of the *Index Monum. Hist. Brit.*, identify the *Cancanorum promontorium* as *Brachypull point*, in Carnarvonshire, which suggests that the *Cangi* may have occupied that county also.

As it is most probable that Domitian did not receive the title *Germanicus* until 84 A.D., we may take this date for this inscription ; and it seems a reasonable conjecture that this was one of a set of blocks prepared for transmission to Rome, with a view to being exhibited at his triumph, which took place in that year. It will be remembered that, on Domitian's accession, Agricola was pursuing his successful career in Britain, and that 84 A.D. was the year of his seventh campaign.

From what has been said it appears that there were three constructions, used in such inscriptions, viz. : the nominative, the

* Mr. Way gives as the date 81—96 ; but Domitian did not obtain the title *Germanicus* until after his reputed victory over the *Chtti*, in the close of 83 or the beginning of 84. Eckhel, *Doc. num. vet.* vi. p. 336, has sufficiently refuted the notion that Domitian assumed this title on his accession.

genitive, and the ablative. In n. (2) TI·CLAVDIVS·CAESAR·
AVG·P·M·TRIB·P·VIIII·IMP·XVI·DE·BRITAN, we
have the nominative, indicating, as I think, that the object was
taken as spoil: in n. (8) IMP·CAES·DOMITIANO·AVG·
COS·VII. we have the* ablative indicating the time, scil. from
September 13 to December 31, A.D. 81; and in n. (11) IMP·
HADRIANI·AVG· and n. (12) IMP·DVOR·AVG·AN-
TONINI ‖ ET·VERI·ARMENIACORVM we have the genitive, indicating that the blocks were† the property of those
emperors, either as the produce of mines worked for their benefit,
or, rather, as part of the imperial tribute. I have read n.
(7) IMP·DOMIT·AVG·GER·DE·CEANG· in the nomi-
native, conformably to the unquestionable construction of n. (2),
whilst I have preferred regarding nn. (5 and 6) IMP·VESP·
V̄: :T·IMP·III·COS and IMP·VESP·VII·T·IMP·V·COS
in the ablative, indicating the time, although the DE·CEANG
on their sides excited a doubt between that case and the nominative. I shall now proceed to the consideration of the doubtful
portions of the remaining inscriptions,‡ reserving for special

* Mr. Yates, in a valuable "Memoir on the mining operations of the Romans," *Proceedings of Somersetshire Arch. and Nat. Hist. Society, Taunton,* 1852, observes relative to
this inscription: "I conceive that it should be read in the ablative case, *Imperatore
Cæsare Domitiano Augusto consule septimum.* On this supposition the mine may have
been worked by private hands." The first of these remarks is unquestionably correct;
Domitiano, followed by *Cos,* VII., is certainly not in the dative. The latter is probable, as
it is questionable whether under the emperors any mines were worked except for their
benefit, or that of the individuals who rented them.

† Thus Mr. Yates, *On the mining operations, &c.,* p. 2, observes:— "The relocation of
mines by government may account for the inscription found on pigs of lead, such as IMP·
HADRIANI·AVG, in the genitive case, showing that they belonged to the Emperor. In
other instances the name of an individual, occurring in the genitive, shows that he rented
his mine from the government, e. g., L·ARVCONI·VERECVNDI. This implies that the lead
was the property of *Lucius Aruconius Verecundus.*" In article 17 I notice an inscription, having the name in the nominative, on a block, the product, as I believe, of a
rented mine.

‡ From Mr. Yates's Memoir, pp. 21, 22, 23, I learn that two pigs of the Emperor Severus,
probably imported from Britain, have been found in France, one at Lillebonne, the ancient
Julia Bona, and the other at Saussay near Chalons sur-Saone, and far from a Roman Road,
which led to the coast opposite Britain. On one of these are the inscriptions LVICVC and
DL·P. M. Canel, President of the Historical and Archæological Society of Chalons, in a
memoir on the subject, does not attempt to interpret the first of these, but infers from the
accent in the second, whereby L and P are separated, that the letters denote numbers, and
thus interprets DL·P as meaning 550 pounds in weight, P standing, as is common for
Pondo. But as this does not at all correspond with the actual weight of the pig, he "conjectures that it [*Pondo* ?] here denoted the *semis* or *half libra.*" In this way the marked,
and the actual weights agree within 2 kilogrammes and 6 hectogrammes, "the loss of which

notice n. (1) BRITANIC** AVG II, and n. (9) CAESAR
****VADON, which are imperfect, also n. (4) NERONIS
AVG·EX KIAN·IIII COS BRIT, which is unique. These
doubtful portions are (a)* LVT—in

(3) TI·CL·TR·LVT·BR·EX·ARG.
(10) IMP·CAES·HADRIANI·AVG·MET·LVT.
(14) C·IVL·PROTI·BRIT·LVT·EX·ARG·;
(a) MET·LVT·—in n. 10; (a) METAL·LVTVD·—in n.
(13) L·ARVCONI·VERECVNDI·METAL·LVTVD·;
(b) EX·ARG·—in nn. (1) and (14); (c) TR· and BR·—in
n. (3); and (d) T·M·LV· in n. (15).

(a) LVT·, MET·LVT·, METAL·LVTVD·—As these read-
ings seem to be unquestionably correct, I shall offer no criticism
on the interpretations, which have been given, of erroneous readings, such as POT· for LVT· in n. (3), MEM·L·VI for MET·
LVT in n. (10), and LVND for LVTVD in n. (13), but shall
limit my remarks to the explanations, which have been proposed,
of the readings as given above. Mr. Crane, *Archæologia*, xiii.,
405, regards LVT· in n. (3) as standing for LVTVM, and reads
the whole inscription thus: " Ti[berii] Cl[audii] tr[ibutum]
lut[um] Br[itannico] ex arg[ento]—the tribute of Tiberius
Claudius paid out of British money."

Lyson's *History of Derbyshire*, p. ccvi, traces LVT· and
LVTVD· to LVTVDARVM, the Roman Station mentioned
by *Ravennas* as next to *Derrentio*, and believed to be represented
by the modern *Chesterfield*.

Mr. Bateman, *Vestiges of the Antiquities of Derbyshire*, p. 135,
observes :—

---

may very well be ascribed to accident, waste, or abrasion." There is no authority, so far as
I am aware, for the inference from the accent, nor for the use of P or Pondo as denoting
the *semis* or *half-libra*. The accuracy of the readings seems to me very doubtful. Can it
be that the letters, given as LVICVD, are really LVT·CANG?

* Dr. Thoresen, *Historical Etimology of Britain*, p. 109, *Corn. Brit. Dec. 3*, mentions
"the inscription LVTVM EX ARGENT on various British pigs of lead of the date of
Claudius and his successors." There is no authority, so far as I am aware, for this statement: pigs have been found bearing LVT·LVT·EX·ARG·, and EX·ARGENT·, but there is
no example either of LVTVM EX ARGENT·, or of LVTVM alone.

"These inscriptions, [no. (3), (10), and (13)] have given rise to various conjectures, and accordingly to a great display of erudition; but if we allow the LVT· and the LVTVD. to be the contractions of LVTDARVM, the name of a Roman station next in order, according to Ravennas, to Derventio, or Little Chester, and which is supposed to be Chesterfield, much of the difficulty will vanish. The first [n. (10)] will then be found to bear the name of the Emperor Hadrian, in connexion with the name of the metallic district, of which it is probable that Chesterfield was then, as Wicksworth has subsequently been considered, the regulating town; hence this inscription would mean no more than that the block of lead upon which it was stamped belonged to the Emperor Cæsar Hadrian Augustus, from the metallic district of Lutudarum. The second [n. (13)] would, under a similar interpretation, be stamped with the name of its owner, a proprietor of some mines, perhaps, or a merchant, Lucius Aruconius Verecundus, with the addition, as before, of the name of the mining district. The third inscription [n. (3)] appears to mean that the lead upon which it is impressed formed part of the tribute due to Tiberius Claudius from the mines (silver or lead) of the British Lutudæ or Lutudarum. These interpretations [which were first suggested by Mr. Lysons and Mr. Crane] are by far the most conformable to custom and common sense."

The suggestion of Mr. Lysons has also been adopted by Sir Henry Ellis, *Townley Gallery*, ii., p. 290; Mr. Way, *Jour. Arch. Inst.*, 1859, p. 25; and apparently by Mr. Yates, *Mining operations*, p. 10. Mr. C. R. Smith, *Journal Arch. Assoc.*, v. p. 228, is of opinion that LUT· is a contraction of LVTVM or LVITVM, signifying *washed or purified;* and he refers in illustration to the use of *elutia* in Plin. *Hist. Nat.* xxxiv., 16, where it is applied to the washing by water of tin from the vein in the gold mines of Spain and Portugal. Mr. Wright, *Celt, Roman, and Saxon*, p. 238, adopts this opinion as undoubtedly correct.

In favour of the interpretation received by Mr. Smith and Mr. Wright, may be cited the statement of Professor Phillips, whose authority on such points is justly esteemed of high value, that "he is strongly of opinion that much of the lead ore was collected from the surface by aid of water, artificially directed. The process, in fact, is described by Pliny, in terms so exactly applicable to the modern 'hushes' of Swaledale, that no doubt can remain of this custom, which is now esteemed rude and semi-barbarous, being of Roman or earlier date in Britain."—*Ancient Metallurgy in Britain, Journal Arch. Inst.* 1859, p. 17.

As to MET· there is no difference of opinion, all agreeing in tracing it to *metallum*.

(b) EX·ARG·—These letters are found, as we have already seen, in nn. (3) and (14), and an expansion of them appears on the side of the block, n. (4), in the form EX·ARGENT. Mr. Pegge, *Archæologia*, ix., p. 45, read them *ex argent*[o], and regarded them as denoting that the *silver* had been extracted from the lead. He cites in illustration the remarks of Mr. Pennant, *Tour in Wales*, i., p. 58, but notices the difficulty that *ex argento* rather implies the extraction of lead from silver than of silver from lead. Dr. Gifford proposed *ex argent*[ario] and Sir Henry Ellis, *Townley Gallery*, ii., p. 291, suggests *ex argent*-[ariis], the sense intended by each being, I presume, the same, although the number is different, scil. from the silver mine or mines. Sir Henry Ellis remarks—"The known richness of the English lead, with which silver has been sometimes found mixed in large quantities, may serve to explain the word *ex argentariis*."

Mr. Roach Smith, *Journal of Arch. Assoc.* v., p. 228, remarks —"*Ex argent.* refers to the separation of the silver from the ore."

Mr. Wright, *Celt, Roman, and Saxon*, p. 238, observes :

"EX ARG· or EX ARGENT· is explained by a passage of Pliny, who informs us that lead ores are found under two different forms, either in veins by itself or mixed with silver. The latter had to go through a more complicated process of extraction, which is referred to by the words of the inscription—*Lutum ex argento*—and which it seems the Romano-British Metallurgist considered it necessary to specify."

In Professor Phillips's paper, "*Ancient Metallurgy in Britain*," pp. 17, 19, we find the following statement on this point :

"The Romans employed lead in pipes (*fistulæ*) and sheets, which were soldered with alloy, as already mentioned. The lead was previously refined and its silver removed ; the silver, indeed, being often the object of the enterprise."

"The mines of Middleton and Youlgreave (Aldgroove) in Derbyshire, from which the Lutudæ sent not only lead but ' exargentato' (that is to say rectified) lead from which the silver had been removed, use to this day the pig of the same weight of 1½ cwt. of similar shape and similar mark to that of eighteen hundred years' antiquity."

Mr. Yates, *Mining Operations*, p. 19, remarks :

"The letters are supposed to stand for *ex argento*, and to intimate that the lead was extracted from silver. This seems to be the true explanation, although, I think, we might read EX ARGENT]IFODINIS]. Even in the present day, we find that where the galena contains a large proportion of silver, as is frequently the case in the British Isles, the mines are not called lead mines, but silver mines. Also the litharge, which is an impure oxide of lead, formed on the surface of the melted mass during the process of refining, is called *argenti spuma* 'froth of silver,' not froth of lead. It would seem consistent with these ideas to regard the lead as extracted from silver, rather than the silver as extracted from lead, although the ore really contains a far greater proportion of lead than silver."

(c) TR·BR.—These abbreviations are found in n. 3. Mr. Pegge, reading POT· for LVT·, regarded TR· as standing for *Tr*[ibunitia] *i. e., tribunitia pot*[estate]; Mr. Crane proposed *tr*[ibutum]; Dr. Gifford, *tr*[iumviri]; Mr. Yates apparently adopts Mr. Crane's suggestion. As to BR·, Mr. Pegge regarded it as standing for *Br*[itannicus], agreeing with *Cl*-[audius]; Mr. Crane, *Br*[itannico], agreeing with *argento;* Dr. Gifford, *Br*[itannorum] governed by *argentaria;* and Sir Henry Ellis, *Br*[igantum], governed by *argentariis*, in which opinion Mr. Yates seems to concur.

(d) T·M·LV.—No explanation has yet, so far as I am aware, been offered of these *sigla:* I shall consider them in a subsequent part of this article.

As the principal opinions on the doubtful portions of the inscriptions have been stated, let us proceed to enquire to which the preference should be given, and whether any other more probable interpretation can be proposed. As to LVT·, MET· LVT·, and METAL·LVTVD·, there can, I think, be but little doubt that the explanation of Mr. Lyons is to be preferred to those offered by Mr. Crane and Mr. Smith. There is a *prima facie* probability that MET· and LVT· are shorter forms of METAL· and LVTVD· ; moreover, the blocks on which these abbreviations occur, *scil.*, those bearing no. (3), (10), (13) and

---

* I am not sure that this was the construction intended by either : perhaps R was *Lutu-dari Britannorum* and *Lutudari Brigantum, i. e*, at Lutudarum of the Britons or of the Brigantes.

F

(14), have all been found either in Derbyshire, where was the
station "*Lutudarum,*" or in its neighbourhood. *Mansfield,* about
6 miles from which n. (14) was found, is only some 12 miles
distant from *Chesterfield,* which is believed to be on or near the
site of the ancient "*Lutudarum.*" The only exception is in the
case of the four blocks bearing n. (3), which were found in Sussex,
but it may reasonably be inferred relative to these, as to other
pigs under similar circumstances, that they were on their way to
the coast for shipment to the continent, and were probably the
product of mines in Derbyshire, as one bearing the same inscription was found at Matlock in that county. And yet I am inclined
to think that LVT· and LVTVD· on the blocks were not mere
designations of locality. I strongly suspect that they both represent the Celtic term for lead or lead-ore, of which LVTVDA-
RVM was a form, signifying the place where the veins were
found and worked, *i. e.,* the lead mines. This suspicion is strengthened by the fact that we can trace this designation of the metal
in *lood* in Dutch, *loth* in German, *lod* in Danish, *lód* in Icelandic,
lal in Swedish, *lot* in Russian, **luaidh* in Gaelic, and *lced* or *lead*
in Anglo-Saxon, whence our term is derived. It also derives
some support from the remarkable omission in the inscriptions
of the ordinary Latin designation of the metal—*plumbum.*

According to this view the Latinized form of the Celtic word
may have been *lutum* or *lutudu.* When LVT· alone is used I
regard it as the substantive, but in such forms as MET·LVT.,
METAL·LVTVD· I think that it is the adjective.

But a question arises as to *Lutudarum*—in what case is it?
Is it the nominative singular of the second declension? the genitive plural of the first declension? or the genitive plural of the
third declension? Dr. Gifford and Sir Henry Ellis, when they
read LVT· in n. (3) as Lut[udari], seem to have adopted the first
opinion. Similarly Sir Henry Ellis, p. 290, reads LVTVD·
Lutudar[ense], *i. e.,* I presume, deriving this adjective from *Lu-
tudurum* as the nominative. Prof. Phillips, in the passage which
I have cited, p. 40, has adopted the second opinion, but seems to

---

* Can the combination of this and the Gaelic *aithe,* the end of a journey, be the origin of
Lutudu—Luaidhaithe, the lead station?

have mistaken *Lutudæ* for the name of a people or tribe. Mr. Yates is inconsistent on this point, for in the same page, p. 11, he says, "at Lutudarum" and "to Lutudæ," leaving it uncertain whether he adopted the first or third opinion. Similarly Mr. Bateman, p. 31, speaks in one sentence of "the metallic district of Lutudarum," and in another, the next but one, uses the terms— "the mines of the British Lutudæ or Lutudarum." Of these I prefer *Lutudæ*, the nominative plural of the first declension, and hence form *Lutudensis* as its adjective.

Let us now consider the meaning of *metallum Lutudense*, or *metalla Lutudensia.* The words admit the translations :— "Lutudian metal" and "Lutudian mines"; and "Lutudian" may define either the locality—*scil.*, at *Lutudæ*—where the lead was manufactured, or where the mines were situated, or, it may be, "Lutudian" was applied to any lead, wherever produced, that had the characteristics of that obtained (or approved) at *Lutudæ.* There is not one of these interpretations which seems to me satisfactory. I am inclined to regard the words as signifying nothing more than "lead *mine*" or "mines." As to the grammatical †construction, it is not easy to decide which should be preferred of the three that are found on the coins which mention mines. On these we have the genitive singular, as METALLI· VLPIANI and PANNONICI ; the nominative plural, as ÆLI-ANA·PINCENSIA ; and the ablative plural, as METAL· AVRELIANIS. Of these I incline to the ablative plural governed by *ex* understood, just as we have frequently on potters' work, FIG or OF, *i. e., figlina* or *officina* without the preposition. Accordingly I would translate MET·LVTVD· "from the lead mines," and LVT· or LVTVD· alone simply "lead."

Let us now take up the forms EX·ARG· and EX·ARGENT. There can, I think, be no doubt, that the *primâ facie* interpretation of *ex argento* inscribed on an object would be that that object was *made of silver*, as we have *ex arg.* in Orelli, n. 1091 ; now

---

* It is worthy of remark that neither MET· nor METAL is found on the same pig with EX·ARG or EX·ARGENT.

† In the ordinary stamps on some English manufactures, stating the names of the manufacturers or the designation of their works, there is a similar ambiguity.

this is certainly inapplicable to these pigs, for they are, I presume,
unquestionably made of lead. Adopting the same signification of
ex, we may suggest another expansion—*ex argent*[ario plumbo];
but the obvious objection to this reading, otherwise plausible, is
that the *argentarium plumbum* of Pliny was not lead but tin.

The interpretation, which would probably next present itself, is
derived, extracted from silver; and this is adopted as the true
signification by Mr. Yates, who, however, seems to prefer *argent*
[ifodinis]. It may be stated in favour of this view, and also of
the opinions that we should read *argen*' [ifodinis], *argent* [aria],
or *argent* [ariis], that as silver was probably the principal object
that the Romans sought for in these operations, they may have
called their works, " silver mines," instead of " lead mines." Mr.
Yates also suggests : " Even in the present day we find that
where the galena contains a large proportion of silver, as is frequently the case in the British Isles, the mines are not called lead
mines, but silver mines."

The interpretation of EX·ARG· and EX·ARGENT, as
denoting that the silver had been extracted from the lead, seems
more conformable to present usage. A passage in Strabo, p. 198,
ed. Falconer, Oxon. 1807, in which he notices a kind of lead found
in Spain, which contained so little silver that it was not remu-
nerative to extract it, is sufficient to prove that the ancients
were acquainted with some process for effecting this separation ;
and the same inference may be drawn from the obscure statement
in Pliny, *Hist. Nat.* xxxiv., 47, referred to by Mr. Wright :
" *Plumbi nigri origo duplex est : aut enim sua provenit vena nec
quidquam aliud parit ; aut cum argento nascitur mixtisque venis
conflatur. Ejus qui primus fluit in fornacibus liquor stannum
appellatur ; qui secundus, argentum : quod remansit in fornacibus galena, quæ est tertia portio additæ venæ. Hæc rursus
conflata dat* nigrum plumbum *de luctis partibus duabus.*

If these words be taken in their apparent sense, it is evident
that Pliny has made statements on the subject which are wholly
at variance with modern mineralogy and metallurgy. No ore is
known to exist in any part of the world, which at one smelting
process would yield successively *stannum, argentum,* and *galena.*

The only satisfactory explanation of the passage seems to be that suggested by Kopp, *Geschichte der Chemie*, iv., 127, that three different smeltings are referred to, *scil.*, melting out the argentiferous lead, removal of lead by oxidation, and reduction of the so formed litharge or oxide of lead.

But if this reading and interpretation of EX·ARGENT· be adopted, what is the grammatical construction ? It is impossible that the words *ex argento*, if regarded as complete, can express "the silver being extracted," or that the lead was, as Prof. Phillips calls it, "exargentate." The only grammatical explanation which seems at all probable is to regard EX as an abbreviation of the participle of some compound verb, such as *excoquo*, and the construction as that of the ablative absolute, *scil.*, *ex*[cocto] *argent*[o].

After the best consideration that I have been able to give to this perplexing phrase, I am disposed to prefer *ex argent* [aria] (*scil.*, *vena* or *fodina*), or the equivalent *argent* [ifodina], but in the sense that the marks EX·ARG· or ARGENT· indicated that those blocks, on which they were inscribed, were the product of a mine of argentiferous lead—that they were made from a vein which had been found to yield silver, and consequently that these marks were a sort of guarantee that the blocks which bore them contained the precious metal in combination with the lead of which they were composed. The grounds of this interpretation are that as the Romans were acquainted with a process for extracting silver from lead, the blocks of lead would command a higher price, if they were known to contain silver—and that British lead varies so much in this respect, some veins, as in Derbyshire and elsewhere, containing but a trace, that it was necessary to use such distinctive marks, in order to enhance the market value. But we have yet to consider TR·BR· and T·M· LV. As there is but one example of each of these abbreviations—*scil.*, n. (3) and n. 17—we shall take up the inscriptions themselves.

TI·CL·TR·LVT·BR·EX·ARG·

---

* And yet *excoctum argentum* is used in the sense—refined silver.

Another conjecture has occurred to me relative to EX·ARG·, that it may be connected with the provincial *denciter dieri of argenti*. See *Mommsen, Inscrip., Neapol.*, n. 8540.

The following readings having been proposed:— *Ti*[berii *Cl*[audii] *Tr*[ibutum] *Lut*[um] *Br*[tannico] *ex ar*[gento], by the Rev. T. Crane; *Ti*[berii] *Cl*[audiani] *Lut*[udari] *Br*[ituunorum] *ex arg* [entaria], by Dr. Gifford; and *Ti*[berii] *Cl*[audiani] *Tr*[iumviri] *Lut*[udari] *Br*[igantum] *ex arg*[entariis], by Sir Henry Ellis.[*] The first question which presents itself here is, does this inscrip tion refer to the Emperor Claudius? I must confess that I have doubts on this point. [†]The absence of any title whatever in this case, whilst in every other instance in which an Emperor is named, we always have some one or other, suggests the suspicion, that the reference to the Emperor Claudius is erroneous, and that TI. CL. TR. are the initials of some private individual, such as those named in nn. (13) and (14).

We have an example of similar abbreviations on the medicine stamp found at Wroxeter in 1808. According to Mr. Wright's readings, *Celt, Roman, and Saxon*, 2nd ed., p. 249, the name of the empiric who prepared it, was TIB·CL·M·, *i. e.*, *Ti*[berii] *Cl*[audii] *M*[edici], but both his readings and expansion seem very doubtful. In the *Celt, Roman, and Saxon*, 1st ed., p. 244, he read IBCLM, and thus Mr. Way and Dr Simpson, the latter of whom proposes the expansion *J*[ulii] *B*[assi] *C L*[o]=[cutis]. Similarly also we find the abbreviations of names on potters' work, in Fabretti, p. 503, and Orelli, ii., p. 372. It is of course impossible to surmise for what *cognomen*, according to this sup position, TR· stands, but it may have been such as *Tr*[ophimus] or *Tr*[ajanus] of which we have examples with *Ti*[berius] *Cl*[audius]. And yet n. (15), IMP·CAES·HADRIANI· AVG·T·M·LV, favours the interpretation of TR· as *tributum*, for I know no more probable expansion of T. As to M·LV· there can, I think, be but little doubt that these letters stand for MET·LVT as in n (10).

On comparing nn. (3) and (14) a difference of order—LVT·BR· and BRIT·LVT·—is observable, but this is, I think, nothing more than the variety of collocation of the adjective, which is often found. It, however, proves that Mr. Crane's construction Br[itannico] agreeing with ar[gento] is erroneous.

I would read nn. (3), (14) and (15) thus :—

Ti[berii] Cl[audii] Tr[****]+Lut[**] Br[itannicum] ex arg [entaria];

C[aii] Jul[ii] Proti Brit[annicum] +Lut[**] ex arg[entaria].

Imp[eratoris] Caes[aris] Hadriani Aug[usti] t[ributum] m[etallis] Lu[tudensibus].

In the first two I regard LVT·BR and BRIT·LVT· as meaning " British lead." There may, of course, be either construction —the nominative, or the ablative governed by ex understood. The third I interpret as signifying that it was one of those that belonged to Hadrian as ‡tribute from the lead mines. According to my view the blocks of lead manufactured by proprietors of mines were stamped either with their own names or with those of the reigning emperor—the former being for sale, the latter belonging to the *fiscus* as tribute or as a royalty.

We may now proceed to nn. (10) and (13).

IMP· CAES· HADRIANI· AVG· MET· LVT·

Imp[eratoris] Cae[saris] Hadriani Aug[usti] [Met[allis] Lut-[udensibus.]

L· ARVCONI· VERECVNDI· METAL· LVTVD·

L[ucii] Aruconi[i] Verecundi Metal[lis] Lutud[ensibus].

The second of them I interpret as denoting that the block was from the lead mines owned or rented by Lucius Aruconius Vere-

---

† I have given asterisks for the termination, as I am not sure what it was in the Latinised form. The name Br[itannicum] is equally uncertain.

‡ I am aware of the difference between *tributum* and *vectigal*, and yet offer this interpretation. The distinction is not always observed, and *tributum* seems more suitable to the circumstances of Britain at the time.

cuinlus. The first may mean that the block was either from the mines worked for the benefit of the emperor Hadrian or belonged to him as tribute or royalty. I prefer the latter.

Mr. Yates, p. 11, remarks : " Aruconius appears to be a name of British origin. Perhaps this Lucius had removed to Lutudar from Ariconium, the modern Weston in Herefordshire, and an important mining station of the Romans." If there be any connexion between *Aruconius* and *Ariconium*, it seems more probable that the name of the place was derived from the name of the person than *v. v.*

Nn. (1) and (9) remain for consideration before we proceed to n. (4).

*(1) BRITANNIC**AVG II.

Mr. Way, who was the first that noticed this pig, refers the inscription to Britannicus, the son of Claudius, and assigns the "date about A.D. 41–48." In confirmation of this reference it is stated by Mr. Way that "Mr. Franks, [who had opportunities of examining the block in the British Museum] informed him that the inscription may be read BRITANNIC :: :: :: AVG F:: (Augusti filius)." Mr. Yates, p. 17, remarks : "On examining the object itself, I was satisfied that the last letters are FIL, which is the reading adopted by Mr. Roach Smith, and not II or IMP*, as other antiquaries have supposed. Hence, I conclude that the inscription, which is of unusual historical interest, may be thus restored :

BRITANNICI CLAVDII AVGVSTI FILII."

As the wood-cut, illustrating Mr. Way's remarks, presents II · after AVG ·, I have so represented these letters in the copy which I have given, but I concur in Mr. Yates's reading and expansion.

It seems probable to me that this block was prepared at the same time as n. (2), and with a similar object—to grace the ceremonies in honour of the enlargement of the *pomœrium*.

---

* On the side of this pig are the letters V·EI·C cc, as they are otherwise read, V·EIP·C or V·FTP·C, which, Mr. Way observes, probably denote its weight. The only ground for this opinion seems to be the occurrence of P. which may stand for *Pondo*. I at one time doubted whether they might not be a misreading for V·EID·O, marking the time, *scil.*, *quinto idus Idus Octobres*; but I am now inclined to regard them as the manufacturers' marks, as we have EIPC on the handle of an amphora. See Wright's *Celt, Roman, and Saxon*, p. 473.

N. (9) CAESAR*****VADON.

Mr. Smith, *Journal of Archæol. Assoc.*, v., p. 558, observes :

"Unfortunately the inscription, which originally had been well cut, has so perished from oxidation, that its restoration cannot with safety be proposed, especially as it exhibits a reading different from those of a similar description, which are yet preserved or on record. Camden mentions, that several of these pigs of lead had been found in Cheshire, inscribed IMP· DOMIT·AVG·GER·DE·CEANG·, and IMP·CAES·DOMITIAN·AVG·COS· VII·BRIG· One similar to the latter of these was found, in the last century, at Hayshaw Moor, in Yorkshire, and one on Hints Moor, near Tamworth, reading IMP·VESP·VII·T·IMP·V·COS·DE·CEANG· The specimen [bearing CAESAR*****VADON] was most probably inscribed to Domitian."

Mr. Smith justly regarded the restoration of the fragment as hazardous. In addition to its imperfection, it has peculiarities which are not found in the other extant inscriptions on pigs of lead. But there are no grounds, so far as I can see, for his reference of it to Domitian. The absence of IMP· and AVG· would certainly suit his position at one period of his life, but it is impossible to make out his name from the extant letters. DO are the first two letters, but they are followed by a form which seems necessarily to be either N. or VA.* I have myself nothing further to suggest than that it is possible that the last word may have been DOVA, another form of DEVA.

We now proceed to n. (4), the inscription on the block represented in the subjoined †wood-cut.

(Weight nearly 156 lbs ; upper, or larger, surface, 21 in. by 5 in. ; inscribed surface, 21 in. by 8½ in. ; thickness, 5 in.)

---

* In the original, the transverse line is not in the same position as in N, but connects the other extremities of the perpendiculars, i. e., as if it were VA ligulate, without the bar of the A.

† Copied from a wood-cut, in *Journal Arch. Assoc.*, vol. v., illustrating an article, by Mr. C. Roach Smith, which contains much valuable information relative to these blocks.

G

In *the Journal of the Archæological Association*, v., p. 227, Mr. C. Roach Smith offers the following remarks on it :—

" It is inscribed on the top, in letters an inch in length, NERONIS·AVG· EX·RIAN·IIII COS·DRIT·; on one side ΠVLPMCOS·; on the other EX· ARGENT· and CAPASCAS·; with the numerals XXX. This inscription is peculiarly interesting as referring to the Cangi at an earlier date [than on the pigs of the time of Vespasian and Domitian, A.W.] the name being spelt as pronounced, *Kiangi*, and just previous to the reverses of the Romans in Britain, from the courage and skill of the heroic Boadicea. Nero was the fourth time Consul the year before; and this pig of lead would seem to have been on its way from the country of the Cangi towards the south, for exportation, composing probably part of the tribu e, the harsh exaction of which was one of the causes of the insurrection. The *Brit.* must be considered as referring to the metal or the province, and not intended for *Britannicus*, as before observed on the *Br.* in the inscription of Claudius. The lateral marks are not altogether [at all?] to be satisfactorily explained, except the *ex argent.*, which occurs in other instances and refers to the separation of the silver from the ore."

In Mr. Wright's *Celt, Roman, and Saxon*, p. 237, we have an additional observation by Mr. Smith on this inscription :

" As Nero never assumed the title of Britannicus, and as the numerals precede the *cos*, I suspect the inscription should be read —

(Plumbum or Metallum) Neronis Ang. cos, IIII. Ex. Kian. Brit.

The P·M·Cos· may belong to the above, and the rest to the name of some superintendent."

The obscurity of this singular inscription fully justified Mr. Smith's resort to conjecture, and the suggestions which he offers are, as is usual with him, worthy of consideration. But the tone of his remarks is likely to mislead; and perhaps did mislead Mr. Yates, when he regarded this inscription as "evidently referring to the Ceangi." Mr. Smith says that "this inscription is peculiarly interesting as referring to the Cangi at an earlier date, the name being spelt as pronounced, *Kiangi*." Now this statement, as to pronunciation and orthography at an earlier date, is wholly conjectural, without any authority to support it.

Nor is the suggested transposition of *ex Kian.* and iiii *cos* warranted by precedent, or at all probable. Moreover a very strong objection to Mr. Smith's reading is derived from the difference of the propositions. In other blocks where the *Ceangi* are named we have the proposition *de*, whilst here we have *ex*. Again, in these other blocks we have *Ceang.*, but here K is substituted for C, *i* for *e*, and *g* is omitted.

But if we give up the reading *ex Kiangis*, what solution is there of the difficulty? The only conjecture which I can offer on the subject is, that the words EX·KIAN express a date, *scil.*, EX·K[ALENDIS] IAN[VARIIS].

It is scarcely necessary to say, that there are examples of K·IAN· being used for *Kalendis Januariis*; and the only enquiry which seems necessary, relative to this reading, is as to the reason of the date being stated in the inscription.

We know from Pliny, xxxiv., ch. 17, that there was a law prohibiting more than a limited production of lead in Britain—*ne plus cer'o modo fiat*—and it seems probable that with a view to this law, the blocks, at least in some reigns, bore marks of the time at which they were made, so that it might be known what blocks were manufactured, and consequently what quantity of lead was produced during the year. The mention of the consuls, or not unfrequently of one, especially the Emperor, was, as is well known, the recognised mode among the Romans of distinguishing the year. But it may be asked—why mention *Kalendis Januariis* when that day was commonly known to be the first of the consular year? To this it may be answered that it was not uncommon for the Emperors to enter on the consulship at different periods of the year, and hence it may have been necessary to specify in this case the date of the commencement of the Emperor's fourth consulship. Another reason, peculiar to Nero, for this specification, may be, that it conveyed a flattering reference to his having rejected the proposition of the Senate, that the year should begin with the month of December. Tacitus, *Ann.* xiii., 10, notices this fact:—*Quanquam censuissent patres ut principium anni inciperet mense Decembri, quo ortus erat, veterem religionem Kalendarum Januariarum inchoando anno retinuit.*" But there is another and simpler solution, which I shall offer after the consideration of the lateral inscription.

Such forms as $\overline{\text{IIII}} \cdot \text{COS} \cdot$, instead of $\text{COS} \cdot \overline{\text{IIII}} \cdot$ —a transposition which Mr. Smith notices—are rare : but both forms seem to have been used. In Henzen, n. 6770, we have :—DOMIT·IANO·$\overline{\text{II}}$·COS·, VESPAS·$\overline{\text{X}}$.COS·, DOMIT·$\overline{\text{VIIII}}$·COS·, DOMIT·$\overline{\text{XIIII}}$·COS·, NERVA·$\overline{\text{II}}$·COS. It may, however, be inferred, as I think, when the numeral is placed before instead of after COS·, that the date of the inscription is not during but after the expiration of the consulship.

BRIT· I regard as standing for BRIT[ANNICVM], as is common, and agreeing with *lutum* understood. The pig was, most probably, thus marked to distinguish it as the product of Britain, from others manufactured elsewhere, as in Spain.

We now proceed to consider the lateral inscriptions. Mr Smith reads these marks as HULPMCOS· on one side, and EX ARGENT· and CAPASCAS· with the numerals XXX on the other ; and thus they were also read by the writer in the *Gentleman's Magazine*, liii., p. 936. In the *Monum. Hist. Brit.* they are given :—

HUL P M CO, EX ARGE N
       CAPA OC? IV
           XXX

and from the wood-cut it seems probable that some letters are effaced before IVLPMCOS. In such uncertainty regarding the true readings, it might, perhaps, be more judicious for me to follow Mr. Smith's example in the *Journal*, and leave them as I found them. But as in such cases even an attempt may be useful, I venture to offer some suggestions. From IVI. and COS·, I draw the conjecture, that there may be a reference to the circumstance, that Nero held his fourth consulship only for six months. His colleague in that year (A.D. 60) was Cornelius Lentulus, and in their places Vellaius Paterculus and Pedanius Salinator were *suffecti* on the Calends of July. See Borghesi, *Bull. Inst. Archæol.* 1846, p. 174, and Henzen, 5407. This conjecture leads to another, that the date mentioned here indi-

cates the end, as *ex Kalendis Januariis* denoted the beginning
of the period during which the set of pigs, of which this was one,
were manfactured. Thus in *Mommsen., Inscrip. Neopol.,* n. 697,
we have the time marked by the consuls and EX K·IAN·
AD·K·IVL. But what of PM? It is plain that the ordinary interpretation of these *notæ* as *pontifex maximus* is inapplicable here, and that we must look for some other more
appropriate expansion. They may, possibly, stand for *posuit
modum,* in the sense of "put an end to," "gave up," and COS for
consulatui; but I do not recollect having met with a similar
form. Or perhaps, P·M·COS· may stand for *post mensem consul-
atum,* and the phrase may have been used in accordance with the
ordinary *ante diem (tertium, &c.,) Kalendas, &c.,* where *ante*
governs *Kalendas,* and *diem* is placed in the accusative, although
the context would sometimes require a different case. As to
CAPASCAS—if that be the true reading—the only conjecture
which I can offer, is that it is possible that CAPAS—of which
C·AS may be a repetition in a shorter form—may be for CAPI-
TARIVS AS, *scil.,* as for *tributum, i. e.,* the capitation tax.
It is scarcely necessary to say that the *tributum* was of three
kinds : *secundum capita, secundum censum,* and *extra ordinem.*

On the whole, I am inclined to suggest as the most probable
reading of the principal inscription :—

NERONIS AVG[VSTI] EX K[ALENDIS] IAN[VARIIS]
QVARTVM CO[N]S[VLIS] BRIT[ANNICVM]

whilst it seems not improbable that the lateral inscription
IVLPMCOS may stand for IVL[IAS] P[OST][M]ENSEM
CO[N]S[VLATVM], some such form as K or N or I being lost
before IVLIAS ; and it is possible that CAPASCAS may denote
that the block was one of those prepared in payment of the capitation tax, and XXX may mark the number of the pig. If the
views which I have suggested relative to these obscure inscriptions be adopted, the simplest explanation of the statement of the
time—from the first of January to the —— of July—seems to
be, that it denotes the period for which the imperial tribute
was paid by the set of pigs, of which this was one.

P.S.—To these remarks on the pigs of lead found in Britain, I subjoin some observations on one which, although it was not found in the island, bears an inscription of so great interest as to justify my noticing it.

In 1848, Lord Palmerston presented to the British Museum a pig of lead found at Carthagena in Spain, which bears the following inscription :

M·P·ROSCIEIS·M·F·MAIC.

This inscription is identical with that on the block in the collection of antiquities at the Bibliothèque Impériale at Paris, which was also found in Spain. Mr. Way, *Journal of the Archæological Institute*, 1859, notices a reading *in extenso* suggested by Mr. Newton, *scil.*, *Marcus Publius Roscius, Marci filius, Mæcia [tribu]*. This does not appear to me satisfactory. On comparing it with Henzen's n. 5733, beginning M·P·VERTV-LEIEIS·C·F·, I am inclined to regard ROSCIEIS as an archaic form of the nominative plural, *Roscii*—M·P· as standing for *Marcus et Publius*—and M·F for *Marci filii*. MAEC· may be an abbreviation of MAECII, for we know that *Mæcius* was amongst the names borne by members of the Roscian *gens*, *e. gr.*, Orelli, n. 4952 :

L·ROSCIO·M·F·QVI
AELIANO·MAECIO
CELERI.

But I prefer Mr. Newton's MAEC[IA] *tribu*. Thus we have in Fabretti, p. 240.

L·RVSTICELLIVS·C·SCA [*i. e., Scaptia tribu*]
M·CVSINIVS·M·F·VEL [*i. e., Velina tribu*].

The omission of the cognomen is an evidence of rare antiquity in Latin epigraphy, and the same is indicated by the termination *eis*.

Henzen, (in a paper on the inscription, n. 5733, published in *Bulletin dell' Institut. di Correspond. Arch.* Rome, 1845, and translated by Mr. Key, in *Proceedings of Philological Society*, vi., p. 179) states that he has not met with this form of the nominative plural of the 2nd declension at a later date than about the middle of the seventh century of the city, i. e., about 100 years B. C. Hence we may infer the probable age of the block as about 2000 years, in round numbers.

It may be worth while to observe, that the omission of *et* between the *pronomina* of brothers is not uncommon. We have an example in Henzen, n. 5733,—M·P·VERTVLEIEIS,—i. e, as we express it, *Marcus* and *Publius Vertuleius.* In Orelli, n. 3121, there is a similar form—Q·M·MINVCIEIS Q·F·RVF· i. e., *Quintus* et *Marcus Minucii, Quinti filii, Rufi,* or as we express it, *Quintus* and *Marcus Minucius Rufus, sons of Quintus.*

The inscription on the block I regard as showing that it was from the mines rented by the two Roscii. It is possible that they may have been public officers, but we should then probably have had their official designation.

DURHAM.

---

§ 17. In Horsley's *Britannia Romana*, Durham nn. xi and xii, we have copies of two inscriptions on stones found at *Lanchester :—

(XI.)

```
IMP·CÆS·M·ANT·GORDIA·
NVS·P·F·AVG·BALNEVM·CVM
BASILICA A SOLO INSTRVXIT
PREGNLVCILIANVM·LEG·AVG
PR·PR·CVRANTE·M·AVR
QVIRINO PRE COHLGOR
```

(XII.)

```
IMP·CÆSAR·M·ANTONIVS
GORDIANVS·P·F·AVG
PRINCIPIA ET ARMAMEN
TARIA CONLAPSA RESTITV
IT PER MAECILIVM FVSCVM·LEG
AVG·PR·PR·CVRANTE·M·AVR
QVIRINO PR·COH I·L·GOR.
```

Horsley reads and expands them thus :

(XI.)

"Imperator Cæsar Marcus Antonius Gordianus pius felix Augustus balneum cum basilica a solo instruxit per Oncium Lucilianum legatum Augustalem propraetorem curante Marco Aurelio Quirino praefecto cohortis primae legionis Gordianae."

"Imperator Cæsar Marcus Antonius Gordianus pius felix, Augustus principia et armamentaria conlapsa restituit per Macci-

---

* Horsley regarded this as the *Glana Dewis* of the *Notitia* and the *Glanoventa* of the *Itinerary*; Camden and the Rev. John Hodgson believed it to be the *Longovicus* of the *Notitia*; others identify it with the *Epiacum* of Ptolemy.

lium Fuscum legatum Augustalem propraetorem curante Marco
Aurelio Quirino praefecto cohortis primae legionis Gordianae."

The points obviously open to objection, in these readings and
expansions, are *Gneium Lucilianum*, in n. xi., and *Cohortis primæ
legionis Gordianæ* in both. Instead of " *Gneium*," we should
read *Egnatium*, as proposed by Mr. Ward, and established by
an inscription on an *altar found at High Rochester, in which
the name of *Lucilianus* is given as EGNAT. In the rendering
cohortis primæ legionis Gordianæ, the absence of the number of
the legion at once suggests doubt, and this is strengthened by
the consideration that there is no evidence that any legion, known
to have been quartered in Britain, bore the title *Gordiana*.

As to Mr. Gale's conjecture, that the "legion here called
Gordiana was the *legio sexta victrix*," there is no other ground
than that " the stated quarters [of that legion] were at York,
whilst the other legions had theirs at a much greater distance."
Mr. Smith, *Collect. Antiq.* iv., p. 142, with equally little reason,
refers the inscriptions to "the twentieth legion, apparently the
legio Gordiana."

An examination of the words preceding *legionis Gordianæ*, scil.,
praefectus cohortis, suggests fresh doubt, for there is no authority
for a *praefect* of a legionary cohort, whilst the term is an usual
designation of the commander of an auxiliary cohort. Moreover,
the order of the words—*cohortis legionis*, and not *legionis cohortis*
—is so unusual, if not unprecedented, as in itself to cause dissatis-
faction. Influenced, probably, by these considerations, Henzen,
n. 6626, rejects the expansion—*legionis Gordianæ*—although
accepted by Orelli, n. 975, and suggests *Ligurum*, or *Ligurum
Gordianæ*; but neither of these readings appears to me probable.

I interpret COII·I·L·GOR· as *cohortis primæ †Lingonum
Gordianæ*. We know that there were three, probably four,
cohorts of the Lingones in Britain. Trajan's *tabulæ* inform us

---

* Bruce, *Roman Wall*, 2nd ed., p. 457.

† I do not recollect having seen a similar use of the first letter of the ethnic name of a
cohort; but in this case no confusion could arise, for, so far as we have evidence, there was
no other corps, that served in Britain, whose initial letter was L.

H

that the fourth* was serving in Britain in A.D. 104, and the first
in A.D. 105–106 ; whilst Hadrian's diploma notices the second
in A.D. 124. According to the *Notitia*, the second was stationed
at *Congavata* ; and the fourth at *Segedunum*, near which an
taltar has been found, erected by a Præfect of that corps.

Horsley, *Durham*, xv. gives the following inscription (on a
stone also found at Lanchester), which Dr. Bruce, *Roman Wall*,
p. 461, regards as mentioning the first, not the second, cohort of
the Lingones :—

> GENIO PRAETORI
> CL EPAPHRODITVS
> CLAVDIANVS
> TRIBVNVS CHO
> I LING VLPM

i. e., Genio‡ Prætorii Claudius Epaphroditus Claudianus§ Tribunus cohortis primæ Lingonum votum libens posuit merito.

Dr. Bruce, p. 460, figures a slab, found at High Rochester,
which bears the inscription :—

> IMP·CAES·T·AELIO
> HAD·ANTONINO·AVG·PIO PP
> SVB Q LOL VRBICO
> LEG·AVG PRO PRAE
> COH T LING
> E Q F

Dr. Bruce gives *equitum* as the expansion of EQ ; but the
letters evidently stand for *equitata*—a contraction, of which there

---

* It appears that there is a difference in the number of the cohort between the outer and
inner inscriptions of this diploma. The latter, it is stated, gives IIII and the former III.
It is not easy to decide which is the correct number. Gamers, Henzen, and Böcking
prefer III.

† Bruce, *Roman Wall*, 2nd ed., p. 88.

‡ Horsley strangely interprets—Genius the prætor ; and the author of the Index to the
Inscriptions in *Mon. sm. Hist. Brit.* gives "Genius prætor!" There can be no doubt that
prætorii is correct.

§ Camden and Horsley regarded the cohort, which is named here, as the second, but I
prefer Dr. Bruce's opinion. An objection to my reading—*Præfectus cohortis primæ Lingonum Gordiana*—may be drawn by some from the designation of the commanding officer

are many examples,* and which, in this particular case, is established by the following inscription in Fabretti, p. 486 :—

C·CAESIDIO
C·F·CRV·DEXTRO
EQ·COII·VIII·PRAET
COII·I·LINGONVM
EQVITAT· &c.

Camden gives an inscription, found at Moresby in Cumberland, which mentioned the second cohort—and it is believed that the same corps was noticed in two inscriptions, Horsley's, nn. xiii. and xiv., found at Ilkley in Yorkshire. One of those is so remarkable, that it deserves special notice, and I shall therefore consider it in a separate article. But to return to the Lanchester inscriptions—an obvious suggestion relative to L·GOR is, that it may be a misreading of LINGON· ; but we may not disregard the leaf-stops in n. xii., after COII, I, and L.

There remains but one other point requiring notice—the use of the word principia, of which I have never seen any other example except on a stone found near Bath, on which the letters between PR and PIA are illegible. See my notes on inscriptions found in Somersetshire. Mr. Gale regarded the principia as "either the quarters of the legionary soldiers called the principes, or the place where the ensigns were kept;" whilst Mr. Horsley "rather concludes it to be the General's pavilion." Dr. Bruce interprets the term as denoting "the chief military quarters," or "officers' barracks."

Mr. Smith, *Collect. Antiq.* iv., p. 149, observes :

"The *principia* mentioned in the inscription, it need scarcely be observed, means the quarters of the chief officers, and place of deposit of the standards. The word occurs in an inscription of the time of Elagabalus [?] lately dug up near Bath, and published in the *Journal* of the Archæological Institute."

---

being here *tribunus*, not *præfectus*: but there is no doubt that both terms are applied to the commanding officer of the same auxiliary cohort. In the *Notitia*, the second and fourth of the Lingones are each under a *tribunus*, whilst it appears, from inscriptions on stones found in Britain, that they were each under a *præfectus*.

* In Horsley's *Britannia Romana, Cumberland*, xxi, we have the same mistake. He reads T·O·L·S·EQ *primæ Hispanorum equitum.; it should be *primæ Hispanorum equitum*. In *Cumberland*, liii, and in *Northumberland*, lxxxviii, his reading is *Gallorum equitum*, instead of *Gallorum equites*.

Mr. Smith doubtless inferred the meaning of the word *principia*, as found in the Lanchester and Bath inscriptions, from its signification, when applied to a place in a camp. But there is no authority, so far as I am aware, either in *ancient authors or in inscriptions, whereby this or any other interpretation of the term, as applied to a *building*, can be confirmed.

P.S.—Since the foregoing was in type, I have observed in Henzen's Index, "Coh. I. Lingonum Gordiana," with the reference to Orelli's n. 975=Horsley's *Durham*, n. xii, but it does not appear whether this statement was made through inadvertence or with the intention of correcting the opinion expressed in n. 6626.

§ 18. In the *Archæologia Æliana*, i., p. 142, a sepulchral stone, found near †*Binchester*, is figured. It bears the inscription :

D   M   S
NEMMONTANVS DEC
VIXITANN·XL·NEM
SANCTVSFR·ET·COHERE
EX TESTAMENTO FECERT

Mr. Skene expanded it thus :

" Diis Manibus Sacrum. Nemmontanus Decius vixit annos quadraginta ; Nemmontanus Sanctus frater et cohoredes ex testamento fecerunt." Instead of *Nemmontanus Decius* I would read *Nem*[esius] *Montanus Dec*[urio], and instead of *Nemmontanus Sanctus*, *Nem*[esius] *Sanctus*. *Decurio*, as the designation of a military officer, signified the commander of a *turma*, or, as we may call it, *a troop* of cavalry. It also was used as the designation of a municipal officer. We have examples of both uses in the inscriptions found in Britain.

In Horsley, *Brit. Rom.*, p. 305, we have DEC·AL·AST, *i. e.*,

---

* There is a passage in Tacitus, *Hist.* 3., 43, which at first sight seems to supply an example. The words are—*primani strata sanctissimacorum principis aquilam obstulere*. Plutarch, however, translates it as it is understood by commentators—τῶν πρωτάγων ἀνατειλαντες. See Sallust, *Jugurtha*, 54; Livy, 5., 55, 18., 22.

† The Vinovium of Antoninus.

decurio alæ Asturum. In his n. iii., *Somersetshire*, he finds a *decurio equitum*, who was also a *miles leg·xx·v·v*, but this reading is unquestionably erroneous. See my notes on inscriptions found in *Somersetshire*.

Dr. Bruce, *Roman Wall*, 2nd ed., p. 398, figures an inscribed altar, on which DEC. also occurs:

DIS
MOVNTI
BVSIVL
FIRMIN
VSDECE.

Dr. Bruce remarks "The inscription reads—'To the gods of the *mountains, Julius Firminus, the decurion, erected this.'" In this, as in the preceding inscription, it is uncertain whether *decurio* is used in the municipal or in the military sense. Dr. Bruce understands it in the latter, but the observation in his note does not give a correct impression as to the use of the term in the age in which it is probable that the inscription was cut. His observation is—"Decurion, a commander of a troop of ten men." This originally was the sense of *decurio*, and there were three officers so designated in each *turma*. See Polybius, vi., 25. But between the times of Augustus and Hadrian, it began to be used for the commander of each *turma*, consisting of three decuries. The officers under him in the troop were the *duplicarius* and the *sesquiplicarius*. See Lange, *Hist. mut. rei milit. Rom.*, p. 36. In the *Journal of the Arch. Institute*, 1860, we find the word in its municipal sense in one of the Lincoln inscriptions—AVR·SENECIO·DEC· Thus, also, in Horsley's n. v., *Somersetshire*,—DEC·COLONIÆ·GLEV.

* The rendering of *Dis montibus*, as "the gods of the mountains," or "the gods the mountains," seems to me very questionable. There is no doubt that mountains were worshipped as gods, e.gr., Orelli, n. 2107, but I do not recollect having ever seen an example of the spelling—*montibus*. I suspect that the true reading is *monentibus*. Firminus erected the altar *ex monitu deorum*, but did not know who the gods were that directed him. There are many examples of altars erected to unknown deities, such as those bearing the inscription, *sive deus sive dea*. Of the same class, in my opinion, was that noticed in the *Acts of the Apostles*, xvii., 23, inscribed ΑΓΝΩΣΤΩΙ ΘΕΩΙ.

---

§ 19. Mr. Wright, *Celt, Roman, and Saxon*, p. 252, *remarks relative to †Cirencester in this county :

"Uriconium (*Wroxeter*) appears to have been occupied by Thracians : Cirencester by Thracians and Indians."

There is no doubt that an inscription has been found at each of those places, which furnishes evidence that a horseman of a Thracian cohort was buried in each, but there is no ground for the assertion that there were "Indians" at Cirencester. An inscription, indeed, was found there, commemorating *Dannicius* (or *Dannicus*), a horseman *ala Indiana* ; but this body did not derive its name from the nationality of the men composing it. It was probably called after *Julius Indus*, mentioned in *Tacit. Ann.*, iii., 42 ; and there is reason to believe that the men serving in it were, for the most part, *Treviri.* The *alæ* seem to have received such ‡designations as *Indiana, Frontoniana, Sebosiana*, from the names of the officers who first raised or organized them, and in this respect resembled the military bodies in our own service in the East Indies, known by such names as "Jacob's," or "Hodgson's Horse."

§ 20. The discovery of inscribed stones has made a large addition to the number of the deities in the ancient Pantheon. Besides those noticed in Gruter's great work, Spon made a collection of inscriptions on altars *ignotorum atque obscurorum quorundam deorum ;* and in DeWal's *Mythologiæ Septentrionalis monumenta epigraphica Latina*, we have notices of most of the northern deities, who were known up to the time of the publica-

---

* In the 2nd ed., p. 254, Mr. Wright gives the following modification of this remark— " Cirencester appears to have been occupied by Thracians."

‡ Horsley identifies it with Ptolemy's *Coriniam* and the *Durocornovium* of Antoninus.

‡ *Vide* Hensen, nn. 5412 and 6721; also Roulez, *Mem. de l'Acad. Royale de Belgique* xxvii., p. 12.

tion of the volume in 1847, but no complete list has yet been published. Horsley furnishes an index of "names and attributes of deities," but it is limited to those mentioned in the inscriptions found in Britain which are given in his work, and is not without mistakes, e. gr., "bono generis humani," "genio Romæ." Mr. Roach Smith, *Collectanea Antiqua*, ii., p. 200, introduces a list of the "names of deities occurring in dedicatory inscriptions found on the line of the wall, including some from the Antonine wall," but it also is incomplete and requires emendation, e. gr., "Apollini Granio," "Heroi." In the *Monumenta Historica Britannica* there is an Index—"Deorum dearum et rerum sacrarum nomina quibus templa vel altaria dicata erant in Britannia," —but this is, of course, very limited, relating, merely, to the preceding selection of inscriptions, and is strangely inaccurate—e. gr., "Deæ Melvisiæ," "Nehallenia," "Dea Vagdavera," who are not named in any inscription found in Britain, nor is there any evidence that they had any temple or altar dedicated to them in the island. The most comprehensive catalogue, of which I am aware, is to be found in Hanzen's *Index* to Orelli's Inscriptions, vol. iii., but even it, although very carefully prepared, and giving information up to 1856, is defective. There are some deities, named in inscriptions found in Britain, that are not mentioned in it. Amongst these is a god, whose name appears in three inscriptions found on the site of a Roman villa at Lydney (or Lidney), in this county. The name in one is NODONTI, in the dative case; in another NVDENTE, which seems to be used for NVDENTI in the dative case; and in the third, NODENTI, also in the dative case, and NODENTIS in the genitive case. The only *explanation which I have seen relative to this deity, is contained in "The Romans in Gloucestershire," a Lecture by the Rev. Samuel Lysons, M. A., London, 1860. Mr. L. regards the name of the deity as NODONS or NODENS, and identifies him with Æsculapius, on the following grounds :

"The remains of a very considerable Roman building was discovered on an eminence in Lidney Park, on the forest side of our county, and carefully explored by the late Right Hon. Charles Bragge Bathurst. A very good

---

* The inscriptions are, I believe, given in Lysons' *Reliquia*, but I am not able to consult that work.

series of interesting coins was thus discovered, which is, I believe, still in possession of the present proprietor: but what adds great interest to that discovery was the finding of several votive tablets to a divinity,—which has caused no little speculation among antiquaries—the god Nodens or Nodona. The difficulty was, to identify his name with the statues of the god himself, which were discovered at the same place, and bore all the characteristics of Æsculapius, viz.:—a dog, a cock, and serpents twining round a rod or staff, reminding one of Moses' contest with the magicians of Egypt. Pausanias relates that Æsculapius was represented in his temple at Epidaurus, as leaning on a serpent, with a dog at his feet; and Plato, in his Phaedo, mentions the cock as sacred to the god of Medicine. * * * But a little reflection shows us how the Romans in their later occupation of this island had perverted Æsculapius's Greek attribute of ἀνώδυνος, the alleviator of pain (whence our term anodyne) into the deity Nodens."

The explanation of the name offered by Mr. Lysons, does not commend itself to me: I am not aware of any authority for ἀνώδυνος or νώδυνος as an epithet of Æsculapius.

It is not easy to arrive at any definite conclusion relative to this god—*Nodons*, *Nodens*, or *Nudens*. It seems not improbable that he was a British deity, such as *Maponus*, and *Cocidius*. But it is extremely difficult to draw a distinction between the deities of the native Britons and of the Roman auxiliaries, especially as some of those auxiliaries were of the same stock as the original settlers in the island. On this point Mr. Roach Smith has, in my judgment, pursued the proper course—in looking, in the first instance, to the native countries of the auxiliaries for the origin of the †barbarous deities mentioned in Britanno-Roman

---

* The nominative may also end in on or is, as *Nodon* or *Nodontis*.

† The number of them has, I suspect, been unduly increased by misreadings. Thus in Wright's *Celt, Roman, and Saxon*, p. 293 (p. 297, 2nd ed.), we find the statement that "an altar was found at Newcastle dedicated SANCTO COCIDIO TAVRVNO," from which we would naturally infer that TAVRVNO was an epithet of the god *Cocidius*, or the name of some identified deity. On turning, however, to *Archæologia*, xl., pl. vi., p. 67, we find the inscription, which Mr. Wright misunderstood, as ill:—

SANCTO CO
CIDIO TAVRVNO
FELICISSI
MVS TRIBVN
EX EVOCATO
V·S·L·M

i. e., *Sancto Cocideo T[ibus] Aurund[dius]* (not *Aurunacus*) *Felicissimus Tribun[us] ex Evocato s[olvit] s[ibit] [ibens] m[erito]*. There is another case of a deity supposed to be

epigraphy. It is possible, however, as seems to me, to push this opinion too far. Mr. Wright, *Celt, Roman, and Saxon*, p. 294 (p. 298, 2nd ed.), supplies an example :—

"At Dirrens, in Scotland, is a dedication to a goddess Brigantia, with a winged figure of the deity, holding a spear in her right hand, and a globe in the left. It was supposed that this was the deity of the country of the Brigantes, but I am not aware that this country was ever called Brigantia, and it is not probable that the conqueror would worship the deity of a vanquished tribe. I feel more inclined to suppose the name was taken from Brigantium, in Switzerland, a town which occupied the site of the modern Bregentz. An altar found at Chester was dedicated DEAE NYMPHAE BRIG, which in this case would be ''to the nymph goddess of Brigantium."

As there was a people of Britain called Brigantes, it appears much more probable that Brigantia was their goddess. It is immaterial whether the country was called "Brigantia" or not; and there are many examples of the Roman conquerors worshipping the deities of vanquished tribes.

Prof. D. Wilson, in his valuable work, *Prehistoric Annals of Scotland*, p. 399, seems to have erred on the other side :

"In the obscure gods and goddesses thus commemorated, we most probably recognise the names of favourite local divinities of the Romanized Britons, originating for the most part from the adoption into the tolerant Pantheon of Rome of the older objects of native superstitious reverence."

There can, I think, be no reasonable doubt that the gods and

---

mentioned on an altar, also found in Cumberland, regarding which I have some doubts The following is the inscription, as given by Dr. Bruce, p. 400 :—

DEAE
SETLO
CENIAE
L'ABAE
EVSCE
V·S·L·M·

Dr. B. remarks—" Nothing is known of the goddess *Setlocenia*, to whom the altar seems to have been dedicated by Lucius Abarens, a centurion." Is the true reading that which I suggested in my notes— DEAE S[ANCTAE] ET LOC[I] GEN[IO] T[ITVS AEL[IVS] ABAREVS, &c.? An objection to it arises from the strangeness of the collocation, *loci genio* instead of *genio loci*. De Wal, *Mytholog. Septentrion.*, n. 343, gives the following inscription on a fragment of an altar found at Binchester :—

MANDVS
EX·C·FRIS·
VINOVIE
V· S· L· M·

He expands it thus:—*Amandus ex civitate Frisiorum Vinovia votum solvit lubens merito*. The same view is taken by Dr. Leemans, *Archaeologia*, xxvii, p. 224. who also takes VINOVIE for the name of a goddess. I regard it as another form of VINOVIVM, the ancient name of Binchester, and would expand it thus:—*Amandus ex cohorte Frisiorum*

I

goddesses referred to in this passage, such as VIRADESTHI
RICAGMBEDA, HARIMELLA, and others noticed in altars
erected by auxiliaries, were deities of the localities from which
those auxiliaries came.   At the same time it seems reasonable
to believe that there were some divinities which were peculiar
to the island and were unknown on the continent.   Such a
deity the god noticed in the Lydney inscriptions may have
been, nor can it be denied that there is ground for the designation—"the British Æsculapius"—which has been applied to
him by that able antiquary Mr. A. Franks.   If we turn to
the Roman divinities, the only god, whose name is at all
similar, is *Nadutis* or *Nodutus*, a rural god presiding over
the *nodi culmorum*.   As but very little is known of this deity,
the following references may be found useful : Arnobius, *adversus
gentes*, iv., p. 131, ed. Leyden, 1651—" *Nadutis* dicitur Deus,
qui ad nodos perducit res satas."   Augustine, *de civ. Dei*, iv.,
8, p. 94, ed. *Paris*, 1683—" Præfecerunt ergo Proserpinam fru-
mentis germinantibus, geniculis nodisque culmorum deum *No-
dotum.*"   "Quando *Nodutus*, adjuvaret in bello, qui nec ad
folliculum spicæ, sed tantum ad nodum geniculi pertinebat?"
Another reading of the name is *Nodinus*, which more nearly
approaches that in the inscriptions.   See also Tomasinus, *de donar.
ex tab. vot. c. 26*; Voss, *de Idololatria*, 11, 61; Lexicon Etymol.
in *Nadus*; Rhodiginus, *Ant. Lect.*, xxv., 30, and Struvius, *Ant.
Rom.* 1, p. 151.

Let us now examine the inscriptions found at Lydney.   Of
the three the following seems to be the clearest :—

D·M·NODONTI
FL·BLANDINVS
ARMATVRA
V·S·L·M

which I read,—*Deo Magno Nodonti Flavius Blandinus arma-
tura votum solvit libens merito.*   The epithet *Magnus* suggests
Mithras, but it is also applied to other deities.   See Orelli, n. 3596.
For *armatura* in the sense of *miles*, see Muratori, 801, 6; and

---

Vimeria &c., i. e., Amandus [a soldier] of the cohort of the Friel [stationed] at Vimeria,
&c.   According to this view I suppose the name of the deity to whom the altar was erected
to have been above AMANDVS on a lost portion of the stone.   On this use of ex see
Siebmer, *Inscrip. Rom. Rhen.*, n. 284.

comparo Steiner, i. *Rhen.*, n. 332, and n. 473 ; Henzen, n. 6794 ; and Borghesi (cited by Henzen), *Ann. Inst. Arch.*, 1839, *Iscr. Renane*, p. 5. It is not easy to determine the characteristic of the *armaturæ*. They are mentioned by Vegetius, ii., 7, 15, 17 ; and Ammianus Marcellinus, xiv.,11 ; xv., 4 and 5 ; and xxvii., 2.

According to the former, they seem to have been younger soldiers, lightly armed ; and according to the latter, body-guardsmen. As light infantry, they may have been connected with a legion, as our light company forms a part of one of our regiments. From the *Notitia*, it appears that there was a *cuneus armaturarum* in Britain, at *Bremetenracum*, possibly (as Böcking suggests) detached from the sixth legion. According to this view, *armatura* in the inscription may be translated, a light-infantry soldier ;* according to the other, a life-guardsman.

Another stone found here bore the inscription :

PECTILLVS
VOTVMQVOD
PROMISSIT
DEO NVDENTE
M DEDIT

which I read,—*Pectillus votum quod promisit Deo Nudenti magno (or merito) dedit. Promissit* is used for *promisit*, and *Nudente* for *Nudenti*, by orthographical irregularities not uncommon in epigraphy.

But the most interesting, and most difficult, of the inscriptions is the following, which is engraved on a leaden or pewter tablet :—

DIVO
NODENTI SILVIANVS
ANVLVM PERDEDIT

---

* Some have regarded the *armaturæ* as cavalry; e. g., Camden, *Brit.*, ed. Gibson, p. 835, " these *armaturæ* were horse armed cap-a-pre, but whether they were *duplares* or *simplares* (Veget. II, 7), my author has not told us." Then also Valee, in his note on Ammianus Marcellinus, xv., 4, citing Julian in Orat. I, ad Constantium, p. 44, ed. Spanh. and Orat. II., i. f., *armeria*—" Armaturae equites falso apparet ;" but the examination of the passage, cited by Valee, shows that they do not warrant his inference. The term *cuneus*, however, designating the body at *Bremetenracum*, favours the opinion that they were cavalry, for *cuneus* in the *Notitia* is very rarely, if ever, applied to infantry; although Vegetius, iii., 19, defines it as " multitudo peditum."

DEMEDIAM PARTEM
DONAVIT NODENTI
INTER QVIBVS NOMEN
SENICIANI NVLLIS
PERMITTAS SANITA
TEM DONEC PERF * RA *
VSQVE TEMPLVM NO
DENTIS

Mr. Lysons, *Romans in Gloucestershire*, p. 54, reads and explains the words thus:

"*Divo Nodenti Silvianus annulum perdidit dimidiam partem donavit Nodenti. Inter quibus nomen Seniciani nullis permittas sanitatem donec perferant usque templum Nodentis.* It is, in short, nothing more nor less than a handbill,* issued by a certain Silvianus, for the recovery of a ring which he had lost. He promises to give half its value, on recovery, to the god Nodens, and seems rather to insinuate that a certain Senecianus must know something about it, and threatens him with the loss of health until he shall bring it back to the temple of Nodens; thus identifying that deity with power over the diseases of the body."

To the reading of Mr. Lysons I see no objection, but his explanation does not at all satisfy me. Nor can I understand what construction or translation he proposes for the words *inter quibus nomen Seniciani.*

The interpretation of this singular inscription is a work of no little difficulty. The only sensible suggestion which I can offer is, that the erection of the tablet was the result of a wager. Silvianus made a bet with Senecianus—he put down his ring, as was usual, as his stake or in lieu of the amount that he had bet, and vowed to the deity one-half of the value of the ring. Senecianus won the bet, and refusing to be bound by the vow of Silvianus, left the performance of it to him. Silvianus, lest he should incur the anger of the god by neglect of his vow, erected this tablet recording his prayer for the punishment of Senecianus.

Let us now examine the inscription in detail.

---

* The only example which I have seen of a Latin advertisement of this kind is amongst the *graffiti* of Pompeii, and it does not at all resemble this inscription. *Vide* Wordsworth's *Inscr. Pomp.*, p. 25.

DIVO NODONTI. *Divus* instead of *Deus* is unusual, but not unprecedented. ANVLVM PERDEDIT. The orthography of these words is not rare. Both *annulus* and *anulus* are written, and the use of E for I is common. As to the meaning, there can, I think, be but little doubt that the sense is, *threw away a ring,* i. e., lost it, not accidentally, but through his own fault. If, then, the meaning be *threw away a ring,* the question is—in what way? A probable answer seems to be, by making a foolish bet. The ancient custom of using the ring in bets or wagers may be illustrated from the following passages:—"Celebratior quidem annulorum usus cum fœnore copiæ debet : argumento est consuetudo vulgi ad sponsiones etiamnum anulo exsiliente."—Pliny, *Nat. Hist.* xxxiii., 1 (Arab). "Si quis sponsionis causa, anulum accepit, nec reddidit victori."—Ulpian, *Dig.* xix., 5, 18.

"Provocat me in aleam, ut ego ludam : pono pallium,
Ille suum *anulum* opponit." Plautus, *Curcul.* ii., 3, 76.

DEMEDIAM PARTEM DONAVIT NODONTI. The construction of *donare* either with the accusative of the person and the ablative of the thing, or (as here) with the accusative of the thing and the dative of the person is well known. The plain sense is—" he presented one half to *Nodens ;*" and the words furnish no ground for the interpretation of Mr. Lysons, " he promises to give half its value, on recovery, to the god." The meaning of the words, according to the view that the ring was staked in a wager, seems to be—Silvianus, to obtain the aid of the deity in winning the wager, presented him with one-half of the ring, i. e., vowed that he would give him one-half of its value.

INTER QUIBVS SENICIANI NOMEN NVLLIS PERMITTAS SANITATEM. The construction from *quibus* to *sanitatem* is plain, and the sense is clearly,—grant health to none of those who bear the name Senecianus—*quibus Seniciani nomen est.* But *inter* remains unexplained. Probably the simplest suggestion is, that the construction is, *inter eos quibus,* i. e., *permittas sanitatem nullis inter eos quibus Seniciani nomen est.* But I am not satisfied with *this explanation.

<hr>

* When I first examined these inscriptions, it also occurred to me that possibly INTER might stand for IN-TER[MINO] i. e., *Nodenti in termino,* to *Nodens,* whose terminal

PERFERANT VSQVE TEMPLVM NODENTIS The selection of the words *perferant* and *usque* seems to indicate the distance of the temple, and the consequent labour in reaching it. The use of *usque* without *ad* is well known. But what were they to carry to the temple? According to the view already taken, it was the *dimidia pars* of the value of the ring, which Silvianus had presented to the deity by a vow, the obligation of which Senecianus had refused to acknowledge.

It is right that I should add that I have never met with a *similar inscription, and that I have offered the foregoing conjectural interpretation in the absence of any thing more satisfactory.

figure stands here. This interpretation was suggested by the information which I had received, that two terminal figures had been found on this site, one regarded as that of Pan, and the other probably as that of Diana. From this statement I drew the conjecture that INTES might stand for IN TER[MINO] and that the terminal figure believed to be that of Pan was really that of Nodens. Since that time I have seen the inscription, noticed in the P.S., from which I derive what I believe to be the correct separation of INTES.

* Since the publication of these notes in the *Cumodion Journal* I have observed a notice in the *Archaeologia*, viii. p. 449, which may, perhaps, be regarded as throwing some light on this inscription. The notice is in the following terms:

" Lord Arden exhibited a gold ring of a singular form, which was lately found in ploughing a field at Silchester. The hoop is formed into several squares, in the appearance of which is a head, rudely engraved with the letters VENVS in Roman capitals around it, and in the several other compartments the following inscription:

SE | NI | CIA | NE | VI | VA | S | II | NDE."

On this Mr. Kempe, *Gentleman's Magazine*, 1833, p. 124, remarks:—" The reading of the above legend, either from its blundered or its barbarous Latinity, appears very doubtful. Considering the two Is in the eighth compartment as to be coupled with the N in the ninth, with a slight correction, we have perhaps 'ne vivas in malevolia,' (!) the head being that of Venus Urania, the patroness of pure love and chaste enjoyments." In the *Archaeologia*, xxvii. p. 417, Mr. Kempe very judiciously abandons this reading, and " by comparison with a ring found at Brancaster, Norfolk," suggests another, which, he believes, is right. His words are : " The relic was, I consider, a sort of *annulus Amicitiae*, the gift of some Christian of the Roman times to his friend *Senecianus*; the legend a pious aspiration—'Senecians vivas in Deo.' In the ring was set an antique intaglio of Venus Urania: this addition was merely ornamental." This is a pleasing, but, I fear, untenable exposition. So far as the reading—" Senecians vivas"—it is unquestionably correct, and there is no doubt that there are ancient rings bearing the motto " vivas in Deo." But it does not seem probable that the head and name of Venus would here have been on a ring, " the gift of a Christian;" nor is there any example, so far as I recollect, of two Is standing for one, whilst the use of them for E is common.

I am unable, however, to offer any more plausible reading of IINDE. If we regard the ring as that mentioned in the inscription found at Lydney—and the identity of the name and spelling, etc., SENICIANUS, suggests the conjecture—we shall, of course, be obliged to find explanations for *perdidit, dimidiam portion donavit* and *tinds*, differing from those already noticed. As such explanations can readily be invented, and at best can be but conjectural, it seems sufficient to have called attention to the curious coincidence.

P. 8.—Since the publication of the preceding article, I have had the opportunity of perusing extracts of letters from the late Sir S. Rush Meyrick to the late Samuel Lysons, Esq., and from the late Sir Wm. Drummond to the late Rev. Dan. Lysons, on the subject of the God *Nodons* or *Nodens*.

Sir Samuel Meyrick was of opinion that "Deus Nodens seems to be Romanised British, which correctly written in its original language would be Deus Noddyns, *i. e.*, the god of the abyss, or it may be, 'God the preserver,' from the verb *noddi*, to preserve, both words being derived from *Nawdd* which signifies 'protection:' I think the latter translation best expresses the idea of Silvanus, and it exactly answers to another epithet of the British deity, as mentioned on an altar in Camden, found at Wigton, in Cumberland (Gough's edit. iii, p. 172)—DEO CEADIO, &c. Instead of Ceadio Camden writes Ceaicn, but as in numerous instances he puts IEO for DEO, and such like, I think he may be presumed to have mistaken the *d* for an ι. Duw Ceidiaw is 'God the preserver.'" There are but few, I think, who will view this etymology with any favour.

Sir Wm. Drummond in his first letter on this subject regards the deity as the Roman *Nodutus*, and cites almost the same passages which I advanced in illustration. Subsequently, however, whilst retaining the opinion that the *Nodinus* of Varro, otherwise the *Nodutus* of St. Augustine and Arnobius, was originally the same deity as the *Nodens* of the inscription, he identifies him with Æsculapius. "The emblems," he remarks, "said to have been found along with the inscription, serpents, cocks, and dogs, seem strongly to confirm, nay, even to prove, the truth of this supposition." [Originally advanced by Mr. Bathurst, that the deity in question could be no other than Æsculapius]. This leads him to search for another etymology for the name of the god as given in the inscriptions, and, with the help of certain peculiarities of the Etruscan language and letters, to which he believes the Latin "bore a considerable resemblance until about the 5th century after the foundation of Rome," and the further aid of the fact, that the worship of

Æsculapius was introduced into Rome about that period, *scil.*,
461, A. U. C., he arrives at the conclusion that *Nodens* or *Nodons*
is a corruption of *Nodunos*, *i.e.*, νώδυνος, *alleviator of pain*,
than which "no name or epithet was more likely to be given by
the Greeks to Æsculapius, who was supposed to be the inventor
of medicine, and to whose salutary influence was ascribed the
restoration of health." Of this theory it seems unnecessary to
say more than that there is no authority for the application of
the epithet νώδυνος to Æsculapius, and there is no ground for
questioning the received opinion, that the deity *Nodutus*, or
Nodinus, derived his name from his office of presiding over the
nodi. Since the publication of the preceding article my attention
has also been directed to a notice of the site of the deity's temple
in "*The Proceedings of the Archæological Institute, Bristol,
1851.*" In an elaborate paper on "the British and Roman Roads
communicating with Caerwent," Dr. Ormerod observes : "Between the town of Lydney and Ailburton, it [the road] appears
next as a hollow way between the present road and the hill on the
right crowned with two Roman camps, of which one contains
the remains of the once splendid temple dedicated to a deity of
supposed sanitary powers, and is most rich in antiquities."

To this is subjoined the following note :—

"Within the greater camp, when excavated under directions of its owner,
the late Right Hon. Charles Bathurst, were discovered the foundation walls
of an irregular quadrangle, the sides of which average severally about 200
feet, exclusive of a range of offices along the N. W. side, and of a Palatial
fabric on its upper or N. E. side.

"This fabric, once, possibly, the residence of Flavius Senilis, hereafter
mentioned, had a portico along its west front, and an open court in the
centre, surrounded by corridors, in which, and in various other departments,
tessellated pavements occurred. This building measured about 150 by 135
feet.

"On the north side of this building, separated from it by an open space,
were baths and Hypocausts, with a detached building measuring about 125
feet in length by 70 in greatest breadth.

"Near the centre of the principal quadrangle was (as is supposed) the
temple of the tutelary deity, the "TEMPLUM NODENTIS," mentioned in
the inscription below. It was about 95 feet long by 75 broad, and in it were

three tesselated pavements, the largest having the name of the erector (as in IV.) placed over a fanciful border representing the twisted bodies of salmons, the fish of the Severn.

"The whole was excavated under the direction of its late owner, the relics and coins carefully preserved, plans and drawings taken, and a series of engravings (of very limited number) executed, in which were eleven tesselated pavements. All was then covered again for preservation. Among the relics are coins to the time of Allectus inclusive, a statuette, votive offerings of limbs supposed to be acknowledgments of the sanitary powers of Nodens or Nodons, and three votive inscriptions given below, together with the inscription in the temple. No. III. has been printed by Lysons, the others are not known to have been published, and are given with their errors of grammar and spelling.

I.   D.M.NODONTI.
I.L.BLANDINVS.
ARMATVRA
V.S.L.M

II.   PECTILLVS.
VOTVM. QVOD.
PROMISSIT.
DEO. NVDENTE.
M. DEDIT.

III.   DIVO
NODENTI. SILVIANVS.
ANILVM. PERDEDIT.
DEMEDIAM. PARTEM.
DONAVIT. NODENTI.
INTERQVIDVS. NOMEN.
SENICIANI. NOLLIS.
PERMITTAS. SANITA——
TEM. DONEC. PERFERAT.
VSQE. TEMPLVM. NO——
DENTIS.

IV. Imperfect, but the seeming number of the deficient letters is shewn by points, as follows:

D.A...FLAVIVS. SENILIS. PR. REL. EX. STEPIBVS.
POSSVIT O.... ANTE. VICTORINO. INTER...ATE."

From these statements, it may, I think, be reasonably inferred that this temple was the resort of persons seeking relief from

K

sickness, and that the cocks, serpents, and dogs, as well as the limbs found there, were votive offerings of those who gratefully acknowledged the sanatory powers of the deity worshipped in the place.

The circumstance that limbs were offered, leads to the conjecture that the diseases cured here were such as affect those portions of the body, perhaps rheumatism and gout, the influence of which is felt in the joints, the *nodi*, whence we find *nodosa cheragra* or *podagra*. And this further suggests the query—whether the same deity—*Nodutus*—presided over vegetable and animal *nodi?* But—to turn from mere conjecture to something more certain—the inscriptions marked I., II., and III., are the same as those which formed the subjects of the preceding article, 35, 36, and 37.

The only thing worth noticing regarding them is, that, as given by Dr. Ormerod, they present one or two different readings. They are, however, of no importance; but n. IV. is particularly deserving of attention. The beginning is unfortunately so imperfect, that I can offer no explanation which satisfies me. If the D be regarded as standing for *Deo* or *Dei*, it is not easy to find a suitable word or abbreviation of four* letters, commencing with A. *Aram* or *Ædem* is the most plausible that occurs to me. It is possible that D. A . . . may be *prænomina* of *Flavius Senilis*, *scil.*, Decimus Aulus, the A and V being ligulate. The abbreviations PR·REL· are also doubtful, from the want of authority. It seems probable to me, however, that they stand for PR[ETIO]† REL[ATO], the cost [of the structure or altar] having been obtained *ex stipibus*, i. e., the small pieces of money offered by the votaries of the god, either voluntarily or at the solicitation of the priests, who, like others of their order, during a portion of the day—"*post templi apertionem stipes emendicabant.*" The portion of the inscription—*ex stipibus* [stipibus] *posuit* [posuit]—may be well illustrated by an inscription to *Mercurius Augustus*, found at Yverdun, in Switzerland, Orelli, n. 318,

---

* This limitation excludes the conjecture, otherwise plausible, AGREST· or AGRIC.

† The following may be suggested: pr[æses] p[osuit], or pr[æfectus] re[ligionis].

DONA VENIBVNT
AD ORNAMENTA EIVS
ET EX STIPIBVS
PONENTVR·

This I interpret as meaning that the gifts offered to Mercury, whose statue is referred to in the preceding portion of the inscription, shall be sold to purchase decorations, and the cost of putting them up shall be defrayed from the money-offerings, or what we may call penny contributions.

O .... ANTE · VICTORINO · INTER ... ATE · I regard as standing for OP · CVRANTE · VICTORINO · INTER· AMNATE, *i. e.*, *Opus curante Victorino Interamnate,* [*] Victorinus, an Interamnian—*i. e.*, as I understand it, a native of the country between the rivers, Wye and Severn—or, it may be, the native of a town called *Interamna,* between these rivers—directing the work.

The word INTER .... ATE seems to me to explain INTER, in line six of the third inscription, about the meaning of which I expressed doubts in my article on the subject. I now regard it as an abbreviation of INTERAMNATI, an epithet given to Nodon, from the position of his temple, *i.e.,* NODENTI· INTERAMNATI ; as we find *Hercules Tiburtinus, Juno Albana, Jupiter Poeninus, Apollo Actiacus,* &c.

I avail myself of this opportunity to add what I inadvertently omitted mentioning in my article, that I trace the use of a tablet of lead for this inscription to the fact, that this material was used in recording execrations and for magical *defixiones.* Thus in Tacitus *Ann.,* ii., 69—*nomen Germanici plumbeis tabulis insculptum,* is noticed amongst the *maleficia quiscreditur animas numinibus infernis sacrari ;* and Dio Cassius, lvii. 18, whilst telling the same story of Piso's machinations against the life of Germanicus says : ἐλασμοὶ μολίβδινοι ἀρὰς τινας μετὰ τοῦ ὀνόματος αὐτοῦ ἔχοντες.

---

[*] As Victorinus has no other name, I am inclined to regard him as a native Briton; especially as there is reason to believe that this name was common amongst the *Silures* [*see Archaeologia,* vii., p. 319, Camden's *Britannia, ed. Gough,* III., p. 103. This notion of the birth-place with the name is not uncommon. Thus Sallust, *Catilina,* T., *deptitium quondam Camertem ;* ii., *Volterriam quandam Crotoniensem ;* and Cicero, *pro Milone, C. Cassinius, cognomento Sevis,* Interamnas.]

§ 21. In the same lecture by the Rev. S. Lysons, we find the following account of a tombstone, which was discovered (at Cirencester, I believe) "near the old London road in 1825 or 1826" :—

"On the lower part of the stone was the following inscription—RVFVS SITA·EQVES CHO VI·TRACVM · AN·XI · STIP ·XXII·HEREDES EX S. TEST E · CVRAVE·II · S·E·, may be read thus:—*Rufus Sitorchus Eques cohortis sexti Thracum annos undecim stipendii viginti duo. Heredes ex suo testamento erigere curaverunt.* It may be thus translated:—Rufus, a Commissary-General of the Equestrian Order, and Officer of Cavalry, commanding the Sixth Legion, having served eleven years in the Thracian regiment of cavalry, and twenty-two years in the army, is buried here. This monument his heirs have carefully erected according to the terms of his will."

On this reading and translation it is unnecessary to offer any criticism : it is sufficient to observe that this inscription has been correctly read and translated, by Mr. Wright, *Celt, Roman and Saxon,* p. 315, (p. 319, 2nd ed.)—

" RVFVS·SITA·EQVES·CHO VI
TRACVM·ANN XL STIP XXII
HEREDES·EXS·TEST·F·CVRAVE
II·S·E·

[*i. e., Rufus Sita eques coh[ortis] sextæ Tracum, ann[orum] quadraginta, stip[endiorum] vigintiduorum, hæredes * ex testamento faciendum curaverunt. H[ic] s[itus] e[st].*—J. McC.].

"It may be translated 'Rufus Sita, a horseman of the sixth cohort of Thracians, aged forty years, served twenty-two years. His heirs, in accordance with his will, have caused this monument to be erected. He is laid here.'"

Mr. Lysons seems to think that this horseman was the same as the Rufus, mentioned in St. Paul's *Epist. ad Rom.* xvi, 13, and as Pudens Rufus, the husband of Claudia Ruffina, "a noble British lady, professing the Christian faith." The conjectures have not the semblance of probability to recommend them.

---

* EXS is another form of EX, just as VIXSIT is of VIXIT.

HAMPSHIRE.

§ 22. In the year 1783 a pig of lead was found near Stock-bridge, in this county. It bore the following inscription:

NERONIS·AVG·EX·KIAN·ĪĪĪ·COS·BRIT

On it see my notes on inscriptions found in *Derbyshire*, p. 49.

§ 23. In the year 1789 an ancient ring was found at °Sil-chester, in this county. It bore the following inscription:

SENICIANEVIVASIINDE

On it see my notes on inscriptions found in *Gloucestershire*, p. 70.

LANCASHIRE.

§ 24. Camden, *ed. Gough*, iii., p. 129, gives the following inscription on an altar found at Ribchester in this county :

> SEOESAM
> ROLNASON
> OSALVEDN
> AL.Q.Q.SAR
> BREVENM
> BEDIANIS
> ANTONI
> VS MEG.VI
> IC DOMV
> ELITER

Dr. Bruce, *Journal of the Archæological Institute*, xii., p. 223, figures it and offers the following observations :

"Never, perhaps, was so unmeaning a concatenation of letters submitted to the gaze of a bewildered antiquary. Camden could make nothing of the inscription, but suggests somewhat waggishly that it contained little more than the *British* names of places adjoining. Horsley grappled with Camden's corrupted copy, and elicited one portion of truth. He says, 'I believe the fourth line may be ' Alæ equitum Sarmataruio.' The altar seems soon after its discovery to have been used as a common building stone in the erection of Salisbury Hall. In 1815 it was disentombed and fell into the hands of Dr. Whitaker, who bequeathed it to St. John's College, Cambridge. Dr. Whitaker, (History of Richmondshire, vol. ii., p. 461), thus expands the inscription :—*Deo sancto Apollini Apono ob salutem Domini nostri ala equitum Sarmatarum Bremeten, sub Diunio Antonino centurione legionis sextæ victricis.*"

In a paper on "Roman *Ribchester*," in "the *Journal of the*

* Confidently believed by the authors to be the *Coccium* of the Itinerary and regarded by Mr. Hodgson Hinde as the *Bremetennacum* of the *Notitia* and *Bremetonacum* of the Itinerary. Gough, Camden's *Britannia*, iii., p. 203, remarks : "All antiquaries agree in placing *Bremetonacum* at Overton." This remark is not at present correct. Before Mr. Hinde's statement of the claims of Ribchester, Reynolds *Iter Brittaniarum*, had advanced those of Lancaster. Camden adopted the distinction of *Bremetonacum* and *Bremetu-*

Archæological Association, by John Just, Esq., and John Harland, Esq., vi., p. 293, Dr. Whitaker's reading of the inscription is given thus:—"DEO SANCTO APOLLONI [sic] APONO OB SALVTEM DN AL.Q.Q.SARM . BRENETEN.SVB DIANIO ANTONINO).LEG.VI.VIC.DOMV ELIBER., whilst in the *Archæologia Æliana*, iv., p. 111, Mr. Hodgson Hinde cites as †Whitaker's words:—

"After the most attentive consideration, I think the inscription should be read as follows:—*Deo sancto Apolloni* [sic] *Apono pro salute Domini nostri, Alæ Equitum Sarmatarum Brenetennorum, Didnius Antonius, Centurio Legionis sextæ Victricis, Domu Velitris.* I suspect the word which follows Samatarum to express a subordinate tribe of that widely spread nation, the Sarmatæ Crenetenni; at least I can assign no other meaning to it."

Mr. Hinde, in the paper already mentioned, suggests the emendation (which has been confirmed on closer examination of the stone) BREMETEN for BRENETEN and hence argues that Ribchester was the *Bremetenracum* of the *Notitia*. Mr. Roach Smith introduced another improvement—MAPONO for APONO—regarding Maponus as the British name of Apollo as Belatucader is of Mars. Dr. Bruce adopts both these corrections, and adds another—the substitution of N for A in the 4th line. The whole inscription, as it appears in his wood-cut, may be given thus:

---

rocum. The first he placed at Overborough, the second at Brampton. Horsley, also, making the same distinction, assigns *Bremetonacum* to Overborough, and *Bremeterracum* to all Penrith or Brampton. The similarity of the names favours the opinion of Mr. Hinde that they designated the same place, but an obvious objection to his view that Ribchester was that place is that we are thus obliged to strain the words *per lineam valli* so as to include a station "upwards of eighty miles to the south of it."

* Mr. Wright, *Celt, Roman, and Saxon*, p. 257, 2nd ed., adopts this erroneous reading and translates the inscription thus:—

"DEO SANCTO	To the holy god
APOLLONI [sic] APONO	Apollo Aponus,
OB SALVTEM DN	for the health of our lord (the emperor)
AL EQ SARM	the wing of Sarmatian horse
BRENETEN	of Brenetum,(?)
SVB DIANIO	under Dianius
ANTONINO	Antoninus,
) LEG VI V	Centurion of the sixth legion, called
IC DOMV	the conquering, his native town
ELIBER	was Eliber."

† I am unable to consult Dr. Whitaker's work.

DEO·SAN
POLINIMPON
OSALTED·N
N·EQQ·SAR
BREMETENN
OB·DIANI
+)ANTONI
NVS LEG·VI
VIC·DOMO
MELITENVS·

" Besides the inscription, the altar is sculptured on two of its
sides. The subject of one of these carvings is the youthful
Apollo resting upon his lyre," according to Dr. Whitaker,
" Apollo Aponus, or the indolent Apollo, (or it may be read
Apollo the healer), the god of medicine, who restores health by
relaxation or repose," or " Apollo Aponus," deriving his name
from the *fontes Aponi*, near Padua, " which he supposes to be the
waters from which a cure was in this case supplicated." The other
sculpture represents, as Whitaker thought, " the figures of two
priests in long robes, holding the head of some horned animal
between them ;" but, according to Bruce, " two females, the one
fully draped, the other only partially so," holding some object
between them, which is so much injured as to be undistinguish-
able ; it may have been a basket of fruit or an offering of flowers ;"
or, as seems to me, a male and female.

Let us now proceed to consider the interpretation of this
obscure inscription. Dr. Bruce offers no reading of his own, but
strangely accepts, as in the main correct, Dr. Whitaker's expansion, as cited by him, with the exception of the three emendations already noticed. DEO·SAN[CTO] APOL[L]INI may, I
think, be accepted without doubt. Dr. Whitaker's APONO,
whether as derived from the Greek ἄπονος, or from the Latin,
Aponus, should be rejected, as being without authority and as much
inferior to Mr. Roach Smith's *MAPONO, i. e., as I understand,
MAPON· for MAPONO. The O in the third line may be

---

* This use of the Roman designation of a god with that of the identified barbarian
deity—APOLLINI MAPONA—is common. See my note on inscriptions found in Somersetshire. Sometimes it happened that the barbarian deity was differently identified by
different individuals.

regarded as the last letter of MAPONO, but it seems preferable
to reserve it as an element of the preposition PRO—PR being
regarded as lost by the fracture of the stone. OB seems to me
not as probable, for we have to supply not only B but also *M after
SALVTE. D·N· of course, stand for *Domini nostri*. The
omission of the name of the emperor is not common. In the
fourth line EQQ·SAR are clearly *Equitum Sarmatarum* : this
is confirmed by other inscriptions found here mentioning *ala
Sarmatarum*. But the interpretation of N is not equally certain.
Numerus at once presents itself, but there is a question, *who*
erected the altar ? According to Whitaker's view, as stated by
Bruce, it was the *ala* (or, if we read N, the *numerus*) *sub Dianio
Antonino centurione."* But this is evidently erroneous : there
is not the shadow of authority for *sub*, and besides we have
Antoninus in the nominative case. But it appears from the
extract given by Mr. Hinde, that Whitaker proposed another
reading—*Dianius Antonius Centuria.* If we adopt this, it
would appear that an *et* is to be supplied and the altar was
erected jointly by the *ala* or *numerus* and *Dianius Antoninus.* This seems to me very unsatisfactory ; if Whitaker's
views on the other portions of the inscription be accepted,
the N more probably stands for *nomine*, as in Horsley's *Northumberland*, xcv. His reading *Brennetennorum* should be at
once rejected, as being without authority, and Hinde's †emen-

Bruce I would explain the remarkable fact that on one altar we find DEO MARTI
COCIDIO, on another DEO SILVANO COCIDIO. See a statement by Mr. Clayton, *Gen-
Geman's Magazine*, 1853, p. 53; and my notes on inscriptions found in *Dumfriesshire*,
Dr. Bruce's solution—" that the Roman soldier who was dedicating an altar to one of his
own divinities, pursuing the practice of adopting the deities of the conquered country,
inscribed on the same stone the name of a popular native god, without any particular
inquiry as to his attributes"—does not seem to me probable.

* Not necessarily, for we have examples in inscriptions of the ablative after *ob*, e. gr., *ob
insulibus restitutis*, Orelli, n. 1512; and also of the accusative after *pro*, e. gr., *Pro solu-
tem et victorias*, Orelli, n. 2540.

† Mr. Hinde also suggests an emendation of the passage in the *Notitia*, which deserves
consideration, *viz.,* " supplying the initial S, and making a trifling alteration in the latter
part of the word," i. e., reading *Cuneus Sarmatarum* for *Cuneus Armaturarum*. In
favour of this it may be stated, that the reading of at least five MSS. of the *Notitia* is
armaturum, and that this application of *cuneus* to cavalry is more consistent with the
usage in the *Notitia.* See note p. 17. An objection to the reading may also be drawn
from the usage in the *Notitia*, according to which we should have *equitum* before *Sarmatarum.* Böcking's conjecture that the *armatura* stationed at *Bremetennacum* were a
detachment of the 6th legion supplies an explanation of the presence of ANTONINVS
LEG·VI·VIC· at the place.

t

dation, BREMETENN, adopted. I cannot concur with him,
however, that OR in the next line should be joined to this, as if
Bremetennor stood for *Bremetennoraci*, i. e., another form of *Brem-
etenraci*, the genitive of *Bremetenracum*. But Whitaker's readings, *Dianius Antonius Centurio*, must also be rejected. There
is no authority for the name *Dianius*; the *cognomen*, as is evident from Bruce's wood-cut, is *Antoninus*; and there is nothing
on the stone to warrant *centurio*. There are, indeed, portions of
letters at the beginning of the 7th line, one of which resembles a
reversed C, such as is used for *centurio*, but it is impossible that
this view of it can be correct, as instead of preceding it ought to
follow *Antoninus*. These portions of letters are, I fear, too defective to admit of any certain reading, but they may reasonably be
regarded as representing the name or names of *Antoninus*.
LEG·VI·VIC are, as usual, *legionis sextæ victricis;* and the
omission of *miles* is not uncommon. Whitaker's *domu Eliber* and
domu Velitris are evidently erroneous. The last line is MELI-
TENVS or MELITEN·VS, most probably the former. For
this reading we are indebted, I believe, to Dr. Bruce, but he
does not notice it, and omits in his citation Dr. Whitakers'
domu Eliber. From what has been stated it is plain that the
most obscure parts of the inscription are the sixth line and
the beginning of the seventh. As to the latter, I have already stated the most feasible suggestion which I can offer;
and I now venture to propose a conjecture which seems to
to throw some light on the former. OR·DIANI may be regarded as standing for OR[ESTEAE]·DIANI, i. e., DIAN[A]E,
and it may be urged that this view derives considerable support from the country of *Antoninus*, scil., *Melitenus*, and from
the sculpture of the two figures on one side of the altar. Diana,
as *Orestea Diana*, was worshipped at *Aricia*, to which place
Orestes, with his sister, was reported to have taken her image
from Tauris. See Ovid, *Met.*, xv., 489; Virgil, *Æn.*, vii,
764. At *Comana*, not far from *Melitene*, there was a similar
tradition, that Orestes, with his sister, had brought to the "celebrated temple in that city the sacred rites of Tauropolos Artemis.
See Strabo, xii.; Dio, *Frag.*, xxxvi. Hence Antoninus may
have adopted the deity of *Aricia* as identical with that of *Comana.*

---

* See Cicero, *pro leg. Manil.*, c 9.

Thus the sculpture may represent Iphigenia and Orestes carrying the basket, or casket, containing the sacred symbols or utensils; or, perhaps, the *coma lugubris* to which the name of the city—*Comana*—has been traced; and the altar may have been jointly raised, by a *numerus equitum Sarmatarum* to Apollo Maponus, and by Antoninus to Orestea Diana. According to these suggestions the whole inscription may be read and expanded thus:—

> DEO·SAN[CTO]
> APOL[L]INI·MAPON[O]
> PRO·SALVTE·D[OMINI] N[OSTRI]
> N[VMERVS]·EQ[VITVM] SAR[MATARVM]
> BREMETENN[ACI]
> OR[ESTEAE]·DIAN[A]E
>]] ANTONI
> NVS·LEG[IONIS]·SEXTAE
> VIC[TRICIS] DOMO
> MELITENVS.

i. e., to the holy god [called] Apollo [by the Romans and] Maponus [by the Britons] for the health of our Lord [the Emperor] the detachment of Sarmatian cavalry [stationed] at Bremetennacum : to the Orestean Diana]] Antoninus, [a soldier] of the sixth legion [styled] the victorious, a native of Melitene, [erected this altar].

The union of Apollo and Diana on the same altar is common ; and there are examples of dedications to different deities on the same stone, *e. gr.*, on one found at Rutchester, *Archæologia Æliana*, iv., pl. 1, fig. 4.

It has also occurred to me that G may have preceded the letters in the 6th line, thus forming an epithet of the *equites Sarmatæ*, derived, as is common, from the emperor *Gordian*. Similarly we have in Henzen, n. 6730, NVMERI·EXPLORA-TORVM·DIVITIESIVM·ANTONINIANORVM. If this be adopted, we should regard N· as standing for *nomine*. I am not satisfied that *either of these views is correct, but they seemed not unworthy of notice.

---

§ 25. In the *Journal of the Archæological Association*, vi., p. 341., we have the following account of an inscription on a votive tablet found at Halton in this county :—

"It is as follows (allowing for the letters between parenthesis, and which are doubtful); DEO MART(I) SABI(NVS) P·P· ET MILIT(ES)N·BARC. S . . . EIL V·S·P·O. This is usually read "Deo Marti Sabinus Pater Patrie," [*sic*] or, as Mr. Just read it, pro prætor, "a [*sic*] milites numeri Barcorum [*sic*] (S . . . . EII) voto salato [*sic*] posuit."

The only other notice which I have seen of this inscription is in the same volume, p. 341, in the report of Dr. Johnson's paper on ancient Lancaster. His remarks relative to it are :—

"The name of Sabinus occurs on an altar to Mars, found near a mound two miles above Lancaster, and also on this altar an inscription referring to the Notitia." " Halton the place on the Lone where the altar to Mars was found, in connection with the numerus Barcarii [sic], appears, &c."

It is evident that the author of the account first cited was so imperfectly acquainted with the subject that no reliance can be placed on his reading of the inscription. Enough, however, is clear to prove that Dr. Johnson was correct in referring to the *numerus Barcariorum*, which served in Britain and is mentioned in the *Notitia* in the following terms :—*Præfectus numeri Barcariorum Tigrisiensium Arbeia*. It is difficult to explain the meaning or origin of the terms *Barcarii Tigrisienses*. Horsley, an accurate and diligent enquirer after truth, gives up the search with the remark—"*I can meet with nothing satisfactory about* these Barcarii Tigrisienses." Böcking, p. 863, seems to me to have given the most probable explanation of the term *Barcarii*. He traces it to *baron*, "a barge," and hence interprets "barge-men." We know from various passages that the Romans employed a military and naval force in vessels on the rivers in the provinces. In the *Notitia in partibus orientis* we find mention of *nauclarii, liburnarii,* and *naves amnicæ et milites ibidem deputati*. *Tigrisienses* he traces to *Tigris* either as the designation of a particular kind of vessel, or as the name of a vessel—derived either from the animal, as we apply "the Tiger" to one of our ships, or from the river *Tigris*. Hence he explains the designation as denoting that these *Tigrisienses* served in *barcæ*, either resembling the kind of vessel thus called, or, rather, attending on such vessels.

I am by no means satisfied with Böcking's explanation of *Tigrisienses*. It is, in my judgment, better to trace the designation to the river *Tigris*, with the meaning that these *Barcarii* were from that river on which they had been accustomed to act in that capacity.

The *numerus Barcariorum*, as is plain from this inscription, included soldiers as well as sailors : their duties were discharged in vessels of light draught—probably as Böcking thinks, "lighters" or "tenders"—suitable for river service.

Relative to the inscription itself, I have already stated my belief that no dependence can be placed on the correctness of the copy. As it stands, however, it may be expanded thus :— DEO MART[I] SAB[NVS] P[RAE]POSITVS ET MIL- IT[ES] N[VMERI] BARC[ARIORVM]. *Pater Patriæ* and *proprætore* are unquestionably erroneous: *præpositus* is very probable, as it was a common designation of the commanding officer of a *numerus*. See Henzen, nn. 3100, 3195, 6522, 6749. All after BARC· is doubtful; but from a comparison of Horsley's, n. iii., apparently on a mile-stone, it is possible that SETFE on that stone, and S . . . . EIL on this may indicate a place, perhaps *Setantiorum portus*, which was probably near the mouth of the Ribble. The only other conjectural reading, which I can offer, is—S[VB] [CVRA] EIVS or ILLIVS PO[SVERVNT].

§ 26. Camden, ed. *Gough*, iii., p. 375, gives the following inscriptions found near Manchester :—

OCANDIDI
FIDES·XX
IIII
——
COHO·I·FRISIN
Ɔ MASAVONIS
P·XXIII.

On these see my notes on inscriptions found in *Monmouthshire*.

§ 27. About the year 1776, a cylinder of stone was dug up about two miles to the north of Leicester, near the ancient road called the Fosseway ; it is now preserved in the local museum in that town. According to Mr. Wright, *Celt, Roman and Saxon*, p. 183 (p. 185, 2nd ed.), it bore the following inscription :—

> " IMP·CAESAR
> DIV TRAIAN PARTII F DIV
> TRAIAN HADRIAN AVG
> PONT IV COS III A RATIS
> II "

From this copy it is impossible to extract any sense : PONT is unintelligible, and there is no intimation of the portions which are defective. In the *Monum. Hist. Brit.*, n. 8 a, the inscription stands thus :—

> IMP CAES
> DIVI TRAIAN PARTII F DIV*NEP.
> TRAJAN HADRIAN * * * *   B.
> POT.IV. COS. III. A RATIS*H

From the plate given in the *Archæologia*, vii., p. 85, it would appear that the only legible parts were—

> IMPCAES
> DIVTRAIANPARTIIFDI
> TRAIANHADRIANAVG
> POTIVCOSIIIARATIS
> II

It seems plain that the defects in the style of Hadrian must be thus supplied :—

> IMP·CAES
> DIVI·TRAIAN·PARTII·F·DIVI·NERVAE·NEP·

TRAIAN·HADRIAN·AVG·P·M·TRIB
POT·IV·COS·III

i. e., Imp[erator] Cæs[ar], Divi Trajan[i] Parth[ici] f[ilius], Divi
Nervæ nep[os], Trajan[us] Hadrian[us] Aug[ustus] P[ontifex]
M[aximus] trib[unitiæ] pot[estatis] iv co[n] s[ul] iii, *i.e.*, A. D.
120, after August the 11th. The remaining portions of the
inscription—A·RATIS II—have been correctly explained as
denoting that the mile-stone was distant two miles (*i. e.*, II for II)
from *Rata*, *i. e.*, Leicester. Mr. Newton, *Monum. Hist. Brit.*,
supplies M·P· between RATIS and II : they are often omitted
on mile-stones.

---

§ 28. In 1830, an ancient grave stone was found in excavating the foundations of Mr. J. S. Padley's house in Lincoln. It is figured in the *Gentleman's Magazine* for 1842, p. ii., p. 351; and the inscription is given in the *Monumenta Historica Britannica*, p. cxii. n. 53a; and by Henzen, n. 6676, as follows:

> L·SEMPRONI·FLA
> VINI·MILTIS·LEGVIIII
> Q (?) ALAVDI SEVERI
> AER VIIANOR XXX
> ISPANICA LERIA
> CIVI MA

It is plain that the first two lines are to be read:

> L[ucii] Semproni[i] Fla-
> vini mil[i]tis leg[ionis] nonæ

but there is considerable doubt as to the word or words preceding SEVERI, in the third line. Mr. Padley remarks, that if the first letter in the line be Q, it may stand for *quadrata*, i. e., *legionis nonæ quadrata;* and reads the following word as "Alaudæ (a lark), a name given to legions, the soldiers of which wore tufted helmets, supposed to resemble the crest of the lark." The Editor of the Magazine suggests that the letter is G (not Q), "and is certainly some epithet of the legio Alauda. Perhaps *galeatæ alaudæ*." The rest of the line, I SEVERI, is read by Mr. Padley as *Julii Severi*, and the reading is illustrated by the observation that "Julius Severus was a governor of Britain under Hadrian." Mr. Newton, *Monumenta Historica Britannica*, adopts *Alaudæ*, but doubts whether "I" should be read as *Julius* or *Junius*, as there were two propraetors of Britain named *Severus*; the one, *Julius*, under Hadrian, the other,

Junius, under Commodus. Henzen is of opinion that the latent reading of the line is "*Sub cur A* (or something similar) cLAVDI SEVERI." Henzen's emendation CLAVDI seems very probable, but the *appearance of the stone does not favour it. One of the *cognomina* of the 5th legion was *Alaudæ*; whilst those of the 9th were *Hispanica, Macedonica.* The first letter of the line, which is stated to resemble "the letter *q* inverted," and "the Etruscan G, the Roman G reversed," appears to me to be an inverted C, standing, as it often does, for *centuria*, and denoting that Lucius Sempronius Flavinus was a soldier in that century of the 9th legion, which was under the command of Claudius Severus. To Mr. Padley's reading of the next line, "aerum vii; annorum xxx," there can be no objection, as *aerum* is sometimes used for *stipendiorum*. See Orelli, nn. 3551, 3552; and Henzen, nn. 5202, 6841. The fifth line is read by Mr. Padley as "Ispanica Leria;" and the sixth as "Civitas Materna." Henzen adopts this reading of the fifth line, remarking that Leria was a city of Hispania Tarraconensis; but suggests, for the sixth, instead of "Civitas Materna," "Civi Ma[ximi exempli.]" There are, I think, but few who would regard either of these interpretations of the last line as satisfactory; and on reference to the copy of the inscription in the Magazine, I find that there is no authority on the stone for the second I in CIVI, and that MA is probably an erroneous reading of NIA. It appears to me, then, that we may read the last line thus: C·IVNIA, *curante Junia*, denoting the person who had caused the memorial of Flavinus to be executed. For the reasons which I have stated, I would read the whole inscription *in extenso* thus:

L·SEMPRONI·FLA	L[ucii] Semproni[i] Fla-
VINI·MILITIS·LEG VIIII	vini, mil[i]tis leg[ionis] viiii,
Ɔ CLAVDI·SEVERI	c[enturia] Claudi[i] Severi,
AER·VII ANOR·XXX	aer[um] vii, an[n] or[um] xxx,
ISPANICA LERIA	[H]ispanicâ Leriâ,
C·IVNIA	c[urante] Juniâ.

§ 29. In the *Journal of the Archæologica' Institute*, 1860, there is an interesting and carefully prepared paper by the Rev. Edward and Mr. Arthur Trollope, on "The Roman Inscriptions and Sepulchral Remains at Lincoln." As there are some points on which I differ in opinion from the learned authors, I purpose devoting two or three articles to the consideration of the doubtful readings or interpretations.

In p. 4 we have the inscription:

> D·M
> FL·HELIVS NATI
> ONE GRECVS VI
> XIT ANNOS XXXX
> FL·INGENVA CO
> NIVGI POSVIT

It is thus interpreted:—" To the divine shades,—Flavius Helius, a Greek by nation, lived forty years. The free-born Flavia erected this stone to her husband."

I cannot perceive any reason for rejecting the obvious interpretation of *Ingenua* as a cognomen. It is not rare: Mommsen, *Inscript. Neapol.*, furnishes several examples.

§ 30. In p. 6 we have the inscription that formed the subject of §28 :—

> L·SEMPRONI·FLA
> VINI·MILTIS·LEGVIIII
> *ALAVDISEVERI
> AERVHANORXXX
> ISPANICA LERIA
> CIVMA

The *reading and interpretation of the third line, which seem to be most favourably received by the Messrs. Trollope, are the same as those which I suggested; but a preference is expressed for ISPANI.GALERIA, instead of ISPANICA·LERIA. It is remarkable that, when I first saw the inscription, this reading sug-

* From Holder's article in *Rheinische Museum für Philologie*, n. 1, 1866, p. 18, it appears that Mommsen has anticipated both them and me.

gested itself to me; but although recommended by the circumstance that the Galerian tribe was common amongst the Spaniards,
as noticed by Henzen, n. 5598, I rejected it on the ground, that
there is no example, so far as I am aware, of such a position of
the tribe, not only after the birth-place, but also after the years
of age and of service. But the existence of *Lria*, as a town
of *Hispania Turraconensis*, seems to be questioned apparently
on the ground that it is "not found in Dr. Smith's Dictionary
of Roman Geography." There can be no doubt, however, that
it did exist: it is mentioned by Ptolemy, cited by Cellarius, i.,
p. 106.

The readings *ciris* [or *civitate*] *maximi exempli* for CIVMA
seem to me very improbable. I prefer my own suggestion—C-
IVNIA c[urante] Junia. In support of this it may be added
that the *Junia gens* was common amongst the Spaniards, whence
we may assume that IVNIA was an ordinary name amongst
them. See *Reinesii Syntag*, p. 137.

§ 31. In p. 15 the stone is figured on which is the inscription
given by Horsley, *Brit. Rom., Lincolnshire*, n. 1:—

DIS MNIBVS
NOMINI SACRI
BRVSCI·FNI CIVIS
SENONI·II CARSS
NAE CONIVGIS
＊ ＊ ＊ ＊ ＊ ＊ ＊ ＊

"The memorial has been thus read:—

DIS MANIBVS
NOMINA (or NOMINII) SACRI
BRVSCI FILI CIVIS
SENONII ET CARISS
IMAE CONIVGIS
EIVS ET QVINTI F.

"The slab is broken off just below the last line [marked by asterisks],
and the inscription may be imperfect."

Mr. Ward read the four middle lines: *Nominii Sacri Bruxifili
civis Senonii et charissimæ Vaniæ conjugis.*

Horsley gives the expansion: "Dis Manibus Nominii Sacri Bruscifili civis Senonii et carissimæ Vanio conjugis ejus et Quintio."

Gough, *Camden's Britannia*, ii., p. 374, offers the astonishing note—that the first word in the fourth line "may as well be read LINCOLNI as SENONI."

I am inclined to suggest the reading: *Diis manibus Nominii Sacri *Brusri filii, civis Senonii, et carissimæ conjugis, Lucii Quinti filiæ.* This is favoured by the appearance of the remaining portions of the letters as given in the wood-cut, but it may be LVCIE [*vid.* E for AE]QVINTI F [ILIAE], a reading which is recommended by having the name of the *conjux.*

§ 33. In p. 17 the inscription on the grave-stone presented by Mr. Arthur Trollope to the British Museum, in 1853, is noticed:—

```
        I·VALERIVS·I·F
        CLA·PVDENS·SAV·
        MIL·LEG·II·A·P·F.
        >·DOSSENNI
        PROCVLI·A·XXX
        ΔERA * I D·SP
        II·S·E
```

"The following reading of the inscription may be suggested—Julius (or T.tus) Valerius, Julii (or Titi) filius, Claudia (tribu), Savia, miles legionis II Augustæ (or adjutricis) piæ, fidelis, centuria Dossenni Proculi, annorum xxx, rerum II, de sua pecunia hoc sibi fecit (or hic situs est.)"

The appearance of the letters on the stone, as figured in the *Journal*, leads me to regard *Titus* as more probable than *Julius.* I also prefer *adjutricis* and *hic situs est.* For *de sua pecunia*, I would suggest *de suo peculio*, as in Orelli, n. 5353 ; and for *centuria*, *centuriâ*, as the usual construction seems to have been—the legion, cohort, or *ala* in the genitive, and the century or troop in

---

* The letters BRVSCFIL are inscribed on a piece of pottery found at Doncaster Fort, in Shropshire. See Camden's Brit. ed. Gough, iv. p. 105, Stuart's Caledonia Romana, pl. viii., fig. 4.

the ablative. Thus in Renier, *Inscriptions de'lAlgérie*, nn. 3938, 3939, *centuria* and *turma* are given *in extenso*. On p. 17, the observations of Mr. Franks on this inscription is cited :

" It records Julius Valerius Pudens, son of Julius, of the Claudian tribe, and a native of Savia, a city in Spain; he appears to have been a soldier of the second legion, and of the century of Dessennns Proculus, and to have lived thirty years, two of them as a pensioner."

The tribe, being the Claudian, leads me to prefer, both here and in Gruter, 547, 10, *Saveria*, a town in Pannonia. See Reinesius, cl. viii., n. 5, and Orelli, n. 500. On the same ground I regard SAVA in Steiner, *Cod. In. Rom. Rhen.*, nn. 373, 387, as standing for the same town. The interpretation, "two of them as a pensioner," is liable to the objections, that there is no number on the stone, which can be clearly read, and that there is no authority for "a pensioner." I am not sure that I correctly understand the use of the term by Mr. Franks, but if his meaning be, that Julius Valerius Pudens received pay for two years, as some of our discharged soldiers receive pensions, he has not at all expressed the sense of the Latin. The phrase AERA MERVIT means the same as STIPENDIA MERVIT, *i.e.*, served [the stated number of] years.

But it is more important to notice the construction of the word in this inscription. Instead of AERVM we have AERA, for the last letter seems to be A. The number is so obliterated that it appears scarcely possible to propose a certain restoration ; but perhaps in this injured portion of the stone there was, besides the number, M standing for *meruit.*

Below the inscription is the representation of the *ascia*, so common on tombstones in the south of France. The Messrs. Trollope are the first, so far as I am aware, who have noticed it in Britanno-Roman epigraphy.

§ 33. In p. 19, we find an imperfect inscription, which has been thus read :

```
. . . . . AELIVS·
. . . VS · M · AVRE
. . . VM · ILIB
. . . CINO·
```

```
. . . . XXV ·
. . . . ENIVS·VE
. . . EX·LEG·XIIII
. . . H E·TEST·P·
```

"The concluding formula"—H·E·TEST·P·—"may be thus explained—Hic ex testamento positus, (?)" I prefer "Heres ex testamento posuit," the heir being the veteran named in the sixth line. This inscription is of much interest, as supplying another notice of the 14th legion. The only other stone found in Britain, which mentions this celebrated corps, is that dug up at Wroxeter, and now in the Library of the Grammar School at Shrewsbury.

§ 34. In p. 19 a stone is noticed, which was found at Lincoln during the early part of last year.

"The Inscription, which is perfect, may be thus read :—

```
DIIS·MANIB
C·IVLI·GAL·
CALEN·F·LVC
VET·EX·LEG·VI
VIC·PF·NASEMF
```

"The person here commemorated may have been Caius Julius, of the Galerian tribe, son of Galenus, a native of Lucca (?), and a veteran of the sixth legion, styled *Victrix, pia fidelis* (?). The concluding letters are inaccurately formed, and their import is obscure. *Nepos a suo bene merenti fecit*, has been proposed, but we confess our inability to offer any satisfactory explanation. The sixth legion, however, it must be observed, was styled * *firma* and *ferrata*, which may suggest the more correct reading. It is doubtful whether it was ever styled *pia fidelis*.

The inscription, although apparently plain, and moreover accurately represented in a woodcut prepared with great care from a photograph, presents more than ordinary difficulty. The objections to the readings proposed by Messrs. Trollope for the first three lines, are : that *C. Julius* has no cognomen—that the normal arrangement of the name of the father and the tribe is inverted—and that the sixth letter in the third line seems clearly to be I, not F.

[* There is but one example of this epithet connected with the 6th Legion, *scil.*, in Orelli, n. 564. Henzen emends it by reading *ferrata*.—J. McC.]

I am inclined to suggest the following expansion :—*Diis Manibus Caii Julii, Galeria tribu, Culeni,* (or *Galeni*), *Lugduno, i.e.,* of Caius Julius Calenus (or Galenus,) of the Galerian tribe, a native of Lugdunum. The only objection, worth noticing, which I see to this, is, that in the woodcut there is a mark resembling a point between N and I; but it seems probable to me that the mark is the result of injury or of age. It is remarkable that there is a similar mark between L and I in the fifth line of the inscription noticed in § 32.

LVG is a common abbreviation for *Lugdunum,* and in that city the Galerian appears to have been the ordinary tribe. See Horsley, *Brit. Rom., Monmouthshire,* n. iii, and Orelli, n. 4020.

But the principal difficulty remains for consideration. To the reading of the last line,

·   VIC·PF·NASEMF

the Messrs. Trollope suggest the serious objections, that PIA FIDELIS can scarcely be accepted as an expansion of P·F, as it is doubtful whether the sixth legion was ever styled *pia fidelis;* and that the concluding letters are so inaccurately formed, and their import so obscure, that they are unable to offer any satisfactory explanation. Let us first consider the question as to the application of the epithets *pia fidelis* to the sixth legion. Henzen certainly seems to have been of the opinion that this legion was not styled *pia fidelis,* for, in his index, whilst giving other titles, he omits mentioning these, and corrects two inscriptions in which these letters are found in connexion with the sixth. In his emendations I concur, for the use of CLAVD· in each of these cases shows that LEG·VII was intended; but the opinion that P·F, standing for *pia fidelis,* were never applied to LEG·VI, may be refuted by several examples. In Britain, omitting some instances which may be questioned, we find examples in *Northumberland,* n. xliv.; *Cumberland,* nn. xxiv. and xlii.; and *Westmoreland,* n. vi., of Horsley's collection. In Stuart's *Caledonia Romana,* p. 349, we find an inscription in which the words *pia fidelis,* applied to the sixth, are almost *in extenso.*

Again, in Bruce's *Roman Wall*, pp. 270 and 274, we have other
examples of the application of P·F· to the same. Nor is the
usage limited to Britain. Steiner, n. 611; Lersch, *C. Mus.* i., p.
14; and Dureau de Lamalle, *Annal. dell' Inst. Arch.* iv., 1832,
p. 151, supply examples found on the continent.

In Bruce's *Roman Wall*, p. 250, we have *fidelis* in extenso;
and in Mommsen's *Inscrip. Neap.*, n. 2852, "*fidel.*," but in both
cases without "*pia.*"

As it has now, I conceive, been established, that P·F in the
last line of the inscription under consideration should be read *pia
fideli*, we may proceed to the last letters, read by the Messrs.
Trollope as NASEMF. The ligulate form, read by them as NA,
seems to me to be VM. It is not uncommon, and is noticed by
Horsley in his table of abbreviations. Assuming, then, that
these letters are VM, and adopting the reading of the others by
Messrs. Trollope, I would suggest *vicus monumentum sibi et
maritæ fecit.* But I am not satisfied that E, after S, is the correct reading. The letter, as it appears in the wood-cut, looks
very like P. If this be the fact, then I would suggest:— *Vicus
mandavit sua pecunia monumentum fieri.* According to my view
the inscription may most probably be read thus:

```
    DIIS MANIB[VS]
C[AII] IVLI[I] GAL[ERIA]
CALENI LVG[DVNO]
VET[ERANI] EX LEG[IONE] VI
VIC[TRICE] P[IA] F[IDELI] V[IVVS] M[ANDAVIT]
        S[VA] P[ECVNIA] M[ONUMENTVM] F[IERI].
```

§ 35. In Mr. C. Roach Smith's *Collectanea Antiqua*, i., p. 135, a grave-stone, which was found some sixty years ago in Whitechapel, London, is figured ; and the following explanation is given of the inscription which is on it :

> "D.M.
> IVL.VALIVS
> MIL.LEG.XXVV
> AN.XL.H.S.E.
> C.A.FLAVIO
> ATTIO.HER

Diis Manibus. Julius Valius miles legionis vicesimæ valentis victricis, anno quadragesimo, hic sepultus est. Caio Aurelio herede."

There is no difference between this expansion and that proposed in the *Gentleman's Magazine*, vol. liv., p. 672, excepting the emendation of the number of the legion, which Mr. Smith correctly gives as xx, instead of xxx, and the accidental omission of *Flavio Attio* between *Aurelio* and *herede*.

As there are obvious objections to this rendering, I would read the inscription thus :

D·M·	D[iis] M[anibus];
IVL·VALIVS	Jul[ius] Valius,
MIL·LEG·XX.V·V	Mil[es] leg[ionis] xx V[aleriæ] V[ictricis],
AN·XL·H·S·E	An[norum] xl, h[ic] s[itus] e[st],
C·A·FLAVIO	c[uram] a[gente] Flavio
ATTIO·HER·	Attio her[ede].

§ 36. In the *Journal of the Archæological Association*, ix., p. 91, there is a description of various articles of the Roman period, which were exhibited by Mr. Gunston, who stated that he was informed that they had been found in London. In addition to the reasons which are there given for believing that the infor-

N

mation communicated to that gentleman was incorrect, there
seems to me to be in one of the inscriptions ground for suspicion,
that it was not found in Britain. The inscription, to which I
refer, is

L·AVTRONI
VRBANI·OL·II

The reading of this is evidently:—*Lucii Autronii Urbani ollæ
duæ.* Now there is no example, so far as I am aware, of any
British inscription mentioning the *ollæ,* which are so commonly
noticed in inscriptions found in Italy. The only sepulchral desig-
tions in inscriptions found in Britain, so far as I recollect, are
monimentum, tumulus, and *memoria.* There is, however, a
sepulchral stone, which, if my reading be correct, furnishes a term
that I have never met with in any other inscription. As the
examination of it may be of some interest, I shall devote a separate *article to the consideration of it.

§ 37. In the *Journal of the Archæological Institute*, 1860, p. 270, a tile from *Caerwent is figured, which bears the name BEL-LICIANVS, four times written, in "what may be called the cursive hand [?] of the British Romans. The name Belicianus (with a single *l*) occurs on one of the tomb-stones from Bulmore, near Caerleon, and may possibly refer to the same individual."

To these observations of Mr. J. E. Lee, the following remarks are subjoined:

"The sepulchral stone found at Bulmore, to which Mr. Lee refers, is figured in his *Delineations of Roman Antiquities found at Caerleon*, pl. xxiv., p. 37. It bears an inscription in memory of Julia Veneria; it was erected by Alexander (sic) her husband and Julius Belicianus her son. The upper part of the stone forms a pediment, on which a dolphin is sculptured. The names Bellicius, Bellicinus, Beelicus, and also Bellianus, Bellicuus, &c., occur in inscriptions given by Gruter. Bellicuus was the name of a family of the *Annia gens;* Belliclaqus may have been a name derived from that of the town in Gaul, of some note in Cæsar's campaign against the Allobroges, Bellicium, or Bellex, now known as Belley. It is situated about forty miles E. of Lyons."

I am unable to consult Mr Lee's work, as above referred to; but the inscription, which is cited, is the same as that given in Mr. Wright's *Celt, Roman, and Saxon*, p. 315 (p. 320, 2nd ed.):

" D.M	To the gods of the shades.
IVLIA·VENERI	Julia Veneria,
I·AN·XXXII	aged thirty-three years,
I·ALESAN·CON	Alexander, her husband
PIENTISSIMA	most attached,
ET·I·BELICIANVS	and Julius Bellicious
F·MONIME	her son, this monument
F·O	caused to be made."

With this reading and translation I am by no means satisfied. The I at the beginning of the third line seems to me to be not a

numeral, to be joined to XXXII in the preceding line, but the
ordinary *nota* for *Julius*, scil., "*Julius Alexander.*"   "Her
husband most attached" is evidently a casual slip, as a translation
of CON[IVGI] PIENTISSIMA[E], which, of course means " to
his most attached wife."   The[*] name BELICIANVS may perhaps be nothing more than the ordinary *cognomen* FELICI-
ANVS, the B being used for F.   MONIME is so strange an
abbreviation of MONIMENTUM, that it excites suspicion as to
the correctness of the reading.   I venture to suggest—M·OP·
TIME,—*i.e.* M[ATRI] OPTIM[A]E.   According to this view,
the inscription denotes that "Julius Alexander to his most
affectionate wife, and Julius Felicianus to his excellent mother,
caused [this memorial] to be made."

P. S.—Since the foregoing article was published Mr. Lee
has favoured me with copies of his works—"Delineations of
Roman Antiquities found at Caerleon (the ancient Isca Silurum)
and the neighbourhood, by John Edward Lee," London, 1845;
and "Description of a Roman building and other remains lately
discovered at Caerleon, by John Edward Lee," London, 1850.
I now find, from p. 37 of the first of these works, that Mr.
Wright's translation—"her husband most attached"—was founded
on Mr. Lee's expansion—*conjux pientissima*.   Mr. L. remarks:
"There is some little difficulty with respect to the word *pientissima,* the gender of which is evidently incorrect; but, as it is well
known that the ancients, in their inscriptions, did not always
adhere strictly to the rules of grammar, it probably may be considered as an 'error of the mason."   There can, I think, be no
reasonable doubt that the expansion which I propose—*con*[jugi]
pientissima[e]—is correct.   Mr. Lee's lithographic drawing, however, has satisfied me that his reading of MONIME should not
have been questioned.   The letters are uninjured, and are distinctly MONIME.[‡]

* It is worthy of remark that we have another example of a female named *Julia Veneria*
on an *olla* found at Naples.   See Orelli, n. 4487.

† See note p. 27.

‡ Since this postscript was written, I am indebted to Mr. Lee's courtesy for a copy of his
new work—" *Isca Silurum*"—which "combines the substance of the two former volumes,
with an account of recent discoveries, in the shape of an 'Illustrated Catalogue of the
Museum.'"   From p. 15 of this volume, I perceive that Mr. Lee accepts my first two emenda-

§ 38. Horsley, *Britannia Romana*, p. 321, gives the following inscription, on a stone which was found at Caerleon :—

"PRO SALVTE   *Pro salute*
AVGG N·N·   *Augustorum nostrorum*
SEVERI ET ANTONI   *Severi et Antoni—*
NI ET GETÆ CÆS   *ni et Getæ Cæsaris*
P·SALTIENVS P·F. MAE *Publius Saltienus Publii filius*
                                                      [*Mae-*
CLA THALAMVS HADRI *cia Thalamus Hadrianus*
PRAEF·LEG·II·AVG   *præfectus legionis secundæ Augustæ*
C·VAMPEIANO ET   *Caio Vampeiano et*
LVCILIAN . . . . .   *Luciliano* [consulibus]."

His remarks on it are :—

"Camden gives us this Inscription from a votive altar, out of which the name of *Geta* (as he says,) has been erased, yet so as that some shadows of the letters remain. According to the *Fasti*, it should be *Claudius Pompeianus et Lollianus Avitus*, that is in the year 209. I don't find that in any *Roman* inscription in *Britain Geta* is styled *Augustus*, unless it may have been in some of those in which the name is erased; and then, perhaps, for this very reason it has been struck out."

In the *Monum. Hist. Brit.*, 39 a, we have another inscription found at the same place, which enables us to explain the preceding :

SALVTI RE
GINAE·P·SAL
LIENIVS·P·F·
MAECIAET * *
MVS HAD
PRAEF·LEG·II *
CVM FILIIS SVIS
AMPEIANO ET LV
CILIANO D·D·

tions—acti. I as standing for *Julius*, and CON·PIENTISSIMA for *conjugi pientissima*, but rejects the conjectural reading M·OPTIME, i. e., M[ATRI] OPTIM[A]E. I have already stated my opinion on this last point, since I had the opportunity of seeing a drawing of the stone. Mr. Lee, however, has misunderstood the ground of my "suspicion as to the correctness of the reading and of my venturing to suggest another,"—as he has failed to notice the difference between MONIM· and MONIME. The former is a common abbreviation of *monimentum*, but I had never met with an instance of the latter.

It is evident that these two stones were erected by the same person, a Prefect of the second legion, with his sons. The only doubt about his names arises from a variance in the inscriptions as to his *nomen gentilitium*. From one it appears to be SALTI-ENVS, from the other SALLIENIVS. The omission or insertion of I before the final VS presents no serious difficulty, for there are similar examples, such as ALFENVS or ALFENIVS; but I know not how to explain the difference of T and L. It is strange that the variety should occur in two inscriptions cut in the same place, and not improbably by the same mason, under the eye of the person himself. Has the fourth letter in both been misread? and should it be either V or E? In Mommsen's *Inscrip. Neapol.*, n. 6625, we have SALLIENVS as a *nomen gentilitium*.

The other portions of the Prefect's style are clear, so that we may expand them thus :—P[VBLIVS] SALTIENVS or SALLIENIVS P[VBLII] F[ILIVS] MAECIA [TRIBV] *THALAMVS·HADRIA. Horsley suggests HADRIA[NVS] and Orelli HADRIA[NALIS]. Neither seems to me as probable as *Hadria, scil. Hadria* in Picenum as his birth-place. As to the tribe, see Mommsen, *Inscrip. Neapol.*, nn. 6133, 6138. A very strong argument in favour of my reading is that all the names are thus in the normal order.

From the 7th, 8th, and 9th lines of the second inscription we learn that Horsley's idea, that the persons named in the 8th and 9th of of the first were consuls, is erroneous. It is clear that they were sons of the Prefect, and that their names were *Ampcianus* and *Lucilianus*. From the 7th line of the second we may derive an emendation of the 8th line of the first—*scil.* CVM for C·V, and reject Orelli's conjecture—cu[rantibus]. It is, perhaps, worth while adding that there is no other example, so far as I am aware, of *regina* being applied to *Salus.*

---

* In the 4th line of the second inscription, as given in the *Monum. Hist. Brit.*, there is an E between the final A of MAECIA and the initial T of THALAMVS. I am persuaded that this is a misreading, caused, perhaps, by the accidental prolongation of the bar of the M, which was probably tied to the T. The idea, which is suggested by the reading *et*, that two persons erected the altar cannot for a moment be entertained. Independently of objections to their names—*scil.* P·SALTIENVS or SALLIENIVS·P·F· MAECIA and THALAMVS HADRI[ANVS]—the words *præfectus cum filiis suis* prove that there was but one person mentioned. See p. 4.

P. 8.—On reference to Mr. Lee's *Delineations of Antiquities, &c.*, I find that he accounts for the variance in the *nomen gentilitium*, by supposing "an error of the mason," for "the fourth letter in one case is decidedly T and in the other decidedly L." In the second inscription "an I has evidently been inserted between the N and the V, whereas there is no such letter in the other; but in the former it is rather indistinct and has the appearance of having been partially erased; it is possible that in the [first] inscription there may originally have been a small I joined to the N, but it must be confessed that at present there is no appearance of it." With regard to the ET, rejected in my note, p. 102, Mr. Lee finds it in both inscriptions, and consequently believes the stones to have been erected by two persons—"*Publius Sallienus Publi filius Maccid et Thalamus Hadrianus.* In that given by Camden (although he omits it) Mr. L. discovers it "hidden under certainly a very complicated *nexus*. The T and H are united, and a small obscure letter, which now looks like an I very much widened at the top, is placed above the left upright stroke." In the other on the altar, he regards "the combination of these letters as somewhat different: there is no appearance of any letter above the line, and though the lower parts of the letter are lost, sufficient remains to show that the first letter in the *nexus* is a reversed E (as is evident from the central horizontal stroke), and that the T and H are united; the letter T must therefore stand for the last letter in ET, and the first in THALAMVS." In p. 4, I have noticed errors caused by the intrusion of this conjunction, and will now merely add that sometimes mistakes also arise from assigning a double duty to one letter, as Mr. Lee does here to T, which he regards as at once the final of ET and the initial of THALAMVS. We have an example in Mr. Ward's reading of a part of the inscription given by Horsley, *Somersetshire*, n. iv.—ETVICT. Mr. W. observes—"the T at the beginning of the word TVICTIA is to be twice read, as L in the Middlesex inscription." I have no doubt that the true reading is ET-VICT[ORIA].

I am persuaded that the names in the two inscriptions are not of two persons, but of one; and I cannot but think that Mr. Lee, on *further examination, will find that he is mistaken. In

<hr>

* In his new work—*Isca Silurum*—he adheres to the readings of these inscriptions as

the emendation CVM I have been anticipated by the Rev. C. W. King. p. 42 ; and Mr. Lee also notices the singularity of the epithet *regina* as applied to *Salus.*

§ 39. In the *Monum. Hist. Brit.*, p. cix., n. 26 b, we have a copy of an inscription on a stone found at Caerleon :

> IMPP·VALERIANVS ET GALLIENVS
> AVGG·ET VALERIANVS NOBILISSIMVS
> CAES·COHORTI VII·CENTVRIAS·A SO
> LO RESTITVERVNT·PER·DESTICIVM IVBAM
> VC·LEGATVM AVGG·PR·ET
> VITVLASIVM LAETINIANVM LEG·LEG
> II·AVG·CVRANTE·DOMIT·POTENTINO
> PRAEF·LEG EIVSDEM

[*i. e.*, imperatores Valerianus et Gallienus, Augusti, et Valerianus nobilissimus Cæsar, cohorti septimæ centurias a solo restituerunt, per Desticium Jubam, virum clarissimum, legatum Augustorum, proprætore, et Vitulasium Lætinianum, legatum legionis secundæ Augustæ, curante Domitio Potentino præfecto legionis ejusdem].

The only *difficulties in this inscription are in the words *centurias* and *praef·leg·ejusdem.* C. F. Hermann, *Gött. Gel. Anz.,* 1846, p. 1422, suggests the reading *tentoria* for *centurias,* and this is accepted by Lange, *Hist. Mut., rei. mil.,* p. 89.

Henzen, n. 6746, asks—"num ædificia, in quibus singulæ centuriæ habitabant ?" The explanation, which he has so doubtfully suggested, seems to me to be correct.

---

given in the "*Delineations.*" My opinion, however, remains unshaken, that but one person with his sons erected the altar; nor do I see any reason for changing my views relative to his name. In the *Rheinisches Museum für Philologie*, n. 1, 1856, Dr. K. Hübner has anticipated me by proposing exactly the same reading of the names as I have given. He rejects the ET with the remark; "ET in line 4 is a common evasion of Englishmen, when the nomen *gentilitium* [?] is too much for them." In pp. 3, 4, I have noticed a reading, which proves that the resort to "ET" in difficulties is not peculiar to the island.

* Hübner, *Rheinisches Museum*, n. 1, 1856, p. 6, takes the right view as to *centurias,* and has anticipated me in the reference to the *Museum Veronense.*

In this sense I understand the same term, as it is used by Cicero, *de leg. Agrar.* ii, 13 :—*praeterea mulis, tabernaculis, centuriis, supellectili.* The rarity of this signification is such that Turnebus proposed to substitute for *centuriis, tentoriis,* and Pantagathus read *canteriis,* whilst Professor Long, in his edition of Cicero's Orations, London, 1855, remarks—" there is no meaning in the word."

The difficulty regarding a *legato and a *praefect being at the same time in the same legion leads Lange to suggest the reading—*praef. fab. leg. ejusdem* [*i. e., praefecto fabrûm legionis ejusdem*], as if *fab.* had been omitted by mistake. Henzen regards the inscription as proving that the *praefecti* of legions were under the *legati,* and acted as their deputies. I am inclined to think that *Domitius Potentinus* was *praefectus castrorum,* on whom, from his official position, the duty of superintending the restoration of the soldiers' quarters would devolve. In the *Journal of the Archaeological Institute,* viii., p. 138, an altar to Fortune, which was found at Caerleon, is figured. It was erected by PRAEF CAS-TRO, *i. e., praefectus castrorum. Desticius Juba,* mentioned here, was probably the same noticed in the *Museum Veronense,* p. ccclxxvii, 2 :

T·DESTICIO
T·F·CL
IVBAE·C·V·
PRAETORIO
ORDO·CONCORD
PATRONO

P. S.—Mr. Lee, *Delineations of Antiquities,* p. 13, was the first who correctly interpreted *centurios.* His words are—" the same word may have stood for a century or company, and for its quarters." In his expansion he gives *cohortis,* instead of *cohorti,* which is plainly on the stone. There is no reason for this change, for the Latinity of *cohorti septimae,* in the sense "to or for the seventh cohort," is unexceptionable.†

---

* In Dr. Bruce's reading of an inscription on an altar found at Kirk Steads, Roman Wall, 2nd ed., p. 274, there is a greater novelty—a legion having two legates at the same time. Dr. B.'s reading of KT (which he himself queries), must be incorrect.

† In my copy of the inscription on the opposite page, the second PR·, in the 8th line, is omitted by a typographical mistake.

o

§ 40. In the *Journal of the Archæological Institute*, viii., p. 158, a stone resembling part of a column, or a mile-stone, is figured, bearing the imperfect inscription :

> NCTO
> HRAE
> SFVSTVS
> IIAVG
> M·F

Mr. Lee remarks : "the usual formula, INVICTO MITH-RAE, seems to be discernible." As the first letter seems clearly to be N, the word was more probably *SANCTO, an epithet which is also, though not so commonly, applied to Mithras. In the third line we have the remains of the names of the dedicator, and in the penult there was, perhaps, besides LEG·II·AVG, the designation of his military rank. It is not easy to decide what expansion to give to M·F. If the inscription had been sepulchral, there could be no doubt, but it is evidently dedicatory to Mithras. Of the readings which occur to me the most feasible are *monitus fecit*, and *miliarium fecit*. The erection of altars *ex monitu* was common ; and in Henzen's n. 6134 a we have, I think, an example, of the offering of a *miliarium*.

P. S.—In the *Isca Silurum* Mr. L. observes :—" the first words seem to have been *Sancto Mithræ*, but they may, as Mr. Way appears to think, have been in the usual formula, *Invicto Mithræ*." He passes over M·F in silence and does not even mention II AVG.

§ 41. In Mr. Lee's *Delineations of Roman Antiquities*, &c., plate xi., fig. 3, we find the following inscription on the handle of an amphora :—

> M.ÆMRVS.

---

* The inscription is—

C·FABERIVS·MIL·ET·SEDILIA IVNONI·DAT.

Henzen, in uncertainty about the meaning of MIL·, asks whether it can be Miliarium. I am not sure that I understand what he meant by this word—whether "a milestone" or "a caldron." I have somewhere met with another example of an offering of a *miliarium*, which I conjectured to be a designation of a cylindrical altar or table, but I know no authority for the conjecture. In the *Isca Silurum* Mr. Lee regards the Carrleon stone as " a round altar," as " the top or capital is partially hollowed out."

I am inclined to read and expand the letters thus : M[AR-
CVS] ÆM[ILIVS] RVS[TICVS ?], or M[ANV] ÆM[ILII]
RVS[TICI ?].

§ 42. In plate xiii., fig. 3, is the representation of a fragment
of a tile stamped with the usual legionary impress II AVG, with
the addition of two tied letters followed by T. Mr. Lee observes
that " the whole stamp may be read either IIAVGMVT, or
IIAVGMAT," and adds that the opinion of Mr. King and Mr.
Dunbory were in favour of the first.

Neither MVT nor MAT is intelligible ; I have no doubt that
the *true reading is ANT, i. e., ANTONINIANA. I have not
met with an example of this epithet as borne by the *legio secunda
Augusta ;* but Orelli, u. 2129, supplies one of the *legio secunda
adjutrix pia fidelis,* the same mentioned in one of the Bath and
one of the Lincoln inscriptions.

§ 43. In plate xviii., an altar is figured, bearing the following
inscription:—

> . . . TVNE ETΓBONOEVE
> NTOCORNELI·CASTVSETIVLI
> DELISIM.VS CONIVGES
> POS . . R

" Above this are †two figures, the left one of which is so defaced as
to render it difficult to say whether it was intended for a male or
a female. When Mr. King first saw it, the outline was far more
clearly defined than at present, and he has little doubt that the
two figures represented the men mentioned in the inscription."
Mr. Lee further observes :—

"The inscription may be read as follows:—*Fortunæ et Bono Eventæ
Cornelius Castus et Julius Delisianus conjugesque posuerunt.*

It is singular that this inscription seems never to have been completely finished, although there was sufficient room after the last R for the remaining letters VNT. The lines between which the letters were placed may be traced here very distinctly, but in the other parts of the inscription they have been obliterated; there are also no letters for the que after conjuges, though there appears to be an indefinite mark, as if the workman had begun to chisel out some abbreviation."

Of the worship of *Bonus Eventus* there are many examples; nor is the use of *Evento* for *Eventui* rare. See Orelli, nn. 1783, 1788, &c.

The unauthorised introduction of the *que* does not at all satisfy me. I do not recollect having met in any inscription with such a form as *conjugesque*, or *conjuxque*: either *et conjuges* or *cum conjugibus suis* (as *cum filiis suis*), is more in accordance with epigraphic usage. See Orelli, nn. 1238, 2047, 2504; Zell, *Delectus*, n. 182; and *Museum Veronense*, p. 237. I am inclined to regard the inscription as similar to that noticed in note, p. 4, i. e., as requiring that the word or words (*voverunt* or *votum susceperunt*) meaning "vowed" should be supplied: scil, *Cornelius Castus, et Julius Belisimus voverunt—conjuges posuerunt.* We may, indeed, regard the VS before CONIVGES as standing for v[otum] s[usceperunt], and the one or two letters which are lost before the VS as forming the end of the name BELISIM, but I much prefer my first suggestion.

P. S.—In the *Isca Silurum* Mr. Lee adds the following conjecture:—" Mr. King suggests that this tablet may have been erected by the two individuals named, on taking possession of allotted lands—Fortune being a popular deity, and Bonus Eventus one of the patrons of agriculture (Varro, i.), as a symbol of which he is represented with a patera in his hand holding fruit, or with ears of corn." He also notices other interpretations, whilst both he and Mr. King adhere to that originally given. One suggested by "a leading member of the University of Cambridge" is that *conjuges* refers to the two men named in the inscription in the sense—" intimate friends and companions." It is strange that this view seems to have been so generally received with approval. It is accepted by the author of a critique on Mr.

Lee's work in the *Parthenon*, July 19, 1862, who remarks :
" They were perhaps something like the 'sworn brethren' of the
Middle Ages."

The *author of the review in the *Gentleman's Magazine*,
August, 1862, also receives and defends it.

" To us it seems there is no necessity to suppose either an omission,
[mil. of *que*], or that *conjuges* here implies ' wives' ; or can mean other than
contubernales ' yoke-fellows, friends or companions.' " We therefore submit
an example of this use of the word, from Fabretti, p. 818 :—

DIS·M
PALLADIS
T·STABERI
FAVENTINI·SER·
T·STABERIVS
FAVENTINI·L
CHARITO·CON
IVGI·DE·SE·B·M.
V·A·XXXII.

Here Charito, a *libertus* of T. Staberius calls Pallas, the deceased *servus*
[*serva*] of the same *patronus*, his *conjux*."

This inscription does not prove the point for which it was cited.
Neither in it nor in any other, is one man said to be the *conjux*
of another man.

Relative to such inscriptions, as given by Fabretti, Mr. Lee,
p. 20, had remarked :—" The Rev. C. W. King informs me that
the inscriptions referred to only speak of *contubernales* as people
who have contracted illegal marriages (such as that of a slave
with a freedman), and that there are no instances in Fabretti
of the use of the word *conjuges* in any other than its usual sense."
Mr. King's statement, as given by Mr. Lee, is not accurate.
Fabretti, by a series of inscriptions, beginning at p. 307, and of
which that cited from p. 318 is one, proves that the term *conjux*

---

* From p. 161, I learn that he holds the same opinion that I do as to the erection of the
tablet and altar, noticed in § 23, by one person. The only variance is as to *Hadrianus*.
" As in the engravings no *et* is visible in either, between the words *Marcia* and *Thalamus*,
we suggest the readings as above, [P Sallienus, P. alias Marcia (tribe) Thalamus Hadrianus],
considering P. Sallienus Thalamus Hadrianus as one name, that of the Prefect."

was often applied in cases in which *contubernalis* should have
been used, and even *vice versa*.   As there was no legal marriage
between slaves, neither of the pair cohabiting could be called the
conjux of the other.   The man was said to be the *contubernalis*
of the woman, and the same term was applied to the latter; and
yet, as he shews, this distinction of terms was not observed.

It is in a totally different sense that soldiers were said to be
contubernales.   The term as thus applied means " comrades occu-
pying the same tent."   Neither Fabretti, nor, so far as I am
aware, any other author, furnishes any authority for the use
of *conjuges* applied to two men in the sense " intimate companions" or " yoke-fellows."   In the same review we find the
following passage :

" Mr. Lee and most of his friends, including Professor Mommsen of Berlin, consider the word *que* has been omitted at the end of the third line, ard
they read *conjuges* as " wives." Judging the entire inscription to mean that
Cornelius Castus and Julius Belisimus, with their wives, erected the altar
to Fortune and Bonus Eventus.   Dr. E. Hübner also agrees with Mr. Lee,
and says, ' There can be no doubt about the word *conjuges* being only applicable to a matrimonial couple.'"

There is no evidence in Mr. Lee's published statements on the
subject that either of those scholars agreed with him as to supplying the *que*.   On the contrary, Prof. Mommsen " asks if there
is any probability of the inscription being read BELISAMA
EIVS CONIVGES ; that is (as I understand him) *Cornelius
Castus et Julia Belisama ejus conjuges*—Cornelius Castus and
his Julia Belisama (Julia Belisama his wife), a married couple.
The omission of *uxor* is not uncommon, but I do not recollect
having ever met with an example of *conjuges* applied to both
husband and wife, although *conjux* is an ordinary term for either
separately.   The reading *Belisama* is not warranted by the stone :
the sixth letter seems clearly to be I.

Another view of the inscription has been suggested—that " the
stone was a sepulchral memorial to Cornelius Castus, and Julius
Belisimus, dedicated to Fortune and Bonus Eventus, and erected
by their widows."   Mr. Lee judiciously rejects this extraordinary interpretation : it is wholly unprecedented.

And now, having reviewed the opinions of others, I must express my preference for the interpretation—"Cornelius Castus and Julius Belisimous vowed the altar—their wives erected it." In addition to the example, which I have given, of the omission of the verb in the first clause, I now add another.

In the *Archæologia Æliana*, iv., pl. i., fig. 2, we have the following inscription on an altar found at Rochester :

DEO SOLINVIC
TIBCL DECMVS
CORNELANTO
NIVS·PRAEF
TEMPL·RESTIT

Mr. Thos. Hodgson thinks that the following reading should be adopted : *Deo Soli invicto Tiberius Claudius Decimus Cornelius Antonius præfectus templum restituit* Instead of taking the five names as belonging to one person, I would supply *posuit* or *instituit*, or some such verb after *Decimus*, and regard *Cornelius Antonius* as the names of the prefect, *i. e.*, *Tiberius Claudius Decimus instituit—Cornelius Antonius præfectus templum restituit.*

§ 43. In plate xx. a sepulchral inscription is figured :—

D   M
Q·IVLI·SEVERI·
DINIA·VETERANI
LEG·II·AVG·CONIVX·F·C·

Mr. Lee reads it: *Dis Manibus Quinti Juli Severi Dinia Veterani legionis secundæ Augustæ conjux faciendum curavit.*

To this I would merely add in explanation that *Dinia*, (*scil. Diniâ*), the veteran's *birth-place, was a town in Gallia Narbonensis, now *Digne.*

<hr>

* The author of the review in the *Gentleman's Magazine* observes: " It is not improbable that *Dinia* indicates the birth-place of Julius Severus." It is certain that it does: the use of the ablative of the birth-place without *domo* is common. See Fabretti, pp. 340, 341, and *Reinesii Syntag*, pp. 512, 529.

§ 44. Plates xxi. and xxii. contain delineations of four inscribed stones of the class called "centurial." Previously to entering on the general discussion of this subject, which may be conveniently introduced here, I shall notice plate xxi., fig. 2, as this presents peculiar difficulty. Mr. Lee's observations on it are :—

"This inscription is now on the walls of a ruined bath-house near a small stream, on the lane leading from Caerleon to Malpas; the letters are so rudely executed, and the stone has suffered so much from time, that it is nearly, if not quite, impossible to decipher it. On this account, the greatest care has been taken to give an accurate fac-simile of it on a reduced scale, in order to afford a chance of its being interpreted by some person accustomed to ancient inscriptions."

It appears to me that the stone has been placed in the wall upside down. If we *invert the delineation, we may read the inscription thus :—

Ↄ·C·IVLII
CAECINIANI·

i. e., centuria Caii Julii Cæciniani.

There is a similar rectification of an inverted inscription in Horsley's *Northumberland*, n. iii.

§ 45. The other inscriptions, in plates xxi., xxii., are the following :—

CHOR·V̄I·HAST·PRI·
＞ROESIMODERA

—

CHO·V
＞PAETINI

—

COH·ĪI
＞VALERI·FL
AVI

ASONAL

Mr. Lee's remarks on the first are, "An inscription erected by the sixth cohort, in honour of Roesus Moderatus, the first centurion of the Hastati. *Cohors sexta Hastati primi centurionis Roesi Moderati.*" To these remarks a note is subjoined :

"Horsley, (*Br. Rom.*, p. 207), thinks that when the name of the centurion is in the genitive, the centurial mark is to be read, not '*centurionis,*' but *centuria;* thus making the century or company called after the name of one of its officers ; the present inscription seems to disprove his opinion, as it is difficult to interpret it in any other way than by supplying words for '*In memory*' or '*In honour of*' Roesus Moderatus."

On the second Mr. Lee's remarks are, "A stone erected by the fifth cohort, in memory of the centurion Pactinius [Pactinus] —*cohors quinta centurionis Pactini* ;" and on the third—"Inscription in memory of the centurion Valerius Flavus, by the second cohort : it may be read thus:—

Cohors secunda centurionis Valerii Flavi."

Horsley, *Brit. Rom.*, p. 127, makes the following remark relative to the inscriptions of this class, called "centurial," which have been found in or near the wall of the lower isthmus :—

"These inscriptions were doubtless inserted in the face of the wall, when it was building, and in all probability erected by those centuries or cohorts who built that part of the wall." "These centurial inscriptions," he further remarks "found upon the face of the wall, and a passage in Vegetius mutually illustrate each other. According to Vegetius every century took their share in proportion in digging, building, and other works. His words are, *singulæ centuriæ accipiunt pedaturas.*"

Influenced by this view he supplies in many cases the verb *posuit.* See *Scotland,* n. xxiv., *Northumberland,* i., ii., iii., iv., x., xi., xii., &c., &c. In the following astonishing expansions, p. 301, he varies from both the opinions, expressed by him in pp. 127, and 207 :

" Ɔ CANDIDI	Centurionis Candidi
FIDES. XX	Fidelis annorum viginti
IIII	mensium quatuor.

To the note on the opposite page, I inadvertently omitted mentioning that Mr. Lee has adopted this view and changed the drawing accordingly.

P

The other is thus:

```
      COHO.I.FRISIN.        Cohors prima Frisiogensium
      ;) MASAVONIS             [or Frisonum]
      P. XXIII.            Centurioni Marco Savonis sti-
                           pendiorum viginti trium.
```

If these copies have been rightly taken, the former looks like a sepulchral inscription for a centurion. The XX most probably express the number of years he lived; the IIII either the number of months, or else of days, the number of months being quite effaced. The other also refers to a centurion, and seems to be an honorary monument erected to him by the whole cohort." [!]

For my part I have no doubt that there is not one of such inscriptions that was "in honour" or "in memory" of any one, and that the meaning of the centurial mark, under other circumstances often used for "centurion," stands in all such inscriptions for "century." Nor does Horsley's view of the *pedatura* furnish a satisfactory explanation of the great majority of examples. It is doubtless true that there are inscriptions marking the number of feet—the *pedatura*—in the work appointed to be executed or executed by a century, but there is not one of this kind in Horsley's collection.

As the number of such inscriptions is considerable and much misapprehension seems to exist regarding them, it may be useful to consider the subject at large, and state the varieties, so far as I have noticed them, not only of centuries, but also of legions and cohorts. The legions, as is well known, were distinguished by numbers, i., ii., iii, &c., and when there were more

---

*Horsley, *Northumberland*, Inscr., gives an inscription of this class, in which he regards ⊢ as standing for *centurio*:

```
              ⊢ MVN
              AX?V
```

He expands it—"Centurio Musas votum solvit. In p. lxxv a, we have another of this class:

```
              ⊢ MT
              NATI
              MAX.
```

I have but little doubt that both stones recorded the same century, *mil.*, *centuria Musaei Marini*. In the first we have MVN, for *Musaeii* and the M before MANSV is lost, & a., MANSV(MI) stood for MAXIMI.

than one of the same number, they were distinguished by their epithets or titles—e. gr., LEG·II·AVG·—*legio secunda Augusta* and LEG·II·A·P·F·—*legio secunda adjutrix pia fidelis*. The cohorts of the same legion were also distinguished by numbers from 1 to X, e. gr., COH·X, *cohors decima;* and the cohorts of different legions, when stationed together, by the addition of the legionary mark—e.gr., LEG·II·AVG·COH·X—*legionis secundæ Augustæ cohors decima*. It cannot be inferred, however, from the appearance of the marks of both legion and cohort on a stone, that there was more than one legion in that locality. The centuries of the same legion were distinguished not by number but by the names of their respective centurions, to which the number of their cohorts was sometimes prefixed—e.gr., >VALERI VERI, *centuria Valerii Veri,* *COH·VI·ƆSTATII SOLONIS—*cohortis sextæ centuria Statii Solonis—i. e.,* as we should say, Captain Smith's company of the first or second battalion. When different legions were stationed together it would be necessary to add the legionary marks, but in this case the cohort is scarcely, if ever, mentioned : the type is LEG·II·AVG >IVLI·TERTVLLI-†A[NI]—*legionis secundæ Augustæ centuria Julii Tertulliani*. The names of the centurion, which are usually given, are the *nomen gentilitium* and the *cognomen;* but we sometimes have the *prænomen* also, and there are examples of the *cognomen* alone. There is also another form in which the centurion's name is given —scil., as an adjective formed from his *nomen gentilitium*—thus Ɔ VOLVSIANA—*centuria Volusiana*. It is, perhaps, impossible to give a satisfactory reason for this variety. It may have been on account of the number of officers or men of that *gens* in the century, or that there had been a succession of centurions of that *gens*.

Of the stones which are thus inscribed there are some, of which there can be no question that they were intended to mark work that was executed. There are many examples of such legionary inscriptions of considerable length, which have been found in

---

* There is also another but rare form of this, such as Horsley's *Cumberland*, a. xviii.— ►CASSI PRISCI COH·VI; and a still rarer, *Northumberland*, a. lxiii.—ↄ COH VII [MA]XIM[IANA]

† See Horsley, *Cumberland*, a. xx.

Scotland along the wall of Antoninus; and to this *class also belong the following more briefly expressed :—

LEG	Legio
II	secunda
AVG	Augusta
FEC	fecit.

Horsley, Scotland, ix.

LII·AVG	Legionis secundæ Augustæ
CHO VIII	cohors octava
FEC	fecit.

Horsley, Northumberland, ix.

In the *Archæologia Æliana*, new series, i., p. 257, we have a similar example of an auxiliary cohort :

COH·I·BAT	Cohors prima Bat-
AVORVM F	avorum fecit.

I do not recollect having ever seen in British inscriptions an *undoubted* instance of such a centurial stone, *i. e.*, one designating the work executed, or to be executed by a particular century, except, probably, that given by Mr. Smith, *Journal of Archæological Association*, v., p. 223, *scil.* :

> COH·I·>OCRATI
> MAXIMI ꝶL·M·P

There is not one of those given by Horsley, in the *Britannia Romana*, in which he supplies "*posuit*," nor by Dr. Bruce, in the Newcastle Catalogue, in which he supplies "erected," that seems to me to be a record of this character.

---

* In Horsley's *Cumberland*, n. xlii., we have what appears to be another variety of this class:—

> LEG·VI·
> VIC·VF
> G·P·R·F·

Horsley expands it—" Legio sexta victrix pia fidelis Genio populi Romani fecit:" but G may be a misreading for C, and thus the expansion may be—" Legio sexta victrix pia fidelis romam posuit refecit." See *Northumberland*, cxl., and *Archæologia Æliana*, new series, i., p. 243, n. 30. The letters, however, more probably stand for "Genio Populi Romani feliciter," as they are read by Visconti in the inscription given by Orelli, n. 4947.

The true explanation of such inscriptions, as I think, is, that they were intended to mark the space set apart for quarters in an encampment, *i. e.*, to define the *pedatura* not in the sense in which it is used by Vegetius in the passage cited by Horsley, but in that in which Hyginus employs it. An examination of the varieties bearing numbers will support my opinion.

Ɔ CANDIDI	COHO·I·FRISIN
FIDES·XX	Ɔ MASAVONIS
IIII	P·XXIII

Horsley, *Lancashire*, p. 301.

>VALERI	Ɔ FLORINI	>CLAVDI
CASSIA	PXXII	P·XXX·8
N I I PXIX		

Newcastle Catalogue, no. 57, 73.

>ANTONRIM
N CXX

Welbeloved, *Eburacum*, p. 59.

The P in these examples stands, as I believe, not for *passus* but for *pedes;* and I have but little doubt that in the first of them this word should have been given instead of the misreading FIDES. It appears then that the numbers of feet on these stones are 24, 23, 19, 22, 30 and 120. Now according to the calculation of Hyginus in his distribution of a camp the space to be set apart for a century is 30 × 120 feet. Hence we can at once explain the last two numbers in the inscriptions above given. As to the others they may be regarded as examples of what must have often happened, either that a particular century did not require or could not be allowed the full space. This will seem more probable if we bear in mind that of the 30 feet 6 were left vacant. The arrangement for a century is so well described by Lange, *Hist. mut. rei mil. Rom.*, p. 65, that I subjoin his words:

"Jam igitur apparet, hemistrigia, in quorum latitudine 10 pedes tentoriis, 4 armis, 9 jumentis dantur, 6 vacui manent, contineo pedites contineri debere, si 120 pedes longa sint. Unius autem strigæ hemistrigia ita inter se conjunguntur, ut utriusque hemistrigii jumenta contigua sint, et, cum seoi pedes vacui singulorum hemistrigiorum ante hemistrigia sint, singulae strigae, ubi via viclaaria data non est, pedibus 12 vacuis dirematæ sint. In talibus autem hemistrigiis revera non 100 homines tendunt, sed singulæ centuriæ, ita ut, cum singulæ centuriæ 80 homimum sint, centurioni quoque in centuriæ pedatura locus assignari possit. Singulæ autem centuriæ octona tentoria habent, ita ut in singula 10 homines, qui contubernali ejusdem sunt, computentur, quorum tamen bini quoque tempore in excubiis sunt. Ex hac centuriarum distributione sequitur, ut singulis cohortibus legionariis 6 hemistrigia pedum 120 danda sint."

I would read the inscriptions thus :

Ɔ CANDIDI PEDES·XX IIII	*Centuria Candidi pedes xxiiii.
COHO·I·FRISIN Ɔ MASAVONIS P·XXIII	Cohortis primæ †Frisiouum centuria Masavonis pedes xxiii
>VALERI CASSIA N I I PXIX	Centuria Valerii Cassiani [?] pedes xix.
Ɔ FLORINI PXXII	Centuria Florini pedes xxii.
> CLAVDII P·XXX·S	Centuria Claudii pedes xxx. ½s[emis ?] .
>ANTONE ? M N CXX	Centuria Antonii §R ? m ? n[i] pedes cxx.

But we have yet to consider—

COH·I·>OCRATI
MAXIMIßL·M·P

As far as MAXIMI all is plain, *scil.*, Cohortis primæ centuria Ocratii Maximi, but the difficulty begins with the next letter, which resembles a Q with two tails. Mr. Roach Smith observes relative to the inscription :—

"It resembles in character the centurial commemorations on the stones of the great northern wall, and, like them, apparently refers to the completion of a certain quantity of building."

As it seems almost impossible that any building of a single century could be 50 miles long, it is better to separate the L from the M·P so that the latter shall mean but one mile, *scil.*, *mille passus*. I would then take *L* as standing for L[IMITIS] and regard the letter before it either as O for *opus*, or as Q the *symbol of the direction of the *limes*, either from east to west or *v. v.* See Facciolati in *limes*, and Mr. Yates's paper on the *limes Rhætia transrhenanus*, in the *Proceedings of the Arch. Instit.*, 1852, p. 104. The whole may thus be read : Cohortis primæ centuria Ocratii Maximi Q limitis mille passus, and the meaning would be that this century was to execute or did execute one thousand paces of the boundary running from east to west or west to east.

Let us now take up the inscription in Mr. Lee's delineations :

CHOR·VI·HAST·PRI

> ROESIMODERA

He regards it as "an inscription erected by the sixth cohort

---

to expound it—Cohortis sextæ Legio Fabric posuit. I incline to the opinion of Dr. Hunter, noticed but rejected by Horsley, that the words should be read *locus aversis*, and think that they were used ironically, as the Tarentian *locus sacris*. The use of *locus* favours my opinion that such stones were used to mark the spaces that were set apart for each cohort or century.

† This is doubtless the *cohors prima Frisiaonum* of the *tabulæ honestæ missionis* of Trajan, 1056, and of Hadrian, 124, and the *cohors prima Frisigorum* of the Notitia. *Frisii* is also written *Frisii* and *Frisei*, and we also find *Frisiaeones*. See Dr. Lavmana, *Archæologia*, xxvii, p. 224.

‡ See my notes on inscriptions found in Scotland.

§ Mr. Wellbeloved, p. 20, strangely reads "ANTONius PRæfectus Militum." The defaced letter after ANTON seems plainly to have been S, and the other letters probably formed the cognomen.

* I know no authority for regarding it as such. In the difficulty I have resorted to conjecture.

in honour of Roesus Moderatus, the first centurion of the Hastati;—*Cohors sexta Hastati primi centurionis Roesi Moderati.*" This expansion is unquestionably erroneous—but the correct reading is by no means clear. In Horsley's *Cumberland*, n. xxxviii., we have an exactly similar inscription :

COH IIII PR·POS
> IVL·VITALIS.

He has wholly mistaken its meaning, for he expands it— "cohortis quartæ prætorianæ posuit centuria Julii Vitalis;" whereas it is evident that as HAST·PRI denote the *hastatus primus*, or *prior*, so PR·POS denote the *princeps posterior*.

It seems then that in the first inscription we have the *hastatus primus*, or *prior*, of the 6th cohort, and in the second the *princeps posterior* of the 4th cohort. Thus in Orelli, n. 3452, we find PRINCIPEM POSTERIOREM and ASTATUM POSTERI-OREM of the 1st cohort of the XIth legion. But it must be observed that all such designations of centurions apply strictly only to those belonging to the first cohort. Thus, if we find *hastatus primus* alone, we understand by it the centurion who commanded the first century of the *Hastati* in the 1st cohort. But here we have COH·VI·HAST·PRI, whence it would appear that this was another form of HASTATVS SEXTVS. See p. 17. But, again, the terms admit two interpretations. By the *hast. pri.* of the 6th cohort may be meant either the centurion commanding the first century of the *hastati* of the 6th cohort; or that *ordo* itself, for the terms are used for either centurion or *ordo*. See Livy, xlii., 34, and Cicero, *de Divinat.* i., 35. Similarly by the *pr. pos* of the 4th cohort may be meant either the centurion commanding the second century of the *principes* of the 4th cohort; or that century itself. Thus we may render the first line of one inscription—the first *hastatus* of the 6th cohort, and of the other—the second *princeps* of the fourth cohort, with either of the two significations above mentioned. As it seems almost certain that the centurions named in the second lines were respectively the *hastatus primus*, or *prior*, and the *princeps posterior*, the construction may have been *hastati primi*, or *prioris*, and *principis posterioris*, in apposition with their names : but I am inclined to prefer regarding them as standing for the *ordines*, or centuries, and consequently take the construction to be *cohortis sextæ hastatus primus* (or *prior)—*centuria Roesi Moderati*—and *cohortis quartæ princeps posterior*—*centuria Julii Vitalis*

P. S.—In the *Isca Silurum*, Mr. Lee offers the following observations on the subject :—

" The general opinion now seems to be that the reversed C stands not for *centurionis* but for *centuria*, as Horsley considered it when the name was in the genitive. (Br. Rom. p. 207). In this case the company or century would be called after the name of its officer, and the centurial inscription will simply mean that a certain portion of work was done (as in the inscriptions on the Roman wall) by such a century, or that the stone pointed out its quarters."

In p. 6, Mr. Roach Smith's opinion is given that "it was set up on account of some work done by order or direction of Roesius, a centurion *primus hastatus* in the sixth cohort." I have no doubt that > stands for century, not for centurion ; and I am persuaded that the stone marked the space set apart for the quarters of that century of the 6th cohort. As to the change of *Roesus* for *Roenus*, I can see no reason. I would prefer either *Roesius* or *Roesius*, as the name is the *nomen gentilitium*.

§ 46. Mr. Lee, in his observations on the sepulchral inscription in pl. xxiii., fig. 1, notices the great age of the veteran—100 years. There is no other example, so far as I am aware, in Britanno-Roman epigraphy of so great an age. Indeed, as Mr. Wright remarks, "the average at which the Romans in Britain died, seems to be not much more than thirty." This remark is confirmed on examination of twelve sepulchral inscriptions as they appear in the plates of the *Britannia Romana*. A remarkable contrast is presented by the inscriptions in Algeria. If we take the first

* I prefer *prior* as the expansion of *pri.* in this inscription to Mr. Lee's *primus*, as I am not aware of any authority for the use of *hastatus primus* as denoting any other than the centurion commanding the first century of the *hastati* in the first cohort. He was also called simply *hastatus*, i. e. "the" *hastatus*, as the centurion commanding the first century of the *principes* in the first cohort was called *princeps*. See p. 17. Hence, n. 571, gives an inscription, from which some might infer that he was also called the *hastatus prior* of the legion. It is possible that he may have been, but the inscription, as given by Henzen, does not prove it.

Q

twelve, as they appear in Renier's collection, at *Lambæus, Vere-cunda, Cirta,* and *Sitifis* we find the average for the first place 39, for the second 50, for the 3rd 49, and for the fourth 40— *i. e.,* an average for the four of over 44. But it is not safe to draw inferences from small numbers.

§ 47. In pl. xxv., fig. 2, is the representation of a tombstone. It bears the following inscription :—

> . . . . AIDERNAVX·S
> TANNOSXVIMESSEXF
> CFLAFLAVINAMATER

Mr. Lee reads it thus :—*Julia Iberna vixit annos sexdecim menses ser faciendum curavit Flava Flavina mater.* For *Flava* read *Flavia.*

§ 48. In pl. xxvi., fig. 2, we have a very defective sepulchral inscription :—

> AL
> EG·II·AVG
> ˜E'RO·SE IV
> ECIANVS
> F·   C

" Fortunately, however, an exact [1] copy was taken by Mr. Jones at the time it was found, which shows it to be a sepulchral inscription for some person connected with the second legion : it is as follows :

> M
> GENIALIS
> EG·II·AVG·EX
> FERO* SE   IV
> NECIANVS
>   FC   "

I am inclined to suggest as a conjectural reading :

> D M
> I GENIALIS
> LEG·II·AVG·EX
> T·HERS·SEC·I·IV
> MECIANVS
>   F· C

*i. e., Diis Manibus ? Genialis legionis secundæ Augustæ ex
testamento heres secundus ? Julius Merianus faciendum curavit.*
I am not satisfied with it, however, as the collocation is objec-
tionable.

§ 49. In plate xxvi., fig. 3, is the representation of a fragment
of a tombstone, which bears the following imperfect inscription :—

M
ORVI
NISXVII

Mr. Lee reads it :—"*Dis Manibus* * * * *orvi annis sep-
tendecim.*" OR is more probably the ending of a name, such as
Victor, and VI the beginning of VIXIT.

§ 50. On p. 53, Mr. Lee copies the restoration of an imperfect
inscription, found at Caerleon, as given by Camden, ed. *Gough*,
iii., p. 109 :—

IMp
M AV*relio*
ANTO*nino*
AVG
SEVER L*ucii*
FILIO
LEG II Aug p.

*i. e., Imperatori Marco Aurelio Antonino Augusto Severi Lucii
filio legio secunda Augusta posuit.* It is impossible that the
reading *Lucii* can be correct. I suspect that the letter read
as L was really I, *i. e.*, SEVERI, and that AVG followed it.

P. S.—In the *Isca Silurum*, pl. vii., the stone is figured, from
which it appears that the letters in the 5th, 6th, and 7th lines are
now so injured that no reliable reading can be given of them.
Hübner, *Rhein. Mus.*, n. i, 1856, p. 6, suggests the following
restoration :—

IMp caes
M AVr antonino
AVG
SEVERI aug
FILIO
LEG II Aug

If he had adhered to the model which he proposed, viz. : n. 5943 of Mommsen's *Inscrip. Neapol.*, his restoration would have more nearly accorded with the Caerleon stone, for ANTONINO forms in both a separate line.

§ 51. In the same page the following *inscription is given :—

<pre>
          DEDICATV
            VRF
        OG   ES
            VE   NIO
          MAXIMOIE
           FVRPANo
            COS
</pre>

It is evident that the inscription records a dedication or inauguration, probably of a building. In the 2nd and 3rd lines the day seems to have been mentioned, for it is not improbable that the third should be read—OCTOBRES. The fourth probably contained the names of the dedicator ; and the remaining stated the year, for there can, I think, be but little doubt that the 5th and 6th are misreadings of MAXIMO II ET VRBANO, who were consuls in A.D. 234.

§ 52. In p. 84 we find a similar inscription, but of a different date :—

<pre>
            DD
           VIIII
           OCCB
           PRCR
           EIML
           COS .
            CVR
           VRSO
           AGTœ
         EI : IVS.
</pre>

DD stand either for DEDICATVM as in the preceding, or are the end of the formula "in honorem D·D", *scil.*, *domus divinœ*.

The 2nd and 3rd lines are plainly VIIII OCTOB., *i. e., September 23rd*, whilst the 4th and 5th are misreadings of letters standing for PEREGRINO ET AEMILIANO, who were consuls in A.D. 244. CVR in the 7th line is probably a contraction of CURANTE, and the last three lines give the names and titles of the individual.

The dates that may be collected from inscribed stones found at Caerleon include about fifty years, from the beginning to the middle of the third century. The notices of Severus and his sons indicate probably the time during which they were in Britain, *i. e.*, between 207 and 211 ; whilst the tablet, naming Valerian, Gallienus, and Valerian the Cæsar, must be referred to some year from 254 to 260. The author of the review of *Isca Silurum*, in the *Gentleman's Magazine*, August, 1862, p. 152, says that "the date of the inscription [on the tablet] must be between A. D. 253 and A. D. 259, just before the revolt of Postumus, in Gaul, when the young Cæsar was murdered." These statements are "erroneous : Gallienus was not associated in the empire until A. D. 254, nor was his son, Saloninus, "the young Cæsar," killed until A. D. 260.

§ 53. On p. 33 there is a most interesting inscription, which, if my reading of it be correct, supplies the Roman designation of *Isca* as a *colonia*.

```
        NN
        AVGG
        GENIO
        LEG      ·
        II AVG
        IN HoNo
        RENMIoT
          M  VA
            FH
            IV
            LE
            SC
              PP
              DD
```

The first five lines are evidently to be read : *Numinibus Augustorum et Genio legionis secundæ Augustæ.* The emperors are, probably, either Severus and Caracalla, or Valerian and Gallienus. The 6th, 7th, and 8th lines, I have but little doubt, are misreadings of the common formula :

IN·HONO

REM·TOT·

DOM·DIVIN.

i. e., *in honorem totius domus divinæ, scil.*. the imperial family. The reading of the next four lines is not so clear, but I strongly suspect that they were—

FEL·

IV

L·E

SC

i. e., *Felix*, or rather *Felicitas, Julia Esca;* *Esca being, as I think, another form of *Isca*.

Of the readings *Felix Julia* and *Felicitas Julia*, I prefer the latter. Thus we have the colonial designation of *Lisbon* in Orelli, n. 810—

SABINAE AVG

IMP·CAES·TRAIA

NI HADRIANI AVGVSTI

DIVI NERVAE NEPOTIS

DIVI TRAIANI·DAC·PAR

FIL·D·D·FELICITAS IVLIA

OLISIPO·PER

M·GELLIVM·RVTILIVM ET

L·IVLIVM AVITVM

It seems not improbable that *Isca* was called *Julia*, after †*Julia Domna,* the wife of Severus, and that we should trace the origin of the name †*Julia*, applied to ‡*strata* in this part of the country,

---

* The E is preserved in Exeter. At Caerleon Isca remains in the name of the river "Usk," on which the town is situated. The Latin word is evidently formed from the old Celtic or British Wysg, signifying " water."

† Thus *Beneventum* was styled in honour of her IVLIA·CONCORDIA·AVGVSTA·FELIX· BENEVENTVM.

‡ Camden traces the name *Julia*, as thus applied, to *Julius Frontinus*, and others perhaps may prefer *Julius Agricola*.

either to it or to her. PP and DD are, I think, to be read
pecuniâ publicâ dono dedit, or *decreto decurionum*.   The reading,
which I have proposed, in itself very probable, is favoured by the
circumstance that *Richard of Cirencester* names *Isca* as one of the
Coloniæ in Britain.

§ 54. In a "description of a Roman building and other remains,
lately discovered at Caerleon, by John Edward Lee," pl. ii., fig. 4,
we have " a mark on the fragment of a mortarium : it is reversed,
and most probably may be read CATTIVS MANSINVS."
Read C·ATTIVS·MANSINVS, *i. e., Caius Attius Mansinvs.*
The cognomen is doubtful.

§ 55. In pl. vii., fig. 1, a sepulchral stone is figured, bearing
the following inscription :—

D   M
TADIA·VALLAVNIVS·VIXIT
ANN·LXV·ET TADIVS EXVPERTVS
FILIVS·VIXIT·ANN·XXXVII·DEFVN
TVS·EXPEDITIONE GERMANICA
TADIA EXVPERATA FILIA
MATRI ET FRATRI·PIISSIMA
SECVS TVMVLVM
PATRIS   POSVIT

There are but two points in this inscription which require
explanation.   One—the meaning of *defuntus, i. e., defunctus*—
has already engaged the attention of Mr. Lee, and of the
Rev. H. H. Knight.   They both prefer interpreting the word as
deceased in the German expedition to *having completed, or served
in the German expedition.*

" In this case," Mr. Lee observes, "the tomb would be merely
a cenotaph to his manes."   On first view it seemed to me more

<hr/>

* Mr. Wright, *Celt, Roman, and Saxon*, p. 313, (p. 329, 2nd ed.) remarks;—" We are in
these inscriptions" (some that he had given in illustration of Roman epitaphs) "how
cautiously a direct allusion to death is avoided. We find an exception to this remark in
an inscription found of late years at Caerleon, in which one of the persons commemorated
is said to have died in a war in Germany." There is no ground for the statement that " a
direct allusion to death is avoided ' in Roman epitaphs. This notion, so far as it relates
to the use of *defunctus*, has long since been refuted by Christo. Biagi, *Monum. Graec. et Lat.
ex Musæo Nanii.*

probable that the stone marked the place of *interment of the three near each other. I was also inclined to prefer the interpretation, " having served in the German expedition to the end of it," as *fungor* with its compounds seems to be the proper term in this connexion. Thus Orelli, n. 3556 :—

OMNIBVS EXPE
DITIONIBVS FVNCTO

and n. 3523 :

OMNIB·EXPEDIT·ET
HONORIB·PERFVNCTO

but Henzen regards the latter as spurious. In n. 3201, also, where we have a notice of death in a German expedition, a different term is used :—

OBIIT IN EX
PEDITIONE GERMANICA

I am now, however, disposed to regard the stone as a sepulchral memorial, placed by the daughter near the grave of her father in memory of her mother and brother, whose bodies were interred elsewhere, probably on the continent. In this change of opinion I am influenced chiefly by the position of *defunctus*. If it had been used in the sense " having served in to the end," or " having completed," it would, I think, have been placed after *expeditione Germanica*.

There were so many German expeditions that it is impossible to determine to which reference is made.

The other point requiring explanation is the use of †VAL-LAVNIVS in the masculine with TADIA in the feminine. The author of the review in the *Gentleman's Magazine*, already referred to, suggests, with a query, *Vallaunium* or *Vallaunusa*, but on the stone there is certainly no A after the S.

---

* Mr. Wright's idea that the body of the son was brought from Germany to Isca is very improbable.

† Mr. Wright, Celt, Roman, and Saxon, p. 254. (p. 258 2nd ed.) remarks—" It is an inscription at Caerleon an adjective in the feminine gender is joined with a masculine name." If his observation refers to this inscription, he has mistaken the adjective, for *Tadia* is certainly not one.

P. S.—Since writing the foregoing, I have had the opportunity of reading the remarks in Mr. Lee's *Delineations of Antiquities*, and have reason to think that Mr. Wright intended to refer to Mr. Lee's reading of CON·PIENTISSIMA, as noticed in article 27.

Marini, *Atti*, i., p. 331, gives the following examples of masculine *cognomina* of females: Ælia *Demetrus*, Cassia *Mus*, Julia *Barachus*, Mucia *Antiochus*, Culidia *Antiochus*, Clodia *Optatus*, Acilia *Carnus*, Sallustia *Helpidus*, Flavia *Chrysophorus*. And yet I am not satisfied with this explanation of VALLAVNIVS. There is no example, so far as I am aware, of a *cognomen* of a female ending in IVS. The word resembles an *ethnic adjective, i. e.*, the Vallaunian, and this view of it may in some degree account for the mistake of gender; but it may also be read VALLA, or rather VALLIA, VNIV·S, *i. e.*, VNIV[IRA] S[ANCTA]. Fabretti, p. 323, gives other examples of this and the corresponding term *virginius*. I am inclined to prefer the view that *Vallaunius* was an ethnic adjective.

P. S.—In the *Isca Silurum* Mr. King remarks—"Unless the stone were a cenotaph the deceased hero must have fallen in the neighbourhood. Now Carausius, whose empire was confined to Britain, boasts on his coins of a 'victoria Germanica,' and displays also a trophy with 'de Germania.' Can these allude to the repulse of any Saxon pirates? The charge brought against Carausius, when admiral of the German ocean, was his allowing the Saxon pirates full impunity to plunder the British and Gallic coasts, and then catching them on their return home and re-capturing their booty for himself. This 'expeditio Germanica' must have been an important event in the British history of the third century for it to appear thus nakedly as a date upon a monument."

I can see no reason for believing that the *expeditio Germanica* mentioned here was more important than other such expeditions noticed in inscriptions. The words of course meant the latest German expedition. See Orelli, nn., 798, 2919, 3201, 3569, 5477, 6482.

§ 56. In pl. xi., we have a copy of what "appears to have formed part of a long inscription:"

CAESARES·L·SEPTI
VG***SEPTIMIVS
ORRVPTVM

Mr. Lee offers the following observations on it :—

" The inscription refers to some building which had gone to decay and had been restored by Severus and Geta his son.   Instances will be found in Gruter (p. 172, No. 6), of a similar use of the word *corruptum* : in the present instance it takes the place in the sentence, which is usually occupied by the word *restituerunt*, or some expression of a similar import.

From a comparison of the space which would have been occupied by the letters wanting to complete the Imperial title, and also the name of Severus, thus,

IMPERATORES

MIVS SEVERVS A

it appears probable that the name of Caracalla has not been mentioned, and that the title AVG refers to Severus only.   If we suppose that the inscription began with the word *Imperatores* there can be little doubt about the matter, and it is rather singular that this supposition is borne out by an inscription recorded by Maundrell in his "Journey from Aleppo to Jerusalem," in 1697, p. 47.   It was found near Sidon and is as follows :—

IMPERATORES

CAESARES

L SEPTIMVS SE

VERVS PIVS PER

TINAX AVG ARA

DICVS ADIADENICVS

PARTHICVS MAXI

MVS TRIDVNICIA

POTES VI IMP XI COS

PRO COS·P·P·

ET M AVREL ANTONI

NVS AVG FILIVS EIVS

It will be observed that the commencement of the inscription in both cases is the same, Imperatores Cæsares ; and also, that in the inscription in Palestine, the name of Caracalla, or Marcus Aurelius Antoninus, as he is usually named, stands alone, his brother's name being omitted, while in the present inscription found at Caerleon there is every probability that the name of Geta has stood alone, that of Caracalla his brother having been omitted.

It is well known that in many inscriptions the name of Geta has been designedly erased * * * [in this] there still remain decided traces of the ET and also of the letter P.

The unhappy disputes in the family of Severus are well known to every one ; they continued for many years, and were a constant source of disquietude to the emperor. We also learn from Herodian, iii., 48, that Severus, when he went northward in Britain took Caracalla with him, leaving Geta his younger son to regulate the affairs of the south of Britain, which was more settled, and for which duty he was better qualified than for the hardships of warfare in the north. While his father and brother were absent, and he had undisputed sway, may not Geta, under a feeling of irritation against his brother, have erected this inscription, leaving out Caracalla's name; in the same manner as his brother, in Palestine, had omitted that of Geta? This seems at least a probable supposition, in endeavouring to account for the omission; the subsequent erasure or attempt at erasure needs no explanation."

I cannot see any grounds for the opinion that in the inscription only Severus and Geta were named. We have examples of Severus, Caracalla, and Geta together and separately, and also of Severus and Caracalla and of Caracalla and Geta together, but there is no instance, so far as I am aware, of Severus and Geta, unless this be taken to be one. In my judgment the AVG of the second line belonged to Caracalla, i. e., M·AVREL·ANTO-NINVS, as in the inscription cited by Mr. Lee, and the inscription when complete contained the names of the three, of which there are well known examples.

The word *corruptum* suggests the conjecture that the building, which was restored, may have been the amphitheatre, of which remains have been found here. Thus in Henzen, n. 6597 :—

IMP CAESARES M AVRELIVS ANTONINVS ET
L AVRELIVS [COMMODVS] AVGG GERMANICI
SARMATICI FORTISSIMI AMPHITHEATRVM
VETVSTATE CORRVPTVM A SOLO REST
TVERVNT, &c., &c.

§ 57. Pl. xv. is a copy of a stone " found in the ruins of the large building," which bears the following inscription :—

PRIMVSTES
ERA

Mr. Lee observes : " It is in memory of the first *Tesserarius*, probably of the Augustan legion, though this is not expressly stated. The actual inscription is *Primus Tesero*, evidently an abbreviation for *Primus Tesserarius*."

There is no ground for the statement that "it is in memory" of the first Tesserarius: to me it seems much more probable that it marked his quarters. Under the emperors there was a *tesserarius* in each century, whose duty it was to communicate the watchword, inscribed on a square piece of wood called a *tessera*, to the men of his century. The *primus tesserarius* would be the *tesserarius* of the first century of the *triarii* of the first cohort.[*]

---

[*] Since the preceding sheets were printed, I have had the opportunity of reading "Letters from Rome," by the Rev. J. W. Burgon, M.A., and now subjoin an inscription given by him, p. 196, as it supports my view that *Felicianus* and *Felicissimus* were merely other forms of *Felicianus*.

"BELLICIA FIDELISSIMA VIRGO IMPACE IIIIX CALENDAS
SENTVRAS SEPTEMBRESQVE VIXIT ANNOS XVIII"

"*Felicia, a most faithful maiden. In peace, 6th of the coming Kalends of September; who lived 18 years.*"

§ 68. In Horsley's *Britannia Romana*, Northumberland, iz. a, we find the following copy of an inscription on a stone found at *Benwell :—

```
VICTORIAE
··GG AIFE
NSSENECIO
N COS FELIX
ALAIASTO
...M          PRA
```

Horsley reads it thus : Victoriæ Augustorum nostrorum fecit nepos Soxii Senecionis consulis Felix alæ primæ Astorum præfectus.

There can, I think, be no doubt that this reading should be at once rejected. It is plain that the names in the second and third lines after AVGG are †ALFENVS SENECIO; and the only real difficulty in the inscription is the initial letter or letters of the fourth line before COS. To me it seems most probable that we should read instead of N either VC or V alone. In a mural tablet found at Risingham, as given by Bruce, *Roman Wall*, p. 287, and Surridge, *Notices, &c.*, Pl. iii., we find the words ALFENI SENECI[O]NIS VCCOS, which, with Henzen, n. 6701, I would read, as here, VC COS, i. e., *vir clarissimus consularis.*

Alfenus Senecio was *legatus Augustorum* in Britain under Severus and Caracalla, the two *Augusti* noticed in the Benwell inscription. He is mentioned also on two other stones found at Greta Bridge and Brough.

As the Risingham tablet gives the 3rd Consulship of Severus

and the 2nd of Caracalla as the date of its erection, it may be inferred that Senecio was in the island at some time between 205 and 207 A.D.

From an inscription found at Naples, and given by Gruter, p. 208, Orelli, n. 4405, and Mommsen, n. 2646, it also appears that he was Sub-Prefect of the fleet at Misenum.

Horsley offers a suggestion as to tracing ASTORVM to Asta in Liguria, not to the Astures, a people of Spain. There can be no reasonable doubt, however, that the latter are intended. In Bruce's *Roman Wall*, p. 110, we have an inscription on a stone found at the same place, Benwell, which is decisive on the point :—

MATRIDVS CAMPEST
ET GENIO ALAE PR HISPANO
RVM ASTVRVM, &c.

As to the grammatical construction of the inscription, which forms the subject of this article, I supply *jussit* after COS, and *curavit* after PRAEF·, i. e., Senecio jussit, Felix curavit.

§ 59. Horsley's n. xviii. is an inscription on a fragment of a grave-stone found at *Halton Chesters :—

IS NORICIAN
ESSORIVS·MAGNVS
RATER EIVS DVPLALVE
SABINIANAE

He expands it thus : " Norici annorum triginta Memorius Magnus frater ejus duplaris alæ Sabinianæ," and offers the following observations :—

" The cut of the letters is neither very good nor exact, nor are they very regular as to their magnitude or distances one from another, and the whole savours of the lower empire. The original of this inscription is now at *Conington*, and there are some defects in the copy which *Cambden* has given us: particularly the S in the beginning of the second line, and the imperfect letters at the top are wholly omitted by him.

* The Horsoum of the Notitia.

Noricus is a Roman name, that occurs several times in *Gruter*. And the same *Nessorius* is found also in an inscription at Risingham in this county. The V in ALVE is manifestly an A inverted by mistake. There appears but one I in *Sabiniana* connected with the last stroke of the N, which, however, must be sounded both before the N and after it, or else we must suppose the former I to be included in the preceding D, as before in the R.

The mark at the bottom looked like a part of a letter, as if this stone had been parted from another, upon which there was some inscription, though perhaps it may be only an accidental flaw. *Camden* supposes that *Sabina, Hadrian's* wife, gave the name to this *ala*. But it seems more probable to me that it was taken from *Sabina*, the wife of the emperor *Gordian*, to whose time this inscription much better agrees."

I have but little doubt that IS are the last two letters of CIVIS, and that NORICI is the ethnic adjective. Neither Camden's nor Horsley's derivation of the name *Sabiniana* seems to me probable. I would trace it, like other similar designations of *alæ*, to *Salinus*, who raised or organised the corps.

§ 60. Horsley, *Britannia Romana*, p. 215, notices "another inscription in *Camden* referred to Hulton Chesters," and gives the following expansion and explanation of it :—

" M·MARI	*Marcus Mari*
VS VELLI	*us Vellia* [tribu]
A LONG	*Longus*
VS·AQVI	*eques*
S HANC	*hanc* [aram]
POSVIT	*posvit*
V·S·L·M	*votum solvit libens merito*

" I take it for granted that AQVIS here is used for EQVES, so EQVIS for EQVES we meet with in other instances : and perhaps A for the E has been an error of the transcriber. This horseman might also belong to the *ala Sabiniana*." AQVIS, in my judgment, is the ablative of AQVAE, the name of the birthplace of *M. Marius Longus* ; and (although it would be agreeable to refer it to the English AQVAE, scil., Bath or Wells), I am inclined to think that it stands for some continental springs, perhaps Aix, which was known as *Aquæ Sextiæ*. See *Marini, Atti*, p. 434, and Steiner, *Cod. In. Rom. Rhen.*, n. 398.

§ 61. Horsley's n. liii. is an inscription on a tablet found at
*Little Chesters. The inscription is imperfect, but the following
portions were legible :—

```
..........................GALIOR
.. .......................VOTANV
..NIEIVS POP IRRIDVS
FVNDAMEN............ERVNT SVB
CL·XENEPHO............EG AV PR
CVRANTE........................
```

He expands it thus :   ....Gallorum........vota
numini ejus principis optimi turribus..........fundamenta
posuerunt sub Claudio Xenephonte legato Augustali propraetore
curante...............

VOTA are plainly the last two syllables of *devota*, and POP,
in my judgment, should have been read POR, *i. e., prae turribus*,
"for the towers of the gate." *Devota* would agree with *cohors*
before *Gallorum*, but it is strange that we have the verb in the
plural—*posuerunt*.

§ 62. Some inscriptions have been found in this county which
seem to warrant the belief that amongst the Roman auxiliaries in
Britain were *cohortes Brittonum*. See Horsley, *Northumberland*,
nn. lxxii., lxxvi., and compare *Scotland*, n. xx., Bruce's *Roman
Wall*, pp. 121, 317, and Camden, *ed. Gough*, iii. p. 236. There can
be little doubt that some of the natives of the island served in it
as auxiliaries of the Romans. A passage in the *Agricola* of
Tacitus, c. 18, favours this view : *lectissimi auxiliarium quibus
nota vada et patrius nandi usus*; and it is probably to such that
the terms *commilitonum barbarorum* in the inscription found at
Carlisle, p. 30, refer. Nor is it improbable that the *cohors prima
Cornaviorum*, mentioned in the *Notitia* as stationed *ponte Ælii*, was
composed of *Cornavii*, the Κορναύιοι or Κορνάβιοι of Ptolemy, in
whose territory *Deva* (Chester) and *Viroconium* (Wroxeter) were
situated. This supposition seems to me much more probable than
that they were either the *Cornavii* of Scotland or the *Cornabii*

Damnonici. See Böcking, p. 902. But whilst I admit that there is sufficient evidence to prove that some of the auxiliary bodies that served in the island were composed of natives of Britain, I am not satisfied that the *cohortes* or *numeri Brittonum*, that served either there or on the continent, were of this character. On the contrary, there is reason to believe that *Britannica* was the proper term for a British corps, whether *ala* or *cohors*, and that *Brittones* denoted a continental people. Thus in a diploma of Domitian's, Henzen, n. 5430, we find I̅ BRITANNICA MILLIARIA immediately followed by I̅ BRITTONVM MILLIARIA, from which Henzen, with justice as appears to me, draws the inference—" Britannos et Brittones diversos esse, hinc apparet."

§ 63. Horsley's n. lxxxvi. is an imperfect inscription on an altar :—

MILC
PRAEEST·M
PEREGRINIV
SVPER·TRIB

He expands it thus : " militum cui praeest Marcus Peregrinius Superstes tribunus." I prefer, instead of *militum*, *miliaria*; and instead of *Superstes*, *Super.* We find this name in Orelli, nn. 455 and 3555. See *Mus. Veron.*, p. cxxiii. There is a similar mistake in the expansion of MIL· in Horsley's nn. xxxvi. and xli. Dr. Bruce, *Roman Wall*, 2nd edit., p. 50, gives the second inscription and corrects the error.

§ 64. Horsley's n. xcv. is an inscription on an altar found at *Risechester :—

D R S
DVPL·N·EXPLOR
BREMENARAM
INSTITVERVNT
N·EIVS C·CAEP
CHARITINO TRIB
V S L M

---

* Otherwise High Rochester, the *Bremenium* of Ptolemy and Antonines. I regard the agreement of the distance between this place and Corbridge or Colorster, with that stated

His expansion and observations are :—

Deæ Romæ sacrum duplares numeri exploratorum Bremenii aram instituerunt numini ejus Caio Cupione Charitino tribuno votum solverunt libentes merito.

"The reading I have given of the body of the inscription is the same with Cambden's, which I take to be right, but nobody (that I know of) has given a satisfactory explication of the DRS at the top: I think it plain that they are to be read *deæ Romæ sacrum*. That they made a goddess of *Rome*, and erected altars and temples to her, needs no proof to those who have any acquaintance with medals, and other *Roman* antiquities.

There is a curious altar at *Elenborough*, erected GENIO LOCI FOR-TVNAE REDVCI ROMAE AETERNAE, &c. I once thought of *diis Romanis sacrum*, but this suits not with *numini ejus* in the body of the inscription; for which reason the learned *Dr. Gale's* reading, *deabus Rumebus sacrum*, cannot be admitted. The altar then is sacred to the goddess *Rome*, erected by the *duplares* of a detachment of *exploratores* or scouts at *Bremenium*, under the command of *Caius Capio Charitinus* the tribuno. *Capio* is a consular name, and we read in the *Notitia* of a *præfectus numeri exploratorum Lavatris*. Whether they were the same with these, I will not undertake to determine. The *duplares* were soldiers who had a double allowance of corn, of which a part of the *Roman* soldier's pay consisted. The *exploratores* were like our scouts, sent to discover the enemy or their country."

The difficulties in the inscription are in D R and N·EIVS. Muratori explained D. R. as *Dianæ Reginæ*, and Orelli doubts between *Deæ Romæ*, *Deæ respicienti*, scil., *Fortunæ*, and *Deæ Reginæ*, citing in favour of the last, Muratori, 112, 9. I am inclined to suggest *Dianæ Reduci*, as more appropriate to the circumstances. Hagenbuch, Orelli, n. 206, explains N·EIVS as standing for *nomine ejus*, scil., *numeri*, i. e., the *duplares* erected the altar, in the name of the *numerus*, acting for the *numerus*. This I much prefer to *numini*. In n. 2166, *Inscriptions de l' Algerie*, N is used in the same sense. Dr. Bruce, *Roman Wall*, 2nd edit., p. 457, gives an inscription on another altar found in, I believe, 1852, at the same place :

---

in the Itinerary to have been between *Bremenium* and *Corstopitum*, as a more satisfactory proof of its ideality with *Bremenium* than the fact that two altars have been found there with the letters BREMEN and BREM inscribed on them. The legitimate inference from such a record of the place in connection with a corps seems to be that the fixed quarters of that corps were in the place thus named, and not that the place in which the record was found was their quarters, for it is possible and even probable that such a record may have been given with the object of marking distance from the usual station.

```
    G D N ET
    SIGNORVM
    COHIVARDVL
    ET N EXPLORA
    TOR BREMCOR
    EGNATLVCILI
    ANVSLEGAVGPRPR
    CVRANTECASSIO
    SABINIANOTRIB
```

He expands it thus :

"G[ENIO] D[OMINI] N[OSTRI] ET   To the genius of our
     SIGNORVM   Emperor and of the standards
CO[HORTIS] PRIMAE VARDVL[ORVM]   of the first
                        [cohort of the Varduli
ET N[VMERI] EXPLORA-   and of the Detachment of pio-
TOR[VM] BREM[ENII] COR[NELIVS]   neers of Bremen-
                       [ium, Cornelius
EGNAT[IVS] LVCILI-   Egnatius Lucili-
ANVS LEG[ATVS] AVG[VSTALIS] PR[O]PR[AETOR]
          anus, the imperial legate, propraetor,
CVRANTE CASSIO   under the superintendence of Cassius
SABINIANO TRIB[VNO]   Sabinianus the Tribune
    aram posuit   erected this altar."

The only doubtful points in this expansion are in line five. I am inclined to think that we should read *Bremeniensium*, instead of * *Bremenii*, both here and in Horsley's reading of the preceding inscription ; whilst my objection to *Cornelius* is that it is never used as a *praenomen*. It may be that *Lucilianus* had two *nomina gentilitia*, as we find in examples cited by Fabretti, p. 203, but we should then, I think, have had his *praenomen*.

There are two other readings of COR• which have occurred to me—GOR•, standing for †*Gordianorum*, or COR•, the first syllable of *Corstopitum*. The latter of these I would regard as denoting that the two bodies occupied *Bremenium* and *Corstopitum*, or had charge of the road between those places. In the *Itinerary* of *Antoninus*, *Corstopitum* is given, in his first route from the wall, as the next place to *Bremenium*, and set

---

* If *Bremenii* be adopted, I would translate, not " of Bremenium," but " of Bremensium."
† See p. 41.

down as M·P·XX. distant from it.   This distance nearly agrees
with the distance of *Corbridge* from *Riechester.*

§ 65. Horsley, n. xcvi., is an inscription on an altar also found
at Riechester :—

> SILVANO
> PANTHEO
> PRO·SAL
> RVFIN·TRIB·ET
> LVCILLAE·EIVS
> EVTYCHVS
> LIB·COS
> V·S·L·M·

Horsley expands it thus: "Silvano Pantheo pro salute Rufini
tribuni et Lucillæ ejus Eutychus libertus consulis votum solvit
libens merito," and supplies *uxoris* after *ejus*, in the fifth line.
The only doubt, which I have as to the accuracy of this expansion,
relates to LIB·COS.   If Eutychus had been a freedman of the
Consul, as Horsley believed, the order, according to usage, would
have been COS·LIB ; and instead of the office, *consul*, the name
of the individual would have been given, for consuls, as such, had
no *liberti*.   I regard LIB· as standing for *Librarius*, and COS·
for *consulis*.   The *librarius* was a book-keeper, who had charge
of the accounts, and is mentioned in many inscriptions, in connection with the officer or body in whose service he was, *e. gr.*,
LIB·PRAEF·*Librarius Præfecti*, LIB·CH., *Librarius cohortis.*

§ 66. Horsley's n. xcviii. is an inscription on a stone found at
Elsdon :—

> B·NOGENERIS
> HVMAN·IMPE
> RANTE·C......
> ....
> AVG·PR·PR·POSVIT
> AC·DEDICAVIT
> C·A·ACIL·

He expands it thus : "Bono generis humani imperante Calpurnio *Agricola legato* Augustali propraetore posuit ac dedicavit
Caius Aulus Acilius ;" and offers the following remarks on it :

" The first words in the fifth line are undoubtedly *Augustali propratore*, which makes it certain that *legato*, and the name of the lieutenant, have gone before, according to the usual form. If we suppose Calpurnius Agricola to be the name that has been designedly erased, I believe that as the letters will exactly fill up the empty space, so that supply will suit very well both with what goes before and what follows. The inscription then, I believe, has been thus:—

> BONO GENERIS
> HVMAN·IMPE
> RANTE·CALPVR
> NIO·AGRICOLA
> AVG·PR·PR·POSVIT·
> AC·DEDICAVIT
> C·A·ACILIVS......

This will make all easy and plain; and there is nothing in the cut of the letters, which is partly good both in this and the next, or any other circumstances of the inscription, but what suits well enough with the time of this legate. And *imperante Calpurnio Agricola*, I take to be the same with *sub Calpurnio Agricola* or perhaps *jussu Calpurnii Agricola*, which so frequently occurs in such sort of inscriptions. Mr. *Gordon* reads it *bono genio humano imperanti;* but this is contrary to the plain letters upon the stone. There is some difficulty in forming a notion of the meaning of an altar erected *bono generis humani;* but this may seem as intelligible as an altar erected *bono fato, bono eventui, &c.*, and perhaps has much the same meaning. There are coins with *Salus generis humani* upon them."

The phrases *bono reipublicæ* or *generis humani natus* were no uncommon compliments of the emperor.

Thus we have in Renier, *Inscriptions de l' Algerie*, n. 109 :—

> BONO GENERIS
> HVMANI PROGE
> NITO D·N·FLAV
> IO CONSTAN
> TIO NOB AC
> FLORENTIS
> SIMO CAES
> &c.

Horsley, *Northumberland*, lix., has—

> BON
> REI
> PVBLIC
> NATO

It seems probable that the same is on the stone found at Wroxeter, said to bear the words BONA REIPVBLICÆ NATVS.
See *Journal of British Archæological Association*, 1859, p. 313.

The order here seems to have been *nato bono generis humani*,
and this was preceded by the name of the emperor, with which
imperante agrees forming an ablative absolute. The name of
the LEG·AVG·PR·PR· in the third and fourth lines was in
the nominative case being the subject of *dedicavit*. C. A. in
the last line stand for *C[VRAM] A[GENTE] or C[VRANTE]
A[VLO], and ACIL are the first two syllables of ACILIO, which
was followed by the cognomen now obliterated.

§ 67. In the year 1726 an altar was found at *Corbridge
which bore the following inscription, as given in the Appendix
to Gordon's *Iter Septentrionale*, and in Horsley's *Britannia
Romana*, Northumberland, n. cviii. :—

LEG·A......
Q·CALPVRNIVS
CONCESSINI
VS·PRAF·EQ
CAESA·CORI
ONOTOTAR
VM·MANV PR
AESENTISSIMI
NVMINIS DEI VS.

The altar and inscription are imperfect, as a portion of the
stone has been broken off at the the top. Horsley supplies the
deficiency in the first line with VG·PR·PR·, and reads the
whole thus :—" Legato Augustali propretore, Quintus Calpurnius Concessinius Præfectus equitum Cæsariensium Corionototarum manu præsentissimi numinis dei votum solvit."

The chief difficulty in the inscription is in the words CAESA·
CORIONOTOTARVM. The author of the letter in Gordon's

* See Horsley, n. G.E.

‡ This, or rather Colcester in its neighbourhood, seems to have been the Curiosolum of Antoninus.

Appendix thinks that we have here a new body of horse, called *equites Cæsarienses* (or *Cæsariani*) *Corionototæ*. The latter designation he supposes to be "a corruption of the Roman name of a people in these parts, perhaps *Curia* or *Coria Otadenorum*, and that *Corbridge* was the place." Horsley rejects the explanation, and proposes three other names, of which the word in the text may have been a corruption: *Coritani*, a people of one of the *Provinciæ Cæsarienses*; *Corioziotæ* in the anonymous *Ravennas*; and *Crotoniatæ*, which last he seems to have preferred. As to the explanation of the rest of the inscription, he adopts the view, that *præsentissimum numen Dei* signifies the emperor, and that *manu* intimates that *Q. Culpurnius* was advanced to his post, by the immediate hand of the emperor, supposed to be *Commodus* or *Caracalla*.

The first doubt which presents itself as to the correctness of this interpretation, arises from the terms *equites Cæsarienses*. So far as I am aware (and I have made a careful search on the subject), there is no example of any *equites* having been denominated *Cæsarienses*. As to the reference, which is made in Gordon's Appendix to Gruter, p. 415, it proves nothing to the point, for in that inscription there is no mention of *equites*. Nor is the well known form *equites singulares* applicable here.

Another doubt is suggested by the meaning given to *manu præsentissimi numinis dei*, as here, too, I have been unable to find any authority for the interpretation, " the immediate hand of the emperor."

Under such circumstances I am inclined to regard *Cæsa* as the participle of *cædo*, and agreeing with *manu*, which I interpret as *band* or *body*. Of the suggestions relative to *Corionototarum* I prefer that which considers it a corruption of *Coriotiotæ*. As to *præsentissimi numinis dei*, I understand the phrase as referring to the god to whom the altar was dedicated, and whose name, along with that of the legate, doubtless appeared on that part of the stone which has been broken off. In construction, *numinis* is governed by *cultor* understood: an ellipsis, which is confirmed by an inscription found in Portugal, and given by Gruter and Orelli :—

DEO ENDOVELICO
PRAESTANTISS
IMI ET PRAESEN
TISSIMI NVMINIS
SEXTVS COCCEIVS
CRATERVS HONOR
INVS EQVES ROMA
NVS EX VOTO.

De Wal also gives this inscription in his *Mythologiæ Septentrionalis Monumenta* (p. 73), and in his interpretation correctly
supplies *cultor* after *numinis*.

I read the inscription thus : Legato Augusti Propraetore, Q.
Calpurnius Concessinius, Praefectus Equitum, caesa Corionototarum manu, praesentissimi numinis dei [cultor] votum solvit.

According to this view, the circumstances under which the
altar was erected were these :—Calpurnius Concessinius before
going into action with a band of Coriototares vowed to some god,
that, if successful, he would erect an altar to him. Having cut
them to pieces he performed his vow in grateful acknowledgment
of the aid of that deity, who had manifested on this occasion his
characteristic of giving most timely and effectual assistance. The
only objection which I see to the interpretation which I propose
arises from the use of *praefectus equitum*, without giving the
designation of these *equites*; but we are not without example of
this omission.

If my interpretation be correct this stone possesses unique
interest, as the inscription is, so far as I am aware, the only one
extant which records an engagement between the Romans and
the Britons.

§ 68. Dr. Bruce, *Roman Wall*, p. 200, 2nd ed., figures a let-
teral stone found at Tynemouth. The following parts of the
inscription are distinctly legible :—

....PVMCVMBAS
ET TEMPLVM
FECIT CIV
MAXIMINVS
LEG VI VI
EX VOTO.

Dr. Bruce's remarks are :—

"About the reading of the first line of this inscription there is some doubt. That active antiquary, Pegge, read it CIPPVM CVM BAS[I], 'a column with a base,' and conceived that an upper line, which has now almost entirely disappeared, contained the name of a deity, probably Mars ; Brand read GYRVM CVMBAS, and translated it 'a circular harbour for the shipping.' He conceived that there was a reference here to the adjoining bay, called Prior's Haven, which he says 'has every appearance of having been one of the artificial harbours of that people.'

No Roman hand, however, made that harbour ; it is manifestly natural ; CYMBAS he conceived to be an equivalent for *cymbas*, boats. But there is no doubt about the other lines, which import that—

Caius Julius Maximinus, of the Sixth Legion Victorious,
In the performance of a vow, erected *this* temple.

The mere circumstance of its selection as the site of a temple proves this to have been a place of some importance in the Roman age.

The name of the builder of the temple fixes, with a near approach to precision, the date of its dedication. Caius Julius Verus Maximinus was a Thracian shepherd of great personal strength ; he attracted, at an early period of his life, the notice of Septimus Severus, and, under Caracalla, attained to the rank of centurion. On the assassination of Alexander Severus, in 285, he assumed the purple, and was himself assassinated in 238. He probably accompanied Septimus Severus into Britain, and on this occasion erected the temple commemorated by the inscription."

Mr. Wright, *Celt, Roman, and Saxon*, p. 175 (p. 177, 2nd ed.), strangely regards this inscription as indicating that " some other buildings (the name is partly obliterated) with a basilica [!] and temple, were built on the site of the modern Tynemouth." As to the true reading he observes that after examination of the stone, he agrees with Mr. Roach Smith that " it seems to be CVPVM (for *cippum*) CVM BASI ET, &c."

The reading *cum basi* is plainly to be preferred, but *cippum* seems to me very improbable. I am inclined to suggest SCYPVM, *i. e.*, SCYPHVM CVM BAS, as we find in Orelli, n. 2504, CANTHARVM CVM VASE SVA. In nn. 1279, 6140, we have examples of *scyphi* as offerings. In *Monum. Hist. Brit.*, the first two letters are read CV, from which a conjecture may be drawn that the letters before CVM BAS may have been CVRIVM,

T

the last three syllables of MERCVRIVM, the first being in the
upper line, which has been obliterated.   This may be supported by
reference to HERCVLEM PVERINVM CVM BASI DEA-
NAE D. D in Murini, *Iscriz, Alb.* p. 49.   It was not unusual to
present as an offering to a god the image of another deity.   See
Morcelli, i., p. 44.   The reading GYRVM suggested to me
TYRVM, the last two syllables of SATYRVM, and this may be
supported by Orelli, n. 1482.   In inscriptions we find not only
basis but *hypobasis :* the only example of this found in Britain is,
I believe, the altar, figured in Bruce's *Roman Wall,* p. 385.   It
is now preserved in the Museum of the Society of Antiquaries,
Newcastle.   The meaning of the double inscription in this case is
that Longinus gave the altar not merely *cum basi sua,* but also
cum hypobasi.

'§ 69. Of the relics found at Risingham (the ancient name
of which is supposed to have been *Habitancum*), one of the
most interesting is an ornamental slab, six feet in length, bearing

---

* This supposition originated with Camden, who formed it on the authority of an altar
which was found there, with HABITANCI on it.   His conjecture derives support from Mr.
Ward's reading of the words that follow HABITANCI, as PRIMA STA(TIONE), which
accord with the position of Risingham, north of the wall on Watling Street.   It must be
borne in mind, however, that there is no notice in any ancient author of any place in
Britain called *Habitancum.*   Mr McLauchlan, in his very carefully prepared " Memoir of a
Survey of the Watling Street," p. 37, is mistaken in calling " the Risingham Station," " the
Habitancum of the Itineraries."   No such name of a place is found in any Itinerary.
But Horsley, *Britannia Romana,* p. 334, remarks : — " It may sometimes so happen,
that the name of a place may be in an inscription which we meet with no where
else.   And of this there is in fact an instance or two in Britain ; namely, *Bra-*
chium at Brugh, in *Richmondshire,* and *Habitancum,* at Risingham, in Northumberland.   To these perhaps may be added *Apiatorium,* in the inscription now in the library at
Durham, which is probably *Newcastle,* if the altar was found there, and also *Alaterva* for
Cramond in Scotland."   The examples, cited by Horsley, prove the danger of depending on
such authority for names otherwise unknown.   *Brachio,* which occurs in the inscription
given by Horsley, p. 333, is plainly not the name of a place, but the designation of " a line
of communication," as Mr. Cole correctly explained it.   See Camden, ed. Gough, iii., p. 331,
and add to the references given there, Livy, iv., 9 ; xxii ,52 ; and xxxviii., 5.   *Apiatorio,* in a-
ligarit, *Northumberland,* is also not the name of a place, but of a person, for it should be
read A PLATORIO ; and the individual named in it is *Aulus Platorius Nepos,* who was legate
under Hadrian.   ALATERVIS, in a. axix, Scotland, is an epithet of the *Dea Matres,* and
seems to me derived from abroad, probably from the neighbourhood of the Meuse or the
Rhine, for the altar was erected by a Tungrian cohort.   Possibly there was some connection
between them and the goddess *Alateivia,* worshipped amongst the *Ingaevones.*   See Homers.
a. 1405.   It is scarcely necessary to add, that there is no ground for the conjecture of Sir J.
Clarke, Pinart's *Caledonia Romana,* p. 171, " that Ptolemy probably made a mistake, when
translating *Alatervum* or *Alatervo castra* into Greek, and that the latter is the true reading
of his αρτεμῶν ἐστρατόπεδον."

P. S. — The following is the inscription, to which I have referred in the foregoing note : —

an inscription which it is more than usually difficult to decipher in consequence of the great number of ligulate letters, and the injuries which the stone has sustained. It is figured in Dr. Bruce's *Roman Wall*, p. 287, and in Dr. Surridge's *Notices of Roman Inscriptions in Northumberland*, pl. iii. ; but the first of these is indistinct from the smallness of the scale ; and the second is disfigured by the introduction of absurd conjectures.* The following is the reading given in the *Monumenta Historica*, p. cxvi., 192 *a* ; and adopted by Henzen, n. 6701 :—

>   *   *   *   ICOMAXI
> COSIII ET M AVREL ANTONINO PIO
>   COS II AVG   *   *   *
> PORTAM·CVM·MVRIS VETVSTATE DI
> LAPSIS IVSSV ALFEN SENECINIS VO
> COS CVRANTE COL ANITI ADVENTO PRO
>   AVGG NN C*I VANGON OPFS
>   CVM AEMI SALVIAN TRIB
>   SVO A SOLO RESTI.

At first sight it is plain, that the emperors named in this inscription are Severus and Caracalla, and that the defect in the

---

Horsley expands it thus :—

MORONT CAD
ET·N·D·N AVG
M·G·SECVNDINVS
BF·COS·HABITA
NCI PRIMA STA
PRO SEETSVIS POS

* Deo Mogonti Cadenorum et Numini Domini nostri Augusti Marcus Gaius Secundinus beneficiarius consulis Habitanci prima stationis pro se et suis posuit.' Camden had read PRIMASTA as primas tua, which Horsley justly rejects on the ground of Latinity. De Wal, p. 125, gives the strange expansion—primas Miulatronum, taking primas in the same sense in which Orelli regarded it, viz., princeps, I have no suggestion to propose with which I am entirely satisfied, but in preference to any of those which have yet been offered, I would read HABITANCI·PRIM·ASTAT, i.e., HABITANCI·PRIM[I;]·[H]ABTATI· Thus the meaning is that Secundinus was of the century of Habitancus the primus hastatus. It is scarcely necessary to add, that there are examples of the omission of the centurial mark before the name of the centurion and also of asterisks for hastatus.

Before leaving this subject I must state my inability to explain the omission of this important station, in the Itinerary of Antoninus. Horsley, p. 397, considers this question but offers nothing satisfactory.

* From Mr. Smith's *Collectanea Antiqua*, vol. iii., p. 4, I learn that "an engraving of this slab illustrates a paper by Mr. Thomas Hodgson, in the *Archæologia Æliana*, vol. iv." I regret that I have not seen it, as I have been unable to procure the work.

line, after COS II AVG, was caused by the intentional oblitera-
tion of the name Geta—an erasure common in similar memorials
of the period. Accordingly, Henzen restores the commencement with the formula: *Impp. Caess. L. Sept. Severo pio
Pertinaci Aug. Arabico Adiabenico Parth*ICO MAXI*mo p. m. tr.
pot.* . . . and supplies the defect in the third line with *et P.
Sept. Getæ nob. Cæs.* As there is no room in the first line for
any addition after MAXI, Henzen's suggestions "*mo p. m.
tr. pot.* . . ." must be rejected; but his reading in the fifth
line, VC. for VO, should, in my judgment, be adopted. See
p. 133. For COL in the sixth line, he proposes CL. . *i. e.*,
Claudio; and O P F S he regards as initials of the *cognomina*
of the cohort, *scil.*, O (for 8 or ϖ) *miliaria*; P, *Pia*; F, *Fidelis*;
and S, *Severriana*; but he admits that there is no authority in
inscriptions for any *cognomen* of this corps.

In the *Monumenta Historica Britannica*, the commencement is
restored by the words: *Impp. Cæss. L. Sever. Pio Pert. P. M.
Arab. Parth. Adiaben* ICO,* and the defect in the third line is
supplied by *Et P. Sept. Getæ nob. Cæs Cos.*† In the *Index
Rerum et Numinum*, p. cxlvi., *viri consularis* seems to be suggested as the explanation of VOCOS, and *C. Antistio Advento* as
another reading of COLANITI ADVENTO.

From what has been stated, it is evident that the parts of the
inscription as yet not satisfactorily explained, are the names COL
ANITI, and the letters O P F S. It appears to me that the
difficulties as to the first of these have arisen from mistaking O
for C, and *vice versa*, i. e., reading COL for OCL; and from
inverting the order of the first three letters in the ligulate group

* Mr. Newton, *Monum. Hist. Brit.*, p. cxvi., doubtless had authority for the restoration
which he engraves of the titles of Severus; but I am not aware of any example of them in
that order. They are usually placed as Henzen gives them in his restoration.

† The addition of COS seems to be justified by the fact, that in the year A.D. 205, Caracalla was Consul for the second time, and Geta for the first. In Dr. Bruce's copy of the
inscription, we have, in the third line, COS I instead of COS II; but this, I presume, is a
mistake. If not we should omit COS from Geta's titles, as the inscription would then be
of A.D. 202-204. The addition of I after COS, instead of COS alone which is the recognised
form for a first consulship, suggests the conjecture, that this style may have been derived
by Caracalla from his father, whose coins of his first consulship present the strange peculiarity of I after COS. Perhaps there was some reference to this in the phrase *ter* of *semel cos*
by which the year 202 was marked. But I must add, that I have never seen an example
in the case of Caracalla, of I after COS on either coins or stones.

N, i. e., reading NIT for TIN ; for I have no doubt that the
individual here named is the same *Adventus* who, some years
afterwards, in A. D. 218, was Consul with the emperor Macrinus.
His *nomen gentilitium* is variously given as *Coclatinus*, *Ocla-
tinus*, and *Oclatinius*. He is named in the following inscriptions :

```
        VICTORIAE·REDVCIS·DD·NN
        *    *    *    *    *    *
        PII·FELICIS·AVG·ET*  *    *
        LIAE *   *    *    *    *    *
        IVGI · D · N · MILITES · LEG · II
        PARTH·  *    *    *    *    *
        AET · Q · M · COCLATINO AD
        VENTO·COS·      &c.  &c.
```

(Fabretti, p. 339, and Relandi *Fast. Consul.* p. 137.)

```
        DEDIC·PR·ID·MART
        IMP  *  *  AVG·COS
              ET
        OCLATINO ADVENTO
```
(Masson, *Hist. Crit.* 6, p. 215, and Orelli, n, 945.)

```
            DIANA
          CARICIANA
        M AVRELIVS CARICVS
        AQVARIVS HVIVS LOC
        CVM LIBERTIS ET ALVM
              NIS
        M · D  *  *  *  D·AUG·ET
          DEDIC·IDID·AVG·
        OCLATINO·ADVENTO·COS·
```

(Muratori, *Nov. Thesaur*, p. 354, n. 1 ; Henzen, n. 6058, and
Marini, *Atti di Frat. Arvali*, pp. 6 48-9.)

Muratori, in a note on the last inscription, enquires whether
the name should be read COCLATINVS or OCLATINVS, and
decides in favour of the latter ; but from the second inscription,
compared with that on the Risingham tablet, I am inclined to
prefer OCLATINIVS. For other notices of this individual,

compare Herodian, *Hist.* iv. 12 and 14 ; and Dio Cassius, *Hist.*, lxxviii., 14,[*] who was probably personally acquainted with him, as they were at the same time members of the senate.   Oclatinius Adventus was one of the most remarkable men of his time.   He entered the army as a common soldier, serving amongst the *Speculatores* and *Exploratores*, who were held in very low estimation, especially as they had occasionally to discharge the duty of executioners.   Then he became successively a *tabularius* and *cubicularius*, from which he was raised to the office of *procurator*.   Subsequently to his serving in England, he accompanied Caracalla in his Parthian expedition as colleague of Macrinus, the *præfectus prætorio*, and was, I suspect, privy to the murder of the emperor. After that, he was despatched by Macrinus to Rome, *ad funus Caracalli ducendum* as Reimar states in his note, but in reality to get rid of his pretensions as a rival aspirant to the imperial throne, for Adventus did not scruple to tell the soldiers, after the death of Caracalla, that the sovereignty properly devolved on him as the senior of Macrinus, but that in consideration of his advanced age he would give place to his junior.   After his return to Rome he was in great favor with Macrinus, who elevated him to the rank of Senator, and to the office of *Præfectus Urbi*, a remarkable elevation, not only with a view to his antecedents, but also because at the time he was not of consular rank.   Then he became consul with Macrinus, and, after the death of that emperor in June, 208, finished his year as colleague of Elagabalus.

Dio Cassius speaks of him very contemptuously, and derides his want of qualifications for the high positions to which he had attained, but his career proves that he must have been a man of very uncommon ability.

This inscription confirms the accuracy of the historian as to his having held the office of *procurator*, and disproves the conjecture of Reimar, that he had been *procurator rei privatæ*.   I have already mentioned Henzen's conjecture as to O P F S ; it is very ingenious, but must, I think, be rejected on the ground, that there is no authority for the application of any one of the

---

[*] Ed. Reimar, Hamburgh, 1752, p. 1322.

designations, *miliaria, pia, fidelis,* or *Severiana* to the first cohort of the Vangiones. I interpret the letters O P F S as the abbreviation of *operibus perfectis,* or *factis,*[*]—i. e., having executed or completed the works. We have a similar form of expression in Gruter, exc. n. 4; OPERIBVS AMPLIATIS RESTITVIT; and also in Morcelli, ii., pp. 129 and 134. I am inclined to venture on the following restoration :

IMPP·CAESS
L·SEPT·SEVERO·PIO
PERTINACI AVG·ARABICO
ADIABENICO PARTHICO MAXI
COS III ET M·AVREL·ANTONINO PIO
COS II AVG·ET P·SEPT·GETAE N·CAES COS·
PORTAM CUM MVRIS VETVSTATE DI
LAPSIS IVSSV ALFEN SENECINIS V·C·
COS CVRANTE OCLATINI ADVENTO PRO
AVGG NN COII I VANGON OPFS
CVM AEMI SALVIAN TRIB
SVO A SOLO RESTI

Imp[eratoribus] Cæs[aribus]
L[ucio] Sept[imio] Severo Pio
Pertinaci Aug[usto] Arabico
Adiabenico Parthico Maxi[mo]
Consuli tertium et M[arco] Aurel[io] Antonino Pio
Consuli secundum Aug[ust]o et P[ublio] Sept[imio] Getæ
N[obilissimo] Cæ[sari] consuli
portam cum muris vetustate di
lapsis jussu Alfen[i] Senec[i]o]nis V[iri] C[larissimi]
Consularis curante Oclatini[o] Advento pro[curatore]
Aug[ustorum] n[ostrorum] coh[ors] prima Vang[i]on[um]
o[peribus] p[er] f[ecti]s
cum Æmi[lio] Salvian[o] trib[uno]‡
suo a solo restituit.

---

* It is scarcely necessary to add, that there are examples of O and OP for *opus,* and of P F and F for *perfecti* and *fecit* respectively.

† Hexaxa, *Index,* p. 72, gives "a.c. 205, seqq.," as the date of this inscription; but this is impossible, according to his reading, for Caracalla was not COS II until 205. The latter year I regard as the date, although COS III of Severus and COS II of Caracalla extended over

P.S.—Since the foregoing article was published, I have had
access to the *Archæologia Æliana*, and have read the paper by
Mr. Hodgson, to which reference is made in my note in page
147. In that paper, after a critical examination in detail of
each phrase or passage of the inscription, Mr. H. proposes the
following reading of it :—

> " IMPP·CAESS.
> L.SEP.SEVERO PIO PERT.P.M.
> ARAB.PARTH.ADIABENICO MAXI.
> COS.III.ET M.AVREL.ANTONINO PIO
> COS.II.AVG.ET.P.SEPT. GETAE.NOB.CAES.COS.
> PORTAM CVM MVRIS VETVSTATE DI-
> LAPSIS JVSSV ALFEN.SENECINIS VO
> COS.CVRANTE COL.ANITI.ADVENTO
> AVG.NN.COH.I.VANGION.——
> CVM AEMI.SALVIAN.TRIB.
> SVO A SOLO RESTI.

Which may thus be explained at length :—

> Imperatoribus Cæsaribus
> Lucio Septimio Severo Pio Pertinaci, Pontifici Maximo,
> Arabico, Parthico, *Adiabenico Maximo*,
> *Consuli tertium*, et *Marco Aurelio Antonino Pio,*
> *Consuli secundo, Augustis,* et Publio Septimio Getæ, nobilissimo
> Cæsari, consuli,
> *Portam cum Muris Vetustate di-*
> *lapsis, Jussu Alfeni Senecinis (Senecionis?) Viri*
> *Consularis, curante Antistio (or Anitistio) Advento, pro*
> *Augustis Nostris, Cohors prima Vangionum ——*
> *Cum Æmilio Salviano, Tribuno*
> *Suo, a Solo restituit.*"

On comparison with the reading which I proposed in p.

205-207. But if the year had been 206 or 207, we should have had, I think, the tribunitian
number (TRIB. POT) of either Severus (*aril.*, xiiii. or xv.) or Caracalla (*aril.*, viiii. or x.), or
of both. I am not satisfied, however, as to the accuracy of the copies which I have seen,
and would suggest a careful re-examination of the stone.

‡ Lucius Æmilius Salvianus was already known as tribune of the 1st Cohort of the
Vangiones from an altar found at Risingham, the inscription on which is given by Horsley,
Northumberland, n. lxxxi.

151, it will be observed that there are several points of difference; but on re-consideration of the subject, I see no reason for changing the opinions which I have expressed in the article and embodied in the restoration. The only question, about which some doubt is suggested, relates to the date. The notice in the inscription of Caracalla as Con. II. of course fixes the date within the cancelli—205, the year of his second consulship, and 208, the year of his third consulship. . Mr. Hodgson argues for 207, assuming that the emperors were at the time in Britain, and adopting Horsley's opinion that "Severus came into the island in the year 207 at latest." He finds confirmation of his assumption as to the presence of the emperors, in the title of Senecio being in this inscription *vir consularis*, instead of *legatus eorum pr. pr.*, as it appears on a stone found at Greta bridge.

Although the conjecture, that the change of title indicates " the exercise in person [by the emperors] of both the military and civil powers of the government, rendering the office of legate no longer necessary," seems plausible, yet there can, I think, be no doubt that both Mr. Horsley and Mr. Hodgson are in error in fixing 207 as the year of the arrival of the emperors in Britain. The statement of Xiphiline, that Severus died in the island " three years after he undertook the British expedition," suggests 208 as the date of his arrival, for he died in 211 (on February the 4th; not the 12th, as given by Mr. Hodgson in a note); and this date (208) is confirmed by reference to coins, e. gr., one of Caracalla's bearing the legend :

PROF.AVGG.PONTIF.TR.P.XI COS.III.

from which it appears that the *profectio Augustorum* took place in the eleventh TRIB. POT. and third COS. of Caracalla, i. e., 208. I am still of opinion, for the reason stated in the note, p 152, that 205 is the most probable date of the inscription, although it is possible that the intention of those who set up the stone may have been to indicate that the work was commenced, carried on, and completed during the time in which Severus was COS. III. Caracalla COS. II., and Geta COS., i. e., 205-207.

U

§ 70. In the *Archæologia Æliana*, new series, i., p. 261, a slab is figured, which bears the following inscription :—

DIISDEABVSQVESE
CVNDVMINTERPRE
TATIONEMORACV
LICLARIAPOLLINIS
COII·I·TVNGRORVM

Dr. Bruce reads and translates it thus :—

"DIIS DEABVSQVE SE-
CVNDVM INTERPRE-
TATIONEM ORACV-
LI CLARI APOLLINIS
COH[ORS] PRIMA TVNGRORVM.

" The first cohort of the Tungrians (dedicated this structure) to the gods and the goddesses, according to the direction of the oracle of the illustrious Apollo."

I have no doubt that I in CLARI stands, as is common, for II ; and that CLARII is the well-known epithet which Apollo derived from *Clarus* (near Colophon, in Ionia), where he had a celebrated temple and oracle. It is scarcely necessary to cite illustrations from ancient authors. Amongst the most obvious are Virgil, *Æn.* iii., 360, " Qui tripodas, *Clarii* lauros, qui sidera sentis ;" and Tacitus *Ann.* ii., 54, " Relegit Asiam appellitque Colophona, ut *Clarii Apollinis oraculo* uteretur."

§ 71. In the same work, p. 226, we find the following inscription on another slab :—

IMP·CÆSMAVR SEVE
RVSALEXANDERPIE
AVG HORREVMVETV
STATECONIABSVMM
COH IIASTVRVM S·A
ASOLORESTITVERVNT
PROVINCIA REG · · ·
MAXIMO LEG · · · ·
· AIMARTI · · · ·

Dr. Bruce reads and translates it thus :—

"IMPERATOR CAESAR MARCVS AVRELIVS SEVE-
RVS ALEXANDER PIVS FELIX
AVGVSTVS·HORREVM VETV-
STATE CONLABSVM M (?)
COHORS SECVNDA ASTVRVM SECVNDVM ARTEM
A SOLO RESTITVERVNT
PROVINCIA REGNANTE
MAXIMO LEGATO............
KALENDIS MARTII ...."

"The emperor Cæsar Marcus Aurelius Severus Alexander, the pious, happy,
and august.—The second cohort of the Astures restored from the ground,
in a workmanlike manner, this granary, which had fallen down through age,
in the kalends of March........., Maximus governing the Province as
(Augustal) Legate."

Dr. Bruce's expansion and interpretation are in the main cor-
rect ; but there are some points which require emendation. I
regard M. at the end of the fourth line, as standing for *MILI-
TES, and COII IL, of the fifth, for COHORTIS SECVNDÆ.
This view is supported by the use of RESTITVERVNT instead
of RESTITVIT. The expansion SECVNDVM ARTEM for
S·A is, in my judgment, very unsatisfactory. I regard the letters as standing, as they often do, for SEVERIANÆ ALEX-
ANDRIANÆ. See Orelli, n. 3359. The reading "PROVIN-
CIA REGNANTE, governing the province," is unquestionably
erroneous. Whether *provincia* be regarded as the ablative, or, as
is most probable, as used for *provinciam*, there is no authority
for the government of either accusative or ablative by *regnare*;
nor for the application of the term to the government of a province by a legato or other Roman officer. I would suggest PRO-
VINCIA[M] † REG[ENTE]. Thus Tacitus, *Hist.* i., c. 48,
"Vinius proconsulatu Galliam Narbonensem severe integroque
rexit ;" c. 60, *rexere* [Britanniam] legati legionum.

Dr. Bruce gives as the date " A. D. 222-235, *viz.*, the period
during which Alexander Severus was emperor—but the precise

* Mr. Newton, *Mon. Hist. Brit.* n. 19 a, has anticipated me.

† This suggestion is favoured by the reading given by Gough, Camden's *Britannia*, iii.,
p. 503—RCENT.

year can be ascertained. The inscription is evidently the * same as that given by Gough, *Camden's Britannia*, iii., p. 503. He gives the last two lines thus :—

MAXIMO LEG·VV·A PRO
SAL MARTI MED·LEGATVSCOII·ET TEXT

There can, I think, be but little doubt that this inscription, as given by Gough, closes with the names of the consuls, and that we should read instead of TVSCOII. ET TEXT—FVSCO II ET DEXT[RO], *i. e.*, A.D. 225. It is not easy to decide on any thing relative to MED·LEGA. I suspect that these and the other words before the names of the consuls should be read—

KAL·MARTIIS·DEDICA

i. e., Ka[lendis] Martiis dedica[tum].

It is scarcely necessary to observe that *dedicare*, as thus used, signifies what we mean by "inaugurate," "formally open."

Of the preceding line there can, I think, be no doubt. It is —

MAXIMO·LEG·AVG·PRF

i. e., Maximo leg[ato] Aug[usti] pr[o] p[retore].

It is strange that we have only the *cognomen* of the *legate*: his other names might have been expected in the preceding line.

It may also be of importance to add, that Dr. Bruce's translation "happy" does not express the sense of *felix* as an epithet of the emperors. It signifies what we mean by "fortunate,"

---

* The only doubt which I have as to their identity arises from the circumstance that the words in the last line of the inscription, as given by Gough, seem, from Dr. Bruce's wood-cut, to be in two lines on the stone in the Newcastle Museum. The remains of this last three lines as there represented are—

MAXIMO LEG
AI MARTI
TVS

Gough's copy of the inscription is disfigured by so many mistakes that I have but little doubt that he has erred even as to the arrangement of the words in them. Dr. Bruce remarks that the stone "is figured in Brand's Newcastle, vol. i., p. 611; Hodgson, lxxxvii. (See also p. 372)." I am unable to consult either of these authorities.

" lucky," and is expressed in Greek by εὐτυχὴς. It was first applied, as is well known, to Commodus, to mark his good fortune in being rid of Perennis, whose treasonable designs were abruptly terminated by his murder by the soldiers.

§ 72. In p. 227, we have the following inscription on another slab :

```
        IMP·CAES·M AVRELIO
        SEVERO·ANTONINO
        PIO·FELICI AVG·PARTHIC
        MAX·BRIT.MAX GERM
        MAX·PONTIFICI MAXIM
        TRIB·POTEST XVIIII IMP·II
        COS IIII PRO COS PP COIII
        FIDA VARDVL CR EQ ∞ ANTO
        NINIANAFECIT SVBCVRA
                         LEGAVGPRP
```

Dr. Bruce expands it thus :—

"IMPERATORES CÆSARI MARCO AVRELIO
SEVERO ANTONINO
PIO FELICI AVGVSTO PARTHICO
MAXIMO BRITANNICO MAXIMO GERMANICO
MAXIMO PONTIFICI MAXIMO
TRIBUNITIÆ POTESTATIS UNDEVIGESIMUM IMPERATORIÆ SE-
                                        [CUNDUM
CONSULARIS QUARTUM, PROCONSULI, PATRI PATRIÆ COHORS
                                        [PRIMA
FIDA VARDULORUM, CIVIUM ROMANORUM EQUITATA [*MILI-
                                        [ARIA] ANTO
NINIANA FECIT SUB CURA...............
. . . . 227. . LEGATI AUGUSTALIS PROPRÆTORIS."

" To the emperor Marcus Aurelius Severus Antoninus, pious, happy, august, *styled* Parthicus M-ximus, Britannicus Maximus, Germanicus Maximus, chief priest, possessed of the tribunitian power for the nineteenth time, of the imperial for the second time, the consular for the fourth time, the father of his country; the First Cohort of the Varduli, *surnamed* the faithful, *composed of* Roman citizens, a military cohort, with its due proportion of cavalry attac'ed, and honoured with the *name* of Antonine, erected *this* under the superintendence of .... or angustal legate and propretor.

"The Antonine here referred to is the eldest son of Severus, commonly known as Caracalla; he was consul for the fourth time A.D. 213."

This is a very unsatisfactory explanation. In the expansion, *imperatoriæ secundum* is a mistake for *imperatori secundum*, and *consularis quartum* for *consuli quartum*. The remark that "Caracalla was consul for the fourth time, A.D. 213," although correct, is likely to mislead, as if that year were the date of the inscription, which it certainly is not. The reading of the 6th line of the inscription must be erroneous. If TRIB·POTEST XVIII be correct, the numerals after IMP· must be III not II, and thus we have A.D. *216 for the date. See Henzen, n. 6700 and Index, p. 74.

§ 73. In the same work (vol. i, p. 251) a stone bearing a funeral inscription is figured :

C·VALERIVS·C·VOL·
IVLLVS·VIAN*MIL
LEG·XX·V·V

Dr. Bruce explains it thus :—

"This inscription may probably be read thus: Caius Valerius Caii (filius) Voltinia (tribu) Tullus vixit annos quinquaginta miles Legionis Vicesimæ Valentis Victricis. (In memory of) Caius Valerius Tullus, the son of Caius, of the Voltinian tribe, a soldier of the Twentieth Legion (styled) Valiant and Victorious (who) lived fifty years. Hodgson's reading is : Caius Valerius Caius Voltinius Julius vixit annos, &c. " " The age of the soldier has been cut upon a nodule of ferruginous matter, which has fallen out : there is not space for two letters, so that there is little doubt that the inscription originally had L."

Dr. Bruce's expansion is a great improvement on Mr. Hodgson's, but I am not satisfied with it. The position of MIL·LEG·, &c., and the absence of any distinguishing mark between VI and AN,† lead me to believe that VIAN [N or A] stands for *Vienna*, his birth-place, especially as it is in the right position, according

---

*Mr. Newton, *Mon. Hist. Brit.*, assigns A.D. 215 as the date, although the numerals, as given by him, are XVIII and II.

† In the original, as figured by Dr. Bruce, there are leaf points after *Valerius*, *C*, *Vol*, and *Tullus*.

to the normal collocation. This conjecture is confirmed by the circumstance, that all the natives of Vienna (scil., Allobrogum), mentioned in inscriptions, belonged to the Voltinian tribe;* e. gr., Orelli, n. 445 :

C·VALERI
VS·C·F·VOL
CAMPANVS
VIENNA MIL
L·XI·C·P·F·
&c. &c. &c.

See also Horsley, Brit. Rom. Yorkshire, n. 8 ; Orelli, n. 453 ; Letronne, Inscr. de l'Egypte, Pl. xxxi. 3, &c.

The form VIANNA for VIENNA is found in the following, given by Steiner, Cod. In. Rom. Rhen. nn. 325 and 397 :—

P·SOLIVS
P·F·VOL·SV
AVIS·VIANNA
&c. &c. &c.

C·DANNIVS·C·F·
VOL·SECVNDVS
VIANNA

I would read the inscription thus : Caius Valerius, Caii [filius], Voltinia [tribu], Tullus, Vianna, miles Legionis xx, Valeriæ Victricis. It is possible that VIANNA, a town of Rhætia or Noricum may be intended, as Reinesius interprets the inscription, which he gives in Class viii., n. 38 (the same as Steiner's n. 325), but as the person named in it was of the Voltinian tribe, I prefer regarding Vianna as another form of VIENNA.

§ 74. In p. 261 of the same work, an altar is figured, which bears the following inscription :—

<hr/>

* I do not mean to say that all the natives of Vienna were of the same tribe. There are examples which prove that some who had the same town as their birth-place were of different tribes. See Orelli, n. 8104 ; and Henzen, n. 6422.

SOLI
APOLLINI
ANICERO.

Dr. Bruce offers no explanation, but remarks :—

"It was found together with three others of Mithraic character. The third line is somewhat obscure, and the subsequent lines are nearly obliterated by the action of the weather. Mr. Thos. Hodgson has described this and the other altars found on the same occasion in the *Arch. Æliana*, vol. iv., p. 6."

On reference to Mr. Hodgson's description, I find that the only letters of the doubtful word, which he attempts to explain, are the first four—ANIO. These he regards as "the dative case of ANIVS, who was the son of Apollo and Rhen," and he cites in illustration (apparently with approval?) one of Mr. Faber's wild speculations, that "Rheo" [thus Mr. F. calls the mother of Anius] "is the same as Rhea, a mere personification of the Ark; Apollo is the solar Noah; and Anius is also the great patriarch, under the title of *Anius*, the *naval deity*."

It appears, from a comparison of the representations of the altar, as figured by Dr. Bruce and Mr. Hodgson, that it is doubtful whether the fourth letter is C or O; and that the last two, read by Dr. Bruce as RO, are not distinct.

I am of opinion that the true reading is ANICETO, and that the word is nothing more than the Greek ΑΝΙΚΗΤΩ [I] in Latin characters, *i. e.*, ἀνικήτῳ, *invicto*, the epithet so frequently applied to Mithras, Sol, and Apollo.

§ 75. Amongst the valuable results of the exploration of the station of *Bremenium*, which was made through the liberality of the Duke of Northumberland, in 1852, was the discovery of several inscribed stones. On one of these, as figured in Bruce's *Roman Wall*, p. 458, is the following imperfect inscription :

```
IMP CAE * * * * * * * * * *
* * * * * * P·F * * * * * * *
* * * * CH·I·F·VARD * * * *
* * * * * BALLIS A SOLO RES
SVB C·CLAP,LINI LEG AVG
INSTANTE AVR QVINTO TR
```

Dr. Bruce remarks :—

"The inscription may be read :—

IMP[ERATORI] CAE[SARI]
P[IO] F[ELICI]
C[O]H[ORS] I F[IDA] VARD[VLORVM]
BALLIS A SOLO REST[ITVIT]
SVB C[AIO] CL[AVDIO] APELLINI[O] LEG[ATO] AVG[VSTALI]
INSTANTE AVR[ELIO] QVINTO TRIB[VNO].

In honour of the Emperor Cæsar,
Pious, happy.
The first cohort of the Vardali, *styled* the faithful,
———— —— from the ground restored,
Under Caius Claudius Apellinius, imperial legate ;
Aurelius Quintus, the Tribune, superintending the work.

"The word *ballis* being peculiar, it would be rash to hazard a hasty explanation of it. It does not occur in Gruter. Is it the termination of some word? Is it a contraction for *balneis ?* or has *b* been substituted for *v*, and should it be *vallis ?* These are the most plausible suggestions which have occurred to me, but I am not satisfied with any of them. I have written the cognomen of the legate, as I think the inscription requires ; it is necessary, however, to state that this name does not occur in Gruter."

In the year 1855, excavations were carried on at the same place, and a slab was discovered bearing the following inscription, as given by Dr. Bruce, in the interesting account published in the *Archæologia Æliana* (new series), vol. i., p. 78 :—

IMP·CAES·M·AV * * *
* * * * * * PIO F * * *
TRIB·POT X COS * * *
P · P · BALLIST·A SO *
VARDVL * * * * * * *
TIB·CL·PAVL * * * * *
PR·PR· FEC.   * * * * *
P·AEL * * * * * * * * *

This inscription, as Dr. Bruce observes, solves the question as to BALLIS in that found in 1852, for BALLIST suggests BAL_LISTARIVM, and we are also enabled to correct the reading of

x

the name of the imperial legate, by substituting *Paulinus* for *Apellinius*. So far every thing seems satisfactory ; but Dr. Bruce adds in a note :—

"A comparison of the two inscriptions does not remove all the difficulties attending the reading of the name of the Proprætor on the slab found in 1852 ; but if the name of this dignitary be not (Tiberius) Claudius Paulinus it is difficult to say what it is."

I am unable to understand the grounds of this remark. The name of the legate on the second slab seems to be, beyond doubt, *Tiberius Claudius Paulinus*, and from this we have to correct the reading on the first slab—*Caius Claudius Apellinius*. The substitution of *Paulinus* for *Apellinius* seems certain. *Claudius* remains in both, the only difference being that in the first we have the abbreviation CLA, in the second only CI,—and all that remains to be done is to get rid of *Caius*, the *prænomen* in the first. Can there be any doubt that the C preceding CLA in that inscription stands not for *Caio* but for *cura*, i. e., that we should read *sub c[ura] ? Paulini*, in the genitive, confirms the expansion. Thus no difficulty regarding the names of this Pro-prætor remains. In one his *prænomen* is given ; in the other it is omitted, as is frequently the case. In the Vieux inscription, given in Mr. C. R. Smith's *Collectanea Antiqua*, iii., p. 95, the names of the same Proprætor also appear without the *prænomen*. Compare the inscriptions 16a, 98, and 102a in *Monum. Hist. Brit.*

But another enquiry remains as to the age of the slabs. Dr. Bruce remarks on this point :—

"The Emperor here referred to is no doubt Heliogabalus. He assumed the same titles as Caracalla ; but the *character of the letters and the evidently intentional erasure of the distinctive part of his name, indicate the latter rather than the earlier monarch. Fortunately the erasure in the second line has not been so effectually performed as to prevent the word ANTONINO being discernible."

---

* This affords a remarkable illustration of the extent to which the professed power of discriminating the age of an inscription by the character of its letters has been assumed by some palæographists. There is no doubt that there are clearly defined distinctions between the earliest and the later Latin inscriptions, one of which, and perhaps the most marked, is the absence or rarity of ligatures in those of older date, but the attempt to assign a definite

Neither of the reasons given by Dr. Bruce seems to me conclusive evidence as to the emperor here referred to being Heliogabalus. Moreover, the examination of the date of the Vieux monument by Mr. Roach Smith, *Collect. Antiq.*, iii. p. 98, does not favour this opinion. He observes :—

"This monument was erected in the first year of the reign of the third Gordian. [In the inscription on the principal face the date is given—ANPIO ET PROCVL-COS—which corresponds to A.D. 288.] The events mentioned in the inscriptions probably occurred a considerable time anterior to the setting up of the monument. M. Huet and the Abbé le Neuf believe that the Ædinius Julianus, præfect of the prætorium, whom Solemnis went to Rome to see, and from whom he received this letter of recommendation [inscribed on the monument], is the Julianus mentioned by Herodian and Capitolinus, who held this high post in the time of Macrinus [i.e., before the commencement of the reign of Heliogabalus]. This was twenty years prior to the reign of Gordian, and as Julianus speaks of Paulinus as his predecessor in Gaul, Paulinus, in this case, must have been in Britain in the reign of Caracalla, possibly of Severus, when the sixth legion was in active service in the north of the island, repelling the Mæatæ and the Caledonians."

In the opinion of M. Huet and the Abbé le Neuf I concur. It seems very improbable that the *Julianus*, who was præfect of the prætorium under Commodus, was the individual named on the monument. I regard the *Ædinius Julianus* of the monument as most probably the same who is mentioned as *M. Ædinius Julianus* amongst the *patroni* of Canusium, in the well-known inscription (of the date A.D. 223) given by Mommsen, *Inscript. Neapol.*, n. 635.

§ 76. Dr. Bruce, *Roman Wall*, 2nd edit., p. 46, figures a slab

---

reign by the special peculiarities of the letters is almost wholly speculative. No more forcible illustration of this can be given than Dr. Bruce's remark, as quoted above, that "the character of the letters indicates the latter rather than the earlier monarch," i.e., Elagabalus rather than Caracalla. This remark is based on the assumption that there was so marked a change in the character of the Latin letters, between April, A.D. 217, and June A.D. 218, that antiquarians can now determine whether an inscription was cut in the reign of Caracalla or of Elagabalus!

The only other ground, which I can conjecture for Dr. Bruce's remark, is his belief that the memorials of Caracalla and Elagabalus, which have been found in Britain, were distinguished by their difference of character; but this cannot be admitted, for no undoubted record, so far as I am aware, of the time of Elagabalus has been discovered in the island, except that given in the *Roman Wall*, pp. 164, 166.

found at *Chesters, on the North Tyne. It bears an inscription, of which a great part is illegible. Dr. B. remarks that "it is a sepulchral stone, and bears at the end of the third and the beginning of the fourth lines the words—

. . . . . . ALAE
II ASTVR[VM] "

The word before ALAE seems to be CVRATORI, designating the office held by the deceased in the *ala*. The notice of this office is so rare that I do not recollect having seen it noticed except in one instance—Renier, *Inscriptions de l'Algérie*, n. 4043:

D   M
VLPIVS·TERTI
VS CVRATOR
ALAEICONTARI
&c.

§ 77. In Mr. Wright's *Celt, Roman and Saxon*, p. 317 (p. 322, 2nd ed.), we have the following inscription, found at Great Chesters :—

"D M	To the gods of the shades,
AEL·MERCV	To Ælius Mercurialis,
RIALI CORNICVL	a trumpeter,
VACIA·SOROR	his sister Vacia
FECIT	made this."

It is not easy to understand how Mr. Wright could have made such a mistake as to translate *corniculario* "trumpeter," especially as in p. 350 (p. 357, 2nd ed.) he remarks relative to this same inscription—"a *cornicularius* is commemorated, but whether he belonged to the departmental court or not is uncertain." Horsley, p. 229, had correctly explained the term as it occurs here, for he remarks : "The name of this officer is upon several monuments in Gruter, and occurs frequently in the *Notitia*. He was a kind of clerk or secretary." In the army, there was a *cornicularius tribuni*, the step above which was the *beneficiarius præfecti*, and the step above that the *cornicularius præfecti*.

---

* The Chairman of the Notitia.

§ 78. Many centurial inscriptions have been found in this
country. On these see my notes on inscriptions found in *Monmouthshire*, § 45.

§ 79. *At Corbridge two altars were found bearing Greek
inscriptions. One of them is figured in Dr. Bruce's *Roman
Wall*, p. 313, and the inscription is thus translated :—

" ΑΣΤΑΡΤΗΣ	Of Astarte,
ΒΩΜΟΝ Μ'	The altar
ΣΣΟΡΑΣ	You see
ΠΟΤΛΛΕΡ Μ'	Pulcher
ΑΝΕΘΗΚΕΝ	replaced."

This translation omits that pleasing characteristic, which is
often found in Greek inscriptions, whereby the object is regarded
as addressing the reader ; and not only is ΜΕ overlooked in the
second and in the fourth line, but the sense of ΑΝΕΘΗΚΕΝ
is not correctly expressed. It does not mean "replaced," but
"set up," "erected," "dedicated." Mr. Wright, p. 269, correctly renders it :—

> " Of Astarte
> the altar me
> you see,
> Pulcher me
> dedicated."

i. e., you see me the altar of Astarte : Pulcher dedicated me. He
also notices the circumstance, that the inscription "forms a line
in Greek hexameter verse." It is strange, that, being aware of
this, he did not observe that a slight and sure emendation will
give the same structure in the inscription on the other altar.
Following Hodgson he reads :—

" ΗΡΑΚΛΕΙ	To Hercules
ΤΙΡΡΙΩ	the Tyrian
ΔΙΟΔΩΡΑ	Diodora
ΑΡΧΙΕΡΕΙΑ	the high priestess."

It is plain that ΤΙΡΡΙΩ destroys the metre, and that the verse
should stand thus :—

ΗΡΑΚΛΕΙ ΤΥΡΙΩ ΔΙΟΔΩΡΑ ΑΡΧΙΕΡΕΙΑ.

i. e.,   Ἡρακλεῖ Τυρίῳ Διοδώρα ἀρχιέρεια.

In another Greek inscription, found at Chester, in, I believe,
1850, we have also an Hexameter, which has escaped the notice
of Dr. J. Y. Simpson, in his paper on the subject in the *Proceedings of the Soc. of Antiq. of Scotland,* vol. ii, p. i, p. 80.   He
reads the words, which form the verse,* thus :—

ΕΡΜΟΓΕΝΙΙΣ
ΙΑΤΡΟΣ ΒΩΜΟΝ
ΤΟΝΑΑΝΕΘΗΚΑ

i. e., ΕΡΜΟΓΕΝΗΣ ΙΑΤΡΟΣ ΒΩΜΟΝ ΤΟΝΑ ΑΝΕΘΗΚΑ.

It is evident that the fourth letter in the third line is not A but
Δ and that the E, which follows it in ΤΟΝΔΕ, is here elided.
Accordingly the verse should be :—

ΕΡΜΟΓΕΝΙΙΣ ΙΑΤΡΟΣ ΒΩΜΟΝ ΤΟΝΔ' ΑΝΕΘΗΚΑ

i. e., I, Hermogenes, a physician, dedicated this altar.

---

* The preceding words [ΣΩΤ] ΗΡΣΙΝ [ΤΙ]ΕΥΜΕΝΕΣΙΝ seem to be a portion of an
irregular pentameter.

---

§ 79. In the year 1752, some *grave-stones were dug up near Wroxeter, the ancient *Viroconium*, † on one of which were three panels, two bearing inscriptions and the third left vacant. According to the copy in Gough's Camden,‡ vol. iii., pl. 1, fig. 5, these inscriptions stand thus :—

D M PLACIDA AN LV CVR AG CONIA XXX	D M DEVCCV S ANXV CVR⁴G RATRE	

The following notice of this slab is given by Mr. Wright, *Celt, Roman, and Saxon,* p. §321 :—

"A monument found at Wroxeter (*Uriconium*) mentions an office, the exact character of which seems to be doubtful, though the *curator agrorum* or *agrarius* may have been the overseer, or bailiff, of the town lands. The monument consists of a tablet in three columns or compartments; that in the middle contains an inscription to the officer; the one on the left has an inscription to the wife; the other is blank, and it has either been left so for a son, or has become erased. The central inscription is :—

---

* They are now preserved in the library of Shrewsbury Grammar School.

† In the MSS. of the Itinerary of Antoninus (see ed. Parthey and Pinder, Berlin, 1848), the name is given also as *Uriconium*, *Uriconium*, *Uroconium* and *Viroconium*. The anonymous Ravennas has *Utriconion*; and in the treatise of Richard of Cirencester, *de Situ Britanniæ*, we find the forms *Uoriconium* and *Viroconium*, besides *Uriconium* and *Uriconum*. It is difficult to decide which should be preferred. Mr. Wright adopts *Uriconium*, and Mr. Scarth *Uriconium*; whilst the weight of authority seems to me to preponderate in favour of *Viroconium*, the *Oὐιροκόνιον* of Ptolemy.

‡ I have omitted points, for I am uncertain whether the marks between certain letters, as they appear in the copy of Gough's Camden, which I use, are intended for points or for representations of defects in the stone, or are blemishes in the engraving or printing.

§ In the 2nd ed., p. 526, the inscriptions, translations and observations are wholly omitted.

D·M	To the gods of the shades.
DEVCCV	Deucous
S·V·AN·XV	lived fifteen (?) years,
CVR·AG	he was overseer of the lands
RA TRE	of Trebonius (?)

" The number of years is perhaps not correctly read from the stone, which seems to be in bad condition.   The other inscription is :—

D·M	To the gods of the shades.
PLACIDA	Placida
AN LV	lived fifty-five years,
CVR·AG	of the overseer of the lands
CON·I A	she was the wife
XXX	thirty years."

Independently of the objections, that there is no authority for the office of *curator agrorum*, and that no account is taken of A in the 5th line of the central inscription, I am unable to perceive any grounds for passing over the obvious interpretation of CVR· AG. *scil.*, cur[am] ag[ente].   The form is found in many sepulchral inscriptions ; and on p. 315 of Mr. Wright's work we have an example :—

> CVRA[M] AGENTE
> AMANDA
> CONIVGE

RATRE is evidently either FRATRE, the F and R being ligulate, or PATRE, the P having been mistaken for R.

In an able and timely *summary of information relative to Viroconium* by the Rev. H. M. Scarth, of Bath, which has recently been published in the *Journal of the Archæological Institute*, this with other inscriptions found at Wroxeter is given, and PATRE is adopted as the true reading of the word in the fifth line, but the letter which follows A in the 4th line is read C instead of G. In the other inscription on this tablet, the I of the fifth line is read by Mr. Scarth as J, and the A in the same line is omitted, whilst the three marks XXX at the bottom are regarded as " more

---

* Wroxeter, in consequence of the discoveries which have lately been made there, is at present regarded with much interest by antiquaries, and " a well organised movement has at length been made for the exploration of the site of Uriconium."

probably merely an ornament, like a leaf introduced at the end
of the next inscription." Adopting his readings, with the exceptions of C for G and J for I, I would give the inscriptions, *in
extenso*, thus :—

D·M	D[iis] M[anibus];
PLACIDA	Placida,
AN·LV	an [norum] LV,
CVR·AG	cur[am] ag[ente]
CONI	conj[uge].

D·M	D[iis] M[anibus];
DEVCCV	Deuccu-
S·AN·XV	s, an[norum] XV,
CVR·AG	cur[am] ag[ente]
PATRE	patre.

If A and XXX be retained in the first inscription, I would
expand the contractions in the 5th and 6th lines, thus :—

CONI A	conjuge annorum
XXX	triginta.

i. e., her husband for thirty years. We have a similar construction in Maffei, *Museum Veronense*, 152, 6 :—

C. CASSIVS. C·F
VESPA
MANLIA. T·F
REPENTINA
VXOR·AN·XXX

It only remains to add, that I concur in Mr. Scarth's opinion,
that the vacant panel was left by the father of Deuccus and the
husband of Placida "for his own name and age at his decease."*

---

* Since the above was written, I observe that the author of a very interesting article on
Uriconium, in *The Gentleman's Magazine* for May, 1859, has adopted Mr. Wright's views,
but I am still of opinion that his interpretation cannot be received.

P.S.—In the *Journal of the Archæological Association*, 1859, p. 213, Mr. Wright courteously
calls the attention of English Antiquaries to my papers in the *Cambrian Journal*, and
adopts my suggestions, relative to these inscriptions and that in § 50. He prefers, however,
CONI·A XXX in the first inscription and FRATRE in the second.

T

§ 80. On another of these grave-stones is the following inscription :—

C MANNIVS	C[aius] Mannius,
CF POL SECV	C[aii] f[ilius], Pol[lia]*tribu*, Secu-
NDVS POLLEN	ndus, Pollen[tia],
MIL LEG XX	mil[es] leg[ionis] XX,
ANORVLII	an[n]oru[m] LII,
STIP XXXI	stip [endiorum] XXXI,
BEN LEG PR	ben[eficiarius] leg[ati] pr[incipalis],
H S E	[hic] [situs] e[st].

Mr. Scarth remarks that this inscription "may be thus rendered :—Caius Maunius Secundus," son of Caius, of Pollentum, a soldier of the twentieth legion, aged 52 years; having served 31 years in the legion and being the beneficiary of the principal legate. He rests here."

Of this rendering I would suggest the following emendations :—the insertion of the words "of the Pollian tribe" after "son of Caius," "Pollentia" for "Pollentum," and †"principal beneficiary of the legate" for "beneficiary of the principal legate." As to the first of these, it is plain that the words proposed to be inserted were inadvertently omitted. The substitution of *Pollentia* for *Pollentum* is recommended by the consideration, that there were three ancient towns so called,—one in Liguria, another in Picenum, and a third in the Balearic isles; whilst there is no authority, so far as I am aware, for *Pollentum*. In the following inscription found at Zurzach in Switzerland, Orelli, n. 455, we have the name almost complete :—

---

* The writer in *The Gentleman's Magazine*, already referred to, gives the name of this soldier as *Caius Marinius Secundus Pollentius*; and adds that he " was also a pensioner of the first legion (i. e., *beneficiarius legionis primæ*), but both these readings are manifestly erroneous.

† The word "principal," as ordinarily used in English, does not convey the meaning of *principalis* as applied to a Roman soldier. The Latin term means that the person so styled was one of the *principales*, a designation given to suboffleers or officials, in contra-distinction to *munifices* or *gregarii*, which denoted the common soldiers or privates. See Veget. de re Militari, ii., c. 7.

....GIACVS
...POLIASVPER
PO .. ENTIA MILES
LEX·XI·C.P.F 7 SALNI
MAXIMI ANNORV
XXXV·STIP...

The third emendation is confirmed by reference to Orelli, n. 3461, where we have PRINCIPALIS BENEFICIARIVS TRIBVNI, and Henzen, n. 6791, where we find PBP for *principalis beneficiarius præfecti*; but the collocation of the abbreviations in this inscription is peculiar.

§ 81. A third stone bore the following inscription :—

M PETRONIVS	M[arcus] Petronius,[*]
L. F MEN	L[ucii f[ilius], Men[enia] *tribu,*
VIC ANN	vic[sit] [annos]
XXXVIII	XXXVIII,
MIL. LEG	mil[es] leg[ionis]
XIIII GEM	XIV gem[inæ],
MILITAVIT	militavit
ANN XVIII	ann[is] XVIII,
SIGN FVIT	Sign[ifer] fuit,
H S E	h[ic] s[itus] e[st]

Mr. Scarth notices the ingenious conjecture of a friend :—

"That Petronius was a bearer of one of the *Signa* of the fourteenth legion in the famous victory over Boadicea, A.D. 61. This legion arrived in Britain in A.D. 43, when Petronius being only twenty years old was a *Miles gregarius,* and subsequently for his valour, perhaps under Ostorius Scapula, raised to the rank of *Signifer.* It could not have been much later, for in A.D. 68 the fourteenth legion was quartered in Dalmatia, (Tacitus). He may have died in consequence of his wounds in the year 61."

It is manifestly impossible to prove the truth of this conjecture, for the fourteenth legion, after their recal from the island under Nero, were sent back in the year 69, and Petronius may have come with them then and died before they were again re-called in

* It is not unworthy of notice, that in an inscription found in Frisheim, Orelli, n. 501, we have the same name of another soldier of this legion, a native of Claudia Celeia in Noricum. He, however, was the son of Caius, and had a brother, whose prænomen was Caius.

the year 70. The conjecture, however, is countenanced by the
coincidence, that his period of service, viz. : 18 years, is the same
as the interval between the first arrival of the legion in A.D. 43,
and the battle in A.D. 61.   But how shall we account for his
burial at Viroconium ?   We have no evidence that the fourteenth
legion was ever stationed there, and it is far distant from the
scene of the battle, which probably took place not far from
London.   Can it have been that the fourteenth legion was with
Suetonius when he crossed over to Mona (Anglesey), and that on
his hurried march back from Wales, Petronius was killed, or died
of fatigue, at or near Viroconium, by which route it is probable
that Suetonius proceeded to London ?   But it is scarcely worth
while to dwell on conjectures formed on such slight foundations ;
it is more important to observe that this inscription is the only
extant British memorial of the "domitores Britanniæ."[*]

§ 82. Blocks of lead, bearing the inscription :—

IMP·HADRIANI·AVG

have been found in this county, about ten miles from Shrewsbury,
seven miles north of Bishop's Castle, and four and a half miles from
Montgomery.   See my notes on inscriptions found in *Derbyshire*.

§ 83. In the *Gentleman's Magazine*, April, 1862, p. 401, a
wood-cut is given of an inscribed stone, which was found at
Wroxeter, in September, 1861.   The inscription which it bears
is evidently funeral, but as some of the letters have been lost by
fracture or decay, and the majority are very indistinct, it is
extremely difficult to offer any satisfactory reading.   The following are the lines as they appear in the wood-cut :—

                    MINIVS T POLIA
               ORVMXXXXVSTIIXXIIMII·IIO·
               IIGEMMIIIIAVIAQNVNCHI S
               LEOITEEFFIIICE VIIAIIVSIIN
                    OVAIIOIIII A
               ADIIISVIVIIED M
                    DATI   IPVS·RONES

From such fragments as these it is plain that but little can be made out : but as I have the advantage of comparing the wood-cut with a carefully executed *photograph of the stone, I am able to offer some probable suggestions relative to those portions which are at all legible. The first line is—

—AMINIVS T·POLIA.

After the L is a mark which looks like a point. I would read the line—

[T. or C. FL]AMINIVS · T[RIBV or ITI· *filius*] POL-[LIA] *tribu* IA[S or SON or SVS] or POLIA for POLLIA *tribu.*

i. e., Titus, or Caius, Flaminius, tribu Pollia, or *Titi* filius Pollia tribu, Ias or Iason, or Iasus ; or Titus or Caius Flaminius, *Titi* filius, *Pollia* tribu. I prefer *Titus Flaminius, Titi* filius, *Pollia* tribu. *filius* and *tribu* being understood, and *Polia* being used for *Pollia.* The second line is clearly,

ORVMXXXXVSTIPXXIIMIL·LEG

i. e, [ANN]ORVM·XXXXV·STIP[ENDIORVM] · XXII· MIL[ES] LEG[IONIS], *annorum xxxxv., stipendiorum xxii. miles legionis.*

Of the third line the beginning and the ending are doubtful, especially the latter : the rest stands thus :

II GEM MILITAVI AQ NVNC—S—

I would read it—

XIIII · GEM[INAE] · MILITAVI·AQ[VILIFER].NVNC · [HIC] S[VM]

i. e., xiiii. geminæ, militavi aquilifer, nunc hic sum.

I prefer the 14th *geminæ*, as another example of this legion was found here. See § 81. The use of the first person in funeral inscriptions is common. On *aquilifer*, see *Orelli*, n. 3389, and on *hic sum*, Orelli, n. 4738, and Henzen, n. 7411.

* For this I am indebted to the Rev. O. H. Scarth, of Bath, who also kindly communicated his views on the subject.

The remains of the fourth line are—

> LEGITE·ET·FELICES·VITA—VS·

I would read it—

> [PER]LEGITE·ET·FELICES·VITA·PLVS

There can, I think, be no reasonable doubt as to our having
here the first four feet of an hexameter, and the long syllable of
the last dactyl : the difficulty is as to the two short syllables of
the dactyl and the final spondee.   The portion of the dactyl
was certainly in this line, but I suspect that the spondee was in
the next.   It opens with letters like IV·A, whence I am disposed to conjecture that the hexameter was—

> *Perlegite et felices ritâ plus minus jutâ,*

but I am not satisfied with it, chiefly on account of the last two
words.   The use of *perlegite* and *felices* in funereal inscriptions is
common.   See Orelli, n. 4818, Henzen, nn., 6813, 7402, 7412,
and Reinesius, xvi., 65.   The remaining letters of the 5th line
are so indistinct that it is almost impossible to make any thing of
them.   In the 6th, however, the letters A·DITIS are plain, from
which we may infer that the preceding portion of the hexameter,
of which IANV[A] or TARTAR[A] or TAENAR[A] (or
some such word with final ä) DITIS formed the ending, was in
the 5th line.   Here a difficulty presents itself as to the letter or
letters in that 5th line, following the letter which stands eighth.
To me this ninth character looks like an inverted E, i. e., Ǝ,
which it is impossible to read so as to obtain a word fit for verse,
unless, indeed, we take it as standing for HVS.   The six letters after
this character look like *AQVATI, but all after this to ADITIS,
in the 6th line, are so indistinct that scarcely one of them can be
identified with probability.   In an attempt to meet the require-
ments of the case I constructed an hexameter, which I subjoin.
It contains many of the apparent letters in order, but I do not
at all suggest it even as a sensible reading of the verse :

----

* The AQ recall *aquatfer* of the 3rd line, but if this view be adopted, the idea of verse must
be given up, at least in this line.   There are then various readings which suggest themselves, but there is not one which appears probable.

OMNIB·ÆQVA·LEGE·ITER·EST·AD·TAENARA·
DITIS

i. e., omnibus æquâ lege iter est ad Tænara Ditis.

The remainder of the inscription is fortunately involved in less obscurity. VIVITE·DVM are plainly the beginning of an hexameter, which ends with TEMPVS·HONESTE in the 7th line, and the letters before TEMPVS resemble DAT as given in the wood-cut. From these *data* then and the appearances of the fragments of letters in the *lacunæ*, I venture to suggest the following verse :

Vivite, dum Stygius vitæ dat tempus, honeste.

On the use of *vivere* and *honeste* in such inscriptions, see Orelli, n. 4807, and Henzen, nn. 6843, 7402, 7407, 7347.[*]

---

§ 84. Of the Roman remains, which are scattered over different parts of Europe, there are probably none which presented so great difficulties to the antiquary as certain small greenish stones of a quadrilateral form, with intagliated inscriptions in Latin on their edges. Schmidt, in "*Antiquitates Neomagenses*," "the Antiquities of Nimiguen," seems to have been the first who directed attention to them, but he was himself unable to decipher them, or to determine their use. Since his time, however, the subject has been explained and illustrated by Spon, Chishull, Caylus, Saxe, Walche, Gough, Tochon, Sichet, Duchalais, Way, and Simpson,* so that there now remains no doubt that they were medicine stamps used by the Roman physicians or empirics for marking their drugs or preparations, especially for diseases of the eyes.

One of the most interesting of these stones, inasmuch as it presents very great difficulties in interpretation, is that which was found at Bath, in a cellar in the Abbey yard, in 1731. "It was shewn to the Society of Antiquaries in London, at that time and twice afterwards. Mr. Lethieullier gave them a cast of it in plaster, and in 1757, the stone itself was the property of Mr. Mitchell. It is square, of a greenish cast and perforated." Dr. J. Y. Simpson, *Edinburgh Medical Journal*, March, 1851, informs us that he "had attempted to trace out the present proprietor of the stamp, with a view of ascertaining, more correctly, the exact nature of the inscriptions; but that these efforts were quite unsuccessful." Fortunately, however, "some manuscript notices of this Bath stamp exist in the minute books of the Antiquarian Society, with an impression taken with ink from the

---

* Dr. Simpson's articles in the *Edinburgh Medical Journal*, January and March, 1851, afford ample and satisfactory information, relative to the stamps found in the United Kingdom.

inscriptions." From a comparison of these notices with the copies of the inscriptions given by Gough, *Archæologia*, ix., p. 228, Dr. Simpson has determined the reading and interpretation of two of the legends with certainty, and of the third with some probability, whilst he states that the fourth side "offers the most puzzling of all the inscriptions hitherto found upon the Roman medicine stamps discovered in Britain." It is to this inscription that I now desire to direct attention. Mr. Gough, *Archæologia*, ix., p. 228, reads it :—

T. IVNIANI HOFSVMADρV
EC VMODELICTA A MEDICIS.

and Dr. Simpson offers the following explanatory remarks :—

"The fourth legend on the Bath stone offers the most puzzling of all the inscriptions hitherto found upon the Roman medicine stamps discovered in Britain. As Mr. Gough gives it, the last words of the inscription (DELICTA A MEDICIS—esteemed by physicians), are alone intelligible. The plaster cast of this side of the seal, contained in the Museum of the Antiquarian Society of London, contains an extremely imperfect copy of the second line, and not an over perfect one of the first ; but we see enough of it to be quite aware of the great carelessness with which Mr. Gough had originally copied the whole inscription. The second last letter in the line is not the Greek ρ, but the Latin Q; and the name of the collyrium is not HOFSVM, as he gives it, but apparently PHOEBVM. At all events there is a P, which he has omitted, before the H ; and the two medial letters, which he has read FS, are seemingly EB. Such is the conclusion to which the examination of the lettering of the cast itself forces me ; and what is much more important, because affording far stronger evidence than mine, Mr. Akerman reads this inscription in the same way. I may add that (as I am informed by the same gentleman) the word is copied and written as PHOEBVM, in the several notices contained in the minute-books of the Antiquarian Society, and to which I have already referred ; and Gough's ρ always given as Q.

Still, with all these emendations, I confess myself quite at a loss to decipher, satisfactorily, the inscription. The spelling of all the inscriptions on this stamp is executed very carelessly,—as in *ersomaelinum* for *erysmelinum* ; *thalaser* for *thalasser* ; and possibly the term QVECVMO may be a mis-spelling, by the engraver, for LEVCOMA. If so, the inscription would stand as :—

T JVNIANI PHOEBVM AD LV
ECOMA DELICTA A MEDICIS.

The Phoebum of T. Junianus for Leucoma, esteemed by physicians.

E

I am not aware that any of the old authors have described a collyrium under the name of PHOEBVM. But it looks like one of those high-sounding titles which the oculists were so fond of selecting and assuming, and we find described in their works collyria with such semi-astronomical appellations, as *Sol*, *Aster*, *Lumen*, *Phos*, &c.

I shall venture only one more remark, viz., the possibility of the term being PHORBIVM and not PHOEBVM. 'The Phorbion,' observes Galen, 'possesses attenuating, attractive, and discutient powers. They apply its seeds mixed with honey to Leucoma, and it is believed to have the power of extracting spicula of wood.'"

The obvious objections to Dr. Simpson's interpretations are :—

1st. That we should have had *delictum* and not *delicto*.

2nd. That the participles *dilecta* or *delecta* are confused with *delicta*.

3rd. That his interpretation requires us to regard *quecumo* as a mis-spelling for *leucoma*.

As the circumstances seem to warrant a resort to conjecture, I venture to suggest QVECVMQ for QVECVMO :—

> i. e., AD QVECVMQ DELICTA A MEDICIS.

If PHOEBVM be the true reading, the designation may have been selected with a view to the supposed superiority of Apollo to his son Æsculapius, and of course to the *medici* the sons of Æsculapius. But perhaps the word may be PHOEDVM, the Latinized form of ΦΟΙΔΟΝ or ΦΩΙΔΟΝ, derived from φωΐζω, whence φοῖδες or φῴδες, used by Aristotle, *Probl.*, 38, 7, Aristophanes, *Plut.*, 535, and Hippocrates, *Œcon.*, p. 494, *ed. Foes.*, already cited by Liddell and Scott, and φῴδον, given by Suidas.

QVECVMQ I regard as a contracted form of *quæcumque*, the E being used for AE, and the final Q for QVE, both of which uses are familiar to those conversant with Latin epigraphy. DELICTA is the participle of *delinquere* ; or is used for *derelicta* from *derelinquere*, as in Ennius "delicto Coelito" (if that be the true reading) for "derelicto Coelito ;" or it may be that the correct reading is RELICTA· In Orelli, n. 1318, we have *derelictus a medicis,* in the sense "given up by the physicians." The word thus admits of two interpretations, either "badly treated" or "given up." The meaning of the inscription, if we adopt PHOEDVM, may be expressed thus: "The blistering (collyrium) of Titus Junianus for such (hopeless) cases as have been given up by the physicians." I prefer PHOEBVM in the sense "radiant" or "Apollinarian."

Another panacea is noticed on the stamp found near Cirencester (the ancient *Corinium*) in 1818, and described by Buckman and Newmarch:

MINERVALIS MELINV [m]
AD OMNEM DOLOREM.

It may, I think, be safely inferred from the Bath inscription, if my interpretation be correct, that the stamp did not belong to a regular *medicus,* but to an empiric, possibly one of the *iatroliptæ.*

The difficulty in interpreting another legend on this stamp arises from the impossiblity of determining the true reading of one of the words. In the books of the Society of Antiquaries the legend is given thus:

T.IVNIANI DIEXVM AD VETeRES CICATRICES.

Dr. Simpson conjectures DIAMYSVM (the name of a well known collyrium) for the inexplicable DIEXVM; but from the copy by Gough it appears that the letters between D and M are in a rude Britanno-Roman character, and that "the disputed word may be more corectly read DRYCVM or DRYXVM," which Dr. S. interprets as a preparation from the bark, acorn, or galls of the *Drys, i. e.,* oak. Can it be that the word is formed from *Druidæ* or *Dryidæ,* and that both the appellation and the characters were adopted with a view to securing its sale among the native population?

§ 85. Horsley's n. ii. is an imperfect inscription on a grave-stone found near Bath:—

C·MVRRIVS
C·F·ARNIENSIS
FORO·IVLI·MO
DESTVS·MIL·
EG·II·AD·P·F
IVLI·SECVNDI
ANNXXVSTI
II

The following are his expansion and remarks :—

"Caius Murrius Caii filius Arniensis (*tribus*) Foro Julii Modestus miles legionis secundæ adjutricis piæ fidelis Julii Secundi annorum viginti quinque stipendiorum—hic *situs est.*"

"The *legio secunda adjutrix* which seems to be mentioned in this monument never was in Britain, or at least there is no proof of it from any other inscriptions or Roman historian. Perhaps this soldier came hither for his health, though the legion was at a distance. The letters A. D. P. F. are so distinct in the original as to leave no room for any suspicion of error. As it does not appear that the *legio secunda adjutrix* was ever in *Britain*, the letters A. D. P. F. in the fifth line may be read *adoptivus filius*. There seems to be no objection to this, but the point between D. and P., for *Manutius* gives us both ADOP and ADP, for *adopticus*, from ancient inscriptions; but that point may be either the remains of an O defaced, or put there through inadvertency. This will make the reading of the sixth line evidently *Julii Secundi*, two names of the person who adopted him.

It is not easy to know what else to make of the sixth line. Some think that the first visible letter may have been a P., and that it has been *manipuli secundi*, the former part of the word *manipuli* being effaced. But the appearance of the original did not in my opinion favour this conjecture; for there were no traces of any more letters in the fifth line after P. F., and the first letter in the sixth line did not seem any way deficient. Besides, it is not usual in such monuments to describe a soldier from the *manipulus* to which he belonged."

There can be no reasonable doubt as to the correctness of the expansion—AD[IVTRICIS] P[IAE] F[IDELIS]. Another soldier of this legion is named on a grave-stone found in Lincoln. See p. 92. IVLI SECVNDI are in the genitive after *centurio* either understood or obliterated, *scil.*, >, and are the names of the centurion under whom he served.

Foro Juli is his birth-place, *scil.*, Friuli, or Frejus, and there is this

peculiarity in its position in the inscription, that it is not in the
normal place. The birth-place, according to usage, follows the
cognomen; here it precedes it. See other examples in *Fabretti*,
pp. 340, 341.

§ 86. Horsley's n. iii. is also an inscription on a grave-stone
found at the same place :—

DIS MANIBVS
M.VALERIVS·M
FILLATINVS CEQ
MILES LEG·XX·AN
XXXV STIPENXX.
H . S . E

The following are his expansion and remarks :—

" Dis Manibus Marcus Valerius Marci filius Latinus centurio
eques miles legionis vicesimæ annorum triginta quinque stipendiorum viginti hic situs est."

" As I read it, this *Valerius* had served in the capacities of a
soldier, an horseman, and a centurion or *decurio equitum* in the
same legion."

Orelli's expansion C[olonia] Eq[uestri], the name of the birth-
place of the deceased, is much to be preferred.

§ 87. Horsley's n. iv. is on a stone with a figure on either side.
He was of opinion that there were three distinct stones, and that
they did not appear to have been ever united. "One of these
figures," he remarks, " is a *Victory* with a palm branch in her left
hand, and a *corona* in her right ; the other, as Dr. Stukely thinks,
has a *cornucopia* in her left hand ; but I am persuaded they have
no reference to the inscription near which they are now placed."
I am inclined to think that the stones, though distinct, were
intended to be placed together, and venture to suggest that the
inscription was, or was reputed to be Christian. The palm
branch and the *corona* are well known symbols of Christianity ;
and I even suspect that the rudely drawn figure with an object
on the shoulders (mistaken for a *cornucopia*) may have been a

a rough representation of "the good shepherd," carrying a lamb.
See Maffei, *Museum Veronense*, p. clxxviii, for a remarkable
illustration of this suspicion. The following is the inscription
on the stone in the middle :

D   M

SVCC·PETRONIAE VIX

ANN·III·M·IIII·D·IX·VᴾᴾO

MVLVS·ETᵛICTSAᴾINA

FIL·KAR·FEC

Mr. Ward's remarks on it are :—

"I am inclined to think the daughter's names here are *Succia Petronia ;*
the father's *Valerius Petronius* . . . . *mulus* or *nuclus ;* and the mother's,
Tuctia or *Tuccia Sabina.* Of these, Petronius is the family name, and therefore given to the daughter. The character at the beginning of it contains
four letters, PETR, of which there are other instances. The names *Tuccia*
and *Sabina* are both found more than once in *Gruter.* The T at the beginning of the word *Tuictia* is to be twice read as L in the *Middlesex* inscription ;
the I has been added after the V to accommodate the spelling to the pronunciation in prolonging the sound, and nothing was more common than the
promiscuous use of C and T in the same word. I cannot but fancy, therefore, that the daughter's name was taken from the mother's, a little softened
by substituting S for T, a thing not uncommon, as we learn from Quintilian ;
and in this case suited to that natural fondness in parents for their children
which the Greeks seem to have happily expressed by the word ὀνοματισμός.
The V in *Succia* is larger than the following letters, very probably to give
it the same force as VI in *Tuictia* by lengthening the sound, which was a
thing very usual."

Horsley gives the following expansion : "Dis Manibus Succiæ
Petroniæ vixit annos tres menses quatuor dies novem Valerius
Petronius et Tuictia Sabina filiæ carissimæ fecerunt."

I am by no means satisfied with this rendering. Instead of
Valerius Petronius I would read *Vettius Romulus*, and instead of
Tuictia Sabina, Victoria Sabina. It is remarkable that all the
names which occur in this inscription are applied to Christians
either in the catacombs of Rome or elsewhere.

§ 88. In the year 1736, a fragment of a grave-stone was
found in Bath, which, according to Dr. Stukeley, *Phil. Trans.*
1748, bore the inscription :—

L·VITELLIVS·MA
NIAI·F·TANCINVS
CIVES·HISP·CAVRIESIS
EQ·ALAE·VETTONUM·CR
ANN·XXXXVI·STIP·XXVI
H·S·E

i. e. "Lucius Vitellius Maximiani filius Titus Ancinus, civis Hispanus Cauriensis equitum alæ Vettonum Curator anno 46 Stipendiorum 26 hic sepultus est."

Mr. Warner, *History of Bath, Append.*, p. 118, reads *Mantani* for *Maximiani*, *Tancinus* for *Titus Ancinus*, *Hispaniæ* for *Hispanus*, *centurio* for *curator*, and *hic situs est* for *hic sepultus est.* He translates the whole inscription thus: "Lucius Vitellius Tancinus, the son of Mantanus, a citizen of Caurium, in Spain, centurion of the Vettonensian auxiliary horse; who died in the forty-sixth year of his age, and the twenty-sixth year of his military service."

The term *centurion* is explained on the supposition that the *ala* "here spoken of was probably attached to the twentieth legion; in this Tancinus bore the office of centurion; a command somewhat analogous to the captaincy of a troop in our service." Mr. Scarth, *Proceedings of Somersetshire Archæolog. and Nat. Hist. Society*, 1852, p. 102, remarks, that "the stone was erected on the place of interment of '*Lucius Vitellius Tancinus*, the son of Mantaus or Mantanus,' a citizen of Caurium, in Spain, a centurion of the Vettonensian horse, who died at the age of forty-six years." Both Mr. Warner and Mr. Scarth observe, in illustration, that Caurium was a town in Lusitania, and that the Vettones were a neighbouring people, who supplied the Romans with excellent heavy-armed horse.

There is no doubt that Mr. Warner's expansion is an improvement on that given by Dr. Stukeley, but it is far from being satisfactory. Of the suggestions which have been offered relative to MANIAI·F, I prefer Mr. Scarth's reading MANTAI·F; but perhaps we should substitute E for I, *i. e.*, MANTAE.*

* From MANTA, as SITA in p. 76. Compare also the inscription given in *Journ. of Arch. Assoc.*, 1847, p. 210, fig. 2.

The reading TANCINVS is supported by the inscription in Gruter, p. cmxvii, n. 8, cited by Mr. Warner; but IIISPANVS, not IIISPANIAE, is conformable to usage. The expansions EQVITVM for EQ· and CVRATOR or CENTVRIO for C· R are unquestionably erroneous. EQ· stands for EQVES, and C·R for CIVIVM ROMANORVM. As to Mr. Warner's suggestion, that the deceased may have been a centurion in an *ala Vettonum* attached to the 20th legion, it is sufficient to observe that there is no authority for a centurion in an *ala*, nor for an *ala* being attached to a legion.

§ 89. In the year 1754 an altar was found in Upper Stall Street, Bath, bearing the following inscription :—

PEREGRINVS
SECVNDI FIL
CIVIS·TREVER
IOVCETIO
MARTI ET
NEMETONA
V·S·L·M.

Mr. Gough, *Camden's Britannia*, i., p. 118, observes, that the altar "was erected by Peregrinus to two new local deities. Jupiter *Cetius* may be the *Ceaicus* or *Ceutius* on an inscription given by Mr. Horsley, 278, in Cumberland, and takes his name from Mount *Cetius* in Noricum, under which was the town of *Cetium*, and Nemetona, one of the many local deities mentioned only in three inscriptions."

Mr. Warner, *Hist. of Bath*, p. 120, *Append.*, remarks : "It is dedicated to three deities, the Cetian Jupiter, Mars, and Nemetona, a local deity. The name of the person who erected it does not appear; for the word *Peregrinus* is merely an appellative, implying that he was a stranger or traveller. We find, however, by the second and third lines, the name of his father *Secundus:* and the city of his residence, Treves in Germany. The last of the deities mentioned in the inscription seems to have been a British one, and known only in the south-western parts of England. The name Nemenotacio (which Baxter considers as synonymous with Nemetomagus) seems in the chorography of Anonymus Ravennas, and is conjectured by Baxter, to be the present Launceston. If this be allowed, the near approach of Nemetona to the town Nemetomagus, will justify the opinion of the former being the local divinity of the latter."

Mr. Scarth, *Somersetshire Archæolog. and Nat. His. Soc.'s Proceedings*, 1852, *p.* 99, mentions the opinions (which have been above stated) relative to Jupiter Cetius and Nemetona, without, however, expressing approval of them, or offering any other explanation.

There can, I think, be but little doubt in the mind of those who have noticed *Marti Leucetio* in Gruter, lviii. 3, that I, the initial letter of the 4th line of the inscription, is a *mistake for L, and that we should read the names of the deities :—

*LOVCETIO
MARTI ET
NEMETONA[E]

In Steiner, 1 Dan. et Rh. 1, n. 472, (cited by Henzen, n. 5899, who also proposes this emendation) we have :—

CVRTELIA·PREPVSA
MARTI LOVCETIO
V·S·L·L·M

and

MARTI·LEVCETIO
T·TACITVS CENSORINVS
V·S·L·L·M

The deities are joined in the following inscription, found at Altripp, *prope Nemetas*, and given by Henzen, n. 5904 :—

MARTI·ET·NEMETO
NAE
SILVIN IVSTVS
ET·DVBITATVS
V·S·L·L·P

---

* Mr. Scarth, on reading this conjecture, examined the stone, which is in the possession of the Bath Institution, and ascertained its correctness. See a paper by him in the *Jour. and of the Arch. Assoc.*, 1861, p. 9.

Leucetius seems to be derived from *Leuci*, and *Nemetona* from *Nemetes*, both being names of peoples in the neighbourhood of the Treviri.* It is scarcely necessary to add, that there is no foundation for Mr. Warner's assertion, that *"Peregrinus is merely an appellative."* The name often occurs in inscriptions ; and it must be borne in mind that the use of but one name was not uncommon among the Gauls. The meaning of CIVIS TREVER, also, is not "a citizen of Treves," but a Trever citizen, *i. e.*, a citizen of the people called Treveri, or Treviri.

§ 90. Restorations of imperfect inscriptions, although subjects of agreeable speculation, are generally very hazardous, excepting those cases in which the extant words or letters are parts of *formulæ*, and then a perfectly reliable reading may be supplied from known examples. It is very different, however, when the attempt is made to complete a fragment by supplying facts supposed to have been stated in the missing or mutilated portions. In such cases the restoration, although sometimes ingenious, is scarcely ever more than plausible. A notable example is presented by Governor Pownall's well-known restoration of the imperfect inscription on stones found in Bath, and believed to to have formed part of the frieze of the ††temple of Minerva in that city. The fragments are figured in Warner's *History of Bath*, pl. 1, fig. 7, and the words on them are thus read by the Rev. H. M. Scarth, *Journal of the British Archæological Association*, 1857, p. 206 :

(1.)	(2.)
LAVDIVS·LICVR	OLEGIO·LONGA·SERIA
E·NIMIA·VETVST	VNIA·REFICI·ET·REPINGI·CVR

---

* Of these derivations, the latter appears to be certain, but the former doubtful, as we have evidence that Jupiter was called *Leucetius*, as the giver of light. See A. Gell. *Noct. Att.* v. 12; Festus, s. h., and Serv. on Virgil, *Æn.* ix. 570. Another derivation, which has been proposed, from *Leuce*, an island in the Euxine, is very improbable.

† The only ancient authority for this temple is the following passage in Solinus :—"*fontes calidi opiparo exornati apparatu ad usus mortalium ; quibus fontibus præsul est Minervæ numen, in cujus æde perpetui ignes nunquam canescunt in favillas sed ubi ignis tabuit, vertit in globos saxeos.*" The identity of the second syllable of *præsul* with the Celtic name of the goddess suggests that Solinus may have referred to it when he used the word, but the suspicion is groundless, as he says in another place, of Angrivarii—*præsul idemtidem.* Mr. Whitaker seems to have attached great importance to this passage in Solinus, and has built up some theories on it. In his estimate of its value I cannot concur ; the facts and the Latinity of Solinus seem to me equally worthless. I am not disposed, however, to question the existence of a temple of Minerva in Bath, as it is otherwise probable.

From these fragments Governor Pownall invented the following restoration :—

[AVLVS·C]LAVDIVS·LIGVR[IVS·SODALIS·ASCITVS
FABRORVM·C]OLEGIO·LONGA·SERIA·[DEFOSSA
HANC·AEDEM·]E·NIMIA·VETVST[ATE·LABENTEM
DE·INVENTA·ILLIC·PEC]VNIA·RFFICI·ET·REPIN-
GI·CVR[AVIT·]

The supplied words and letters I have placed between brackets [ ].

The idea of *Claudius Ligurius* being a member of the college or company of smiths, was evidently suggested, as Mr. Scarth observes, by the inscription to *Julius Vitalis*, in which it is stated that he (*Vitalis*) was *ex *colegio fabrice elatus*. The objections to the use of the words—†*sodalis ascitus fabrorum colegio*—in the connection in which they appear, are, if the word be intended to mean on the occasion of his election or appointment, the money for the repairing and repainting, should, according to usage, have been provided from his own funds ; and if the words be intended merely as an honorary designation, there is no authority, so far as I am aware, for their use in this sense under such circumstances.

---

* It has been inferred from these words, that there was a *fabrica*, i. e., a public factory of arms, in or near Bath, although the *Notitia*, whilst noticing similar establishments in different parts of the empire, does not mention it. This possibly may have been the fact, but it cannot be inferred from this inscription. As *Vitalis* was one of the *fabri* or *fabricenses* attached to the 20th legion, the *collegium*, who manifested their regard for him by a funeral of their expense, was most probably the association of smiths or armourers in that legion. Thus in Orelli, n. 4972, we find mention of the *collegia fraumentariorum* in the 5th and 13th legions. *Notas* (Orelli, nn. 4715, 4716) denotes that the corpse was borne to the place of interment on the shoulders—thus Horace, Sat. ii. 8 :—

Ex testamento sic est elata : cadaver
Unctum oleo largo nudis humeris tulit heres.

Tacitus Ann. i, 8. *Conclamans prius corpus ad rogum humeris suorum ferendum.*

We may also infer that this was a walking funeral, the procession being formed of the members of *collegium* who followed the body on foot. FABRICE may stand either for FABRICE[NSIVM]: or for FABRIC[A]E. Orelli, n. 6079, adopts the latter, referring it, however, to the *fabrica* of the legion.

† Governor Pownall seems to have attached undue importance to membership in a *collegium fabrum*. There were hundreds of such *collegia* or organisations of tradesmen, mechanics, and labourers of every class throughout the Roman Empire. The *collegia fabrum* alone may be counted by dozens ; and we are not without examples of *collegia dendrophororum*, *nautarum et auriearum*, *sauricorum et confectorariorum*, whose members respectively occupied positions in society about the same as English porters, waggoners, and pork-butchers.

The words *seria* and *pecunia* suggested the invention of the story about the money having been found in a vessel. The objections to this application of *longa seria defossa* are—the word *longa* seems inappropriate when applied to *seria*, even though its shape is said to have been *oblonga*; and *defossa* does not signify *dug up*, which seems to have been the meaning intended, but *buried*, so that the translation of the words, as they stand, would be, *a long earthen vessel having been buried*, not *having been dug up*, and moreover, that *Aulus Claudius Ligurius* had himself buried it. If *seria* be the correct reading the most probable *prima facie* reference would be to the *seria* which was kept in temples. Thus :—

Lamprid. *Heliogab. c.* 6. "Penetrale sacrum [Vestæ] est auferre conatus : cumque *seriam*, quasi verum, rapuisset, atque in ea nihil reperisset, applosam fregit."

But it seems not unlikely that either the true reading of the word on the stone is *serie*, or that the final *a* is a mistake in orthography for *e*. We have thus *longa serie*, and if we supply *annorum*, this phrase and *nimia vetustate* will agree well with *refici et repingi*. Thus in Orelli, n. 3300, we have PERMVLTO TEMPORE VETVSTATE CONLAPSVS; and in Renier, *Inscriptions d' l'Algérie*, n. 109, MVLTORVM INCVRIA DILAPSVM ET PER LONGAM ANNORVM SERIEM NEGLECTVM. As to the age of the inscription, a surmise may perhaps be formed with some reason from the use of the word *repingi*, a verb, which I do not recollect having seen in any Latin writer earlier than the 6th century, A.D. On the restoration as a whole, it is unnecessary to say more than that I am persuaded that no one familiar with Latin Epigraphy would mistake it for a genuine inscription : indeed it is not as plausible as many of the Ligorian forgeries.

§ 91. That there was a goddess worshipped at Bath under the name *Sul* there can be no doubt. She is named in inscriptions on four altars, and on a tombstone found in that city. Of the inscriptions on these altars, two of them prove that she was identified with Minerva. The similarity of the name suggests that she may have been the same as *Suliria Idennica Minerva*, in n. 2051, of Orelli's Inscriptions; and also leads to the belief, that there was some connection between her, and the *Sulera*, *Sulevia*, *Silvia*, or *Silvanæ*, mentioned in Orelli's nn. 2099, 2101, 2103. The terms *Suleris et Campestribus* in 2101, and *Silvanob. et Quadribis*, (i. e., *Silvanabus et Quadriviis*) in 2103, favour the opinion, that the *Suleræ* should be classed amongst the *Matres*, traces of whose worship have been commonly found, especially in Germany, Belgium, and Britain. Mr. Scarth, *Journal of the Archæological Association*, 1861, p. 16, regards them as "probably attendant nymphs" of *Sul*; and to Mr. Roach Smith, *Roman London*, p. 38, "they appear to have been Sylphs, the tutelary divinities of rivers, fountains, hills, roads, villages, and other localities, against whom were especially directed, in the fifth and subsequent centuries, the anathemas of Christian councils, missionaries, and princes."

Dr. Thurnam, in the very able dissertation on the "Historical Ethnology of Britain," in *Crania Britannica*, Dec. iv. p. 130, observes :—

"Under that of *Sul*, a Welsh name of the sun, he (Apollo) was worshipped in Brittany, where, under Christianity, he was represented by a pretended St. Sul. There are traces of this name in that of various hills— Solsbury, Sallsbury, Silbory—at Bath, Ribchester, Edinborgh, and Abury, which are so many high places of the Sun-god, or Celtic Apollo." * *
* * *

"The Celts had not only a great male divinity representing the Sun, but likewise a female one symbolising the passive powers of nature, and by whom the Moon (as by the Syrian Astarte or Venus-Urania) was originally intended."

* * * * * * * *

"The goddess worshipped conjointly with Apollo at Aquæ Solis [or, as others prefer, Aquæ Sulis] was clearly the Celtic Minerva, as appears from the epithet SVL., by which she was there known, and which, like that of Baaleemen [Lord of Heaven], had both a feminine and masculine application. The Solimara, [Orelli, n. 2050], worshipped by the Bituriges may have been the same as the British Sul."

§ 91. The following is a copy of the inscription on the Bath altar, in which the *Suleræ* are named :

SVLEVIS
SVLINVS
SCVLTOR
BRV[C]ETI·F
SACRVM·F·L·M

Mr. Scarth remarks :—"In the name of the dedicator we have an instance of the name of an individual derived from the presiding deity of the waters [i. e., Sul.] ; this is also to be remarked on another altar—*Sulinus Maturi fil.*" This account of the etymology of the name seems probable, especially when we call to mind the Greek and Roman usage of forming names of persons from the names of their deities, such as *Hermogenes, Jovinus, &c.*

The *prima facie* interpretation of the three middle lines. *scil.*, " Sulinus Scultor, the son of Brucetus," is liable to the objections, that the *Sulinus* of the other altar has but one name ; and that "the last three lines of this inscription are in letters much smaller, and not so deeply cut as the first two lines," whence " Mr. Hunter thinks that the first two lines are the original inscription and that the others were added afterwards." This peculiarity suggests the the conjecture that the first inscription was left imperfect, and that a different person, 'Scultor, the son of Brucetus' took the vacant space for his inscription consisting of the last three lines. But the Greek and Roman stone cutters seem to have been so capricious as to the size of the letters and the depth of the cutting in the same inscription, that we are scarcely warranted in inferring in this case two inscriptions. I am inclined to think that *Scultor* is not a name of a person, but the designation of an occupation, *scil.*, *sculptor*, the carver or stone-cutter, i. e., " Sulinus the carver."

This conjecture is supported by the use of the rare formula F·L·M·, which I read *fecit libens merito.* If the representation of the altar, as given by Mr. Warner in pl. 2, fig. 6, be accurate, there is reason to suspect the reading BRV[C]ETI·F., as in that representation it seems to be more probably BRVCI·FIL·, or rather BRVSCI·FIL., as in one of the Lincoln inscriptions, noticed in Art. 32 of these notes.

§ 93. The opinion, which I have expressed in the last article, relative to *Sulinus* and *Scultor* is favoured by an examination of the inscription on another altar, scil :

```
        DEAE
       SVLIMI
       NERVAE
       SVLINVS
        MATV
        RIFIL
        VSLM.
```

i. e., Deæ Suli Minervæ, Sulinus, Maturi filius, votum solvit libens merito.

It may, I think, be reasonably inferred, from the apparent etymology of the name *Sulinus*, and from the circumstance, that the individual had but one name, that the dedicator was a barbarian, i. e., a native Briton, or Gaul. This inference derives support from the order of the words SVLI MINERVAE. If the dedicator had been a Roman, or a Romanized provincial, he would probably have conformed to the usage of placing the designation of the Roman deity first, and that of the identified barbarian deity second. There are many examples of this usage. Amongst the most obvious are *Marti Camulo, Apollini Toutiorigi, Dianæ Abnobæ.*

§ 94. The tomb-stone, to which reference was made in art. 91, bears the following inscription :—

```
         D. M.
       C.CALPVRNVS
     [R]ECEPTVS SACER
        DOS DEAE SV
       LIS VIX AN LXXV
      CA[LP]VRNIA TRIFO
     SA[TIIR]EPTE CONIVNX
          F. C.
```

Mr. Scarth's remarks on it are :—

" This is expanded thus by Mr. Lysons :—'Diis Manibus Caius Calpurnius Receptus Sacerdos Deæ Solis, vixit annos septuaginta quinque, Calpurnia

Trifosa Threpte conjunx faciendum curavit.' Mr. Hunter, in the Bath
Institution Catalogue, observes that *Receptus* may be an appellation of
Calpurnius, or it may signify that he was an 'admitted' priest of the
goddess Sul."

Of the two interpretations mentioned by Mr. Hunter, I prefer the former, *scil.*, *Receptus* as a *cognomen*. The omission of
the *cognomen* belongs to an age much anterior to the date of the
grave-stone; and besides if the latter had been intended, the
order would probably have been *Sacerdos receptus.*

The strangeness of the names of his wife might, perhaps, lead
some to question the correctness of the reading, but on examination they will, I think, be found to be free from objection.
According to my view of them, they afford evidence that the
priest married a Greek slave, that was born and brought up in
his own house. TRIFOSA and THREPTE suggests that she
was Greek, and CALPVRNIA and THREPTE that she had
been his slave. TRIFOSA, TRYFOSA, TRIPHOSA and
TRYPHOSA are all Latinized forms of a Greek female name,
taken, as *Sympherusa*, *Prepusa*, *Terpusa* and many others, from
the nominative singular feminine of the present participle active,
i. e., ΤΡΥΦΩΣΑ or τρυφῶσα, from the verb τρυφάω, the
same name that is found in St. Paul's *Epist. ad Rom.* xvi. 12.
THREPTE, or TREPTE as it is otherwise written, is used as
a *cognomen*, but as the female mentioned here already has one,
scil., *Tryphosa*—I regard the word as standing for θρεπτή, the
Greek term corresponding to the Latin *verna.*

It is scarcely necessary to add, that, according to usage, she
took her first name *Calpurnia* from the *nomen gentilitium* of
her master.

It is worthy of observation, that two of the altars, dedicated
Deæ Suli, were erected, probably, by Greek slaves who had been
manumitted, viz., *Aufidius Lemnus,** (*Lemnius?*) and *Aufidius
Eutuches* (*Eutyches?*). These *liberti* took their names *Aufidius*
from their master, *Marcus Aufidius Maximus*, who is mentioned

* In Mommsen's *Inscript. Neapol.* n. 4333, we have LEMNIVS LIBERTVS.

in each of the inscriptions, retaining, according to usage, as cognomina, their servile appellations—*Lemnus* (or *Lemnius?*), probably from his birth-place *Lemnos* in the Ægean, and *Euty-ches*, from ἐυτυχής lucky. It is well known that some slaves were called after their birth-place, e. gr., *Syrus, Geta, Cappadox, &c.*; and others, from reputed or real characteristics. Mr. Warner's supposition (as noticed by Mr. Scarth) that "the name EVTVCHES is EIVS ADOPTATVS HERES" is unintelligible. If his meaning be that the name implies that he was "the adopted heir of his master," there is not the slightest foundation for the supposition, either in the name or in the inscription. Mr. Warner with equally little reason supposes the altar to have been erected by the same freedman. Mr. Hunter and Mr. Scarth infer from the name CALPVRNIVS the rank of this priest as "a member of the noble Calpurnian family." To me there seems to be no ground for this inference; indeed, so far as we know, we may have derived this name, as a *libertus*, from the *nomen gentilitium* of his master. As to his connection with *Quintus Calpurnius Concessinius*, "legate in Britain under Caracalla," it is sufficient to observe, that there was no person of that name who is known to have held the office of legate. Mr. Wright, *Celt, Roman, and Saxon*, p. 358, mentions an individual with the first two of these names as a governor of Britain, "believed to be of the age of Commodus," but this statement is erroneous. The only *Quintus Calpurnius Concessinius*, known in inscriptions found in Britain, was a *præfectus equitum*. See Horsley, *Brit. Rom., Northumberland*, cviii., and art. 67 of my notes.

§ 95. In December, 1854, two coffins, evidently of the Roman period, were found at Combe Down, near Bath. One of these was partly covered by a stone bearing the following inscriptions :

PRO·SALVTE IMP·CES·M·AVR
ANTONINI PII FELICIS INVIC
TI AVG..NAEVIVS AVG
LIB ADIVT PROCC PR..I
PIA RVINA OPRESS·A SOLO RES
TITVIT.

n 2

Mr. Hunter, *Archæological Journal*, March, 1853, supplies M after I in the 4th line, and gives the following explanation :

"For the safety,—or whatever *salus* in this connection, where we for ever find it, may mean,—of the emperor Cæsar Marcus Aurelius Antoninus Pius, happy, invincible, (or unconquered) Augustus, (supply a prenomen where the stone is damaged, probably one represented by two letters, as CN). Nævius, a freedman of Augustus, the adjutor of the procurators, (then comes the doubtful word, which perhaps may be PROVINCIE), restored from its foundations, (this building, temple, or whatever it was, for the edifice was there to speak for itself), when it had been thrown down by an impious act of ruination.

Another reading of the doubtful word may be PRIMARIVS, and I think some one suggested PRETORIVM. I fear the word is too far gone for any one to venture to pronounce conclusively what the reading of it is.

A question arising upon this inscription is, which of the emperors, calling themselves Antoninus, it commemorates. It is a question of about fifty years, A. D. 180-230. On a first view one would refer it to Marcus Aurelius, the immediate successor of Antoninus Pius, the first of the Antonines, and I see not why it should not belong to his reign, unless it can be shown (a point I have not examined) that his name is never found in inscriptions with the additions Felix and Invictus. If it shall appear that his name does not occur with these additions, then undoubtedly it may be assigned to the three years' reign of Heliogabalus, or to any intermediate emperor who called himself Antoninus, and who is known to have used those additions. But at present I see no improbability in assigning it to the emperor so well known by his name of Marcus Aurelius."

Mr. Hunter here offers a conjecture that *impia* may refer to "some religious or political ferment," and cites in illustration the words *locum religiosum per insolentiam crutum*, found in another of the Bath inscriptions.

"Nævius the Adjutor, a Roman officer, to whose duties sufficient attention seems hardly to have been paid by the writers on Roman antiquities, may seem to have been the proper officer to superintend this re-edification.

His name, I believe, is not found in any other inscription discovered in England. But in Gruter, civ., No. 9, we have—P. Nævius, Adjutor, in an inscription found at Tarracona. We find also, in Gruter, ccclxxi., No. 8, Adjutore Proco. Civitatis Senonum Tricassinorum Meldorum, &c., which shows that the Adjutor to the Procurators is not an officer unknown to inscriptions."

In the same number of the *Journal*, we have also Dr. Bruce's observations :—

"As far as my present knowledge goes, I am disposed to expand the inscrip. tion thus:—

Pro salute Imperatoris Cæsaris Marci Aurelli Antonini Pil Felicis Invicti Augusti .... Nævius Augusti libertus adjutor Procuratorum principia ruina oppressa a solo restituit.

It may be translated in something like this form:—For the safety of the emperor Cæsar Marcus Aurelius Antoninus, the pious, fortunate and invincible Augustus .... Nævius, the freedman of Augustus and the assistant of the Procurators restored these chief military quarters, which had fallen to ruin.

The first question that arises here is respecting the emperor, specially addressed. I find that the names and epithets used in this inscription are in others applied both to Caracalla and Heliogabalus, with the exception of the word *invictus*; and in no other instance that I can find is this applied to either of these emperors. I incline to Mr. Franks' opinion, that Heliogabalus is the person here intended, for the following reasons:—1. On the murder of Heliogabalus his name seems to have been erased from inscriptions, or the slabs themselves thrown down. This stone having been used to cover a tomb must have previously been removed from its original position. 2. From the indistinctness of some of the letters, I take it for granted that the inscription is not deeply carved; this, together with the omission of the A in Cæsaris, and the occurrence of tied letters, seems to indicate the *later rather than earlier period. 3. Had Caracalla been the person intended, one of his well known epithets, such as *Parthicus, Britannicus* or *Germanicus*, would probably have occupied the place of *invictus*; so far as I have noticed, Heliogabalus had earned no such distinctions; his flatterers, therefore, on his assuming the purple, would have no resource but to bestow upon him the indefinite title of *invictus*.

The next thing which occurs in it is the name of the dedicator. Mr. Hunter remarked that the name NAEVIVS occurred in Gruter. It is not without interest to observe, that one of the examples furnished by that author (P. civ., No. 9,) contains that name with the epithet *adjutor* appended.

TVTELE
V. S.
Γ. NAEVIVS
ADIVTOR.

The Nævius of the slab found at Bath was a freedman of Augustus, and an assistant or secretary of the procurators of the province. We are not without an authority for the reading *Adjutor Procuratorum*. In Gruter (P., ccclxxvi, No. 8), the following occurs:—

---

* See my note, p. 102.

```
        ....MEMORIÆ AVRELI
        DEMETRI ADIVTORI
        PROCC ....... ...........
```

The word which I conceive to be *principia* presents the greatest difficulty. It appears that the stone is damaged in this part. We are necessarily driven to conjecture in order to supply the vacuity between the N and
the I at the end of the fourth line. The inscription speaks of the restoration of something which had become ruinous. If I correctly read the other
parts of the inscription which seem to be quite plain, this is the only word
left to reveal to us the precise object of the dedicator's exertions. In the
station at Lanchester, a slab has been found (Horsley. Durham. No. xii.),
containing on its third and fourth lines the following words:—

```
        PRINCIPIA ET ARMAMEN
        TARIA CONLAPSA RESTITVIT.
```

Here we have evidence that there was a class of buildings called *principia*, which, like other buildings, would fall into ruin and require restoration.
This word seems best to suit the damaged part of the inscription before us.
The only letters that we require to draw upon the imagination for are the
first I in the word, which has probably been attached to the top of the left
limb of the N, and the C, for which there is sufficient room on that injured
part of the stone between the N and the I. Perhaps the word *principia*
might be translated officers' barracks. The remainder of the inscription
require no remarks."

In the number for June, 1855, Mr. Franks states the grounds
of his conviction that the tablet should be assigned to the reign
of Elagabalus :—

"The inscription can only apply to Caracalla or Elagabalus, but it does
not appear that the epithet *Iuricius* was given to the former. There are,
however, coins of Elagabalus on which he is thus styled. The inscription
may have suffered mutilation in a slight degree, and the popular indigna-
tion, which defaced or destroyed the memorials of the Emperor, may
possibly account for the occurrence of this tablet used as a part of the
cover of a sepulchral cist."

The Rev. H. M. Scarth, by whom the stone was purchased
and presented to the Bath Institution, communicated a very
interesting paper on the subject to the Somersetshire Archæological and Natural History Society, in which he gives full particulars of the discovery of the coffins, and expresses his assent to Dr.
Bruce's interpretation of the inscription.

The only difficulties in the text of the inscription relate to the prænomen of *Navius*, and the word or words between PROCC and RVINA. As to the first it is of but little moment and can never be determined with certainty or probability. It may have been *Publius*, as in Gruter, civ. 9, but it must be borne in mind that in that inscription ADIVTOR is more probably a cognomen and not the designation of an office.

With reference to the word or words between PROCC and RVINA, Dr. Bruce's citation of the inscription given by Horsley, (Durham, n. xii.) seems to remove all doubts on the point. I do not, however, feel quite satisfied with the interpretation of the word *principia*, as "chief military quarters" or "officers' barracks;" or of *ruina oppresso*, as "which had fallen into ruin."

The latter expression, which is so rare that I have been unable to find any other example in inscriptions, seems to me to indicate that the *principia*, whatever they were, were destroyed by the falling of something else,—either the building of which they formed a part, or some adjacent edifice. It is certainly in this sense that the words are used by Cicero, *de Oratore*, ii., 86, "*ea ruina ipsum oppressum cum suis periisse.*

The ordinary form of expression, which is found in inscriptions, relating to the falling of buildings, is *vetustate collapsum.* In Steiner, *Cod. Inscrip. Rom. Rhen.* n. 852, we find the following variety, approaching that in the text :—

DIS·CONSER
VATORIBVS·Q·TAR
QVITIVS·CATVL
VS·LEG·AVG·
CVIVS·CVRA·PRAETOR
IVM·IN·RVINAM
CONLAPSVM·AD·NO
VAM·FACIEM·
RESTITVTVM·

But the principal and most interesting question relates to the emperor, whose names and titles are given.

* See p. 69.

† In Henzen's n. 1397 we have *RVINA PARIETIS OPPRESSVS* applied to a person.

As there were three emperors, each of whom was commonly
known as *Marcus Aurelius Antoninus Pius*, our only hope of
determining to which of them we should refer the inscription, is
in the other epithets *Felix* and *Invictus*. Now there is satisfactory evidence that Commodus was the first Roman Emperor to
whom the epithet *felix* was given, and consequently the question is
limited to Caracalla and Elagabalus.* That the epithet *invictus*
was applied to the first of these cannot be questioned, as the following examples leave no doubt on the subject.

IIII·
IMP·CAESAR
M·AVRELIVS ANTONINVS
INVICTVS·PIVS·FELIX·AVG·
PART·MAX·BRIT·MAX·GERM
MAX·PONT·MAX·TRIB·POTES[T]
XVIIII·IMP·III·COS·IIII·PROCOS
VIAM·ANTE·HAC·LAPIDE[I]AM
INVTILITER·STRATAM·ET
CORRVPTAM·SILICE·NOVO
QVO·FIRMIOR·COMMEANTIBVS
ESSET·PER·MILIA·[PAS]
SVM·XXI·SVA·PECVNIA FECIT
LXXL
(Mommsen, *Inscrip. Neapol.*, p. 354.)

IMP·CAES·M·AVRELIO
ANTONINO·PIO·FELICI
INVICTO·AVG·PARTH
MAX·BRITANN·MAX
PONT·MAX·TRIB·POT·XVI
IMP·II·COS·IV·P·P·PROCOS
DOMINO
INDVLGENTISSIMO
NEGOTIANTES
VASCVLARI
CONSERVATORI·SVO
NVMINI·EIVS
DEVOTI
(Henzen, *Inscrip. Lat.*, n. 7262.)

---

* There are one or two inscriptions, in which Commodus is styled *M. Aurelius Antoninus
Pius Aug. Felix.* and *Invictus*, but, however, the question in the present case seems to be
properly limited to Caracalla and Elagabalus.

From Eckhel, VII., 179, we learn that the epithet was also given to him on coins.

The use of this term in the case of Elagabalus, although probable in consequence of his assumption of other titles of Caracalla,* cannot, so far as I am aware, be established by any inscription clearly belonging to him. But Mr. Franks, *Archæological Journal*, June, states, that "there are coins of Elagabalus in which he is thus styled." I am not aware of any such, excepting those noticed by Eckhel, VII., p. 249, and Rasche II., ii., p. 792, as bearing the legend INVICTVS SACERDOS AVG, where *invictus* seems to be applied to him as priest of Sol, of whom that term is a *perpetuum epitheton*.

If we assign the inscription to Caracalla, a question still remains* as to the date of it. As there is no mention of either Severus or Geta, it is most probable that it was after the death of both. Now Severus died at York in February, A. D. 211 ; and Caracalla and Geta left England in the same year, for Rome, where Geta was murdered in February, A.D. 212. The limits therefore February, 212, and April, 217, when Caracalla himself was murdered. The statement, by Eckhel, that *Felix* did not appear on the coins of Caracalla until A. D. 213, suggested to me that year as one of the *cancelli*, but there is unquestionable evidence that *Felix* was amongst his epithets on stones before that date, not only in conjunction with his father, (of which there are well known examples,) but also separately after his accession.

§ 96. The following inscriptions are on pigs of lead found in different parts of this county :

BRITANNIC * * AVG II

—

TI·CLAVDIVS·CAESAR·AVG·P·M·TRIB·P·VIIII·
IMP·XVI·DE·BRITAN·

IMP·HADRIANI·AVG

———

IMP·DVOR AVG ANTONINI
ET VERI ARMENIACORVM

For remarks on these and other similar relics, see § 16.

---

§ 97. At Hints, in this county, a block of lead was found bearing the inscription

$$\text{IMP·VESP·}\overline{\text{VII}}\text{·T·IMP·V·COS}$$

On this see § 16.

c 2

SUSSEX.

---

§ 98. At Pulborough, in this county, four blocks of lead were found bearing the inscription

TI·CL·TR·LVT·BR·EX·ARG

On this see §16.

---

§ 99. About 200 years ago, a cup made of brass, or bronze, with an inscription round the outer rim, was found in a well at Rudge in Wiltshire. It is figured in Horsley's *Britannia Romana*, and the inscription may be thus represented on a plane surface :

He reads it :—ABALLAVA UXELODUM CAMBOGLANS BANNA A MAIS ; and adopts the explanation offered by Mr. Gale, who supposed " it may have been a *patera*, used in libations by the people of those towns that are mentioned on it." In confirmation of this supposition, it is remarked :

" Sacrifices were generally offered by the ancients, when they met together upon any solemn occasion: sometimes only when they were assembled for mirth and feasting, as is evident from many passages, which mention this custom among them. Why then might there not be an alliance or society form ed among these five neighbouring places, and perhaps a feast annually or more frequently observed by them when they jointly made their libations out of one common *patera*, inscribed with all their names, as a token of their friendship and unanimity ?

> Post Iidem inter se, posito certamine, reges
> Armati, Jovis ante aras, paterasque tenentes
> Stabant, et caesa jungebant foedera porca.

Here indeed each king appears to have had his own *patera*, whereas in the other case it is supposed that one and the same *patera* was common to several places. The gentleman [Mr. Gale], however, would therefore have the inscription read, *A Mais, Aballava, Uxelodum, Amboglanis, Banna;* supposing all the names to be in the *oblative,* governed by the preposition *a,* and that the C before *Amboglanis* has been designed for an O, and is to be joined to *Uxilodum* which therefore makes it *Uxelodune.*"

To this Horsley adds—

" These five places were near to each other, and all of them upon that part of the wall, where probably the inroads were most frequently made; and consequently where the greater danger might make it more necessary for the several garrisons to enter into a stricter confederacy for their mutual strength and relief."

He also notices a conjecture, which he had at one time entertained : —

" This object might have been some way fixed to the top of an *hasta* or military ensign. Somewhat like this does sometimes appear (if I am not mistaken) on the *Roman reulla.* If this could be admitted, we need only suppose, that the cohort to which this ensign belonged had been in garrison and perhaps behaved themselves well at the several places, whose names are inscribed round this ornament; such a matter of fact would be sufficient ground for this inscription."

In answer to the question, " what brought it from Cumberland to Wiltshire" ? he remarks :—

" So small a vessel might easily be transported from one part of the kingdom to another, even the most distant, and that on a thousand occasions which it is needless to mention. The learned Baron Clerk supposes that this *patera* may have been thrown into the well, where it was found, after some solemn libation. In those days wells were esteemed sacred, and sacrificing to them was common."

As to the age of the object, he makes the following observations :—

" It is a little surprising that the name *Banna* on this cup should be exactly the same with what is in the anonymous *Ravennas;* though that name occurs no where else, and the place intended by it be most probably the same that is called *Petriana* in the *Notitia,* as I have shewn in another place. This, and the omission of *Congavata* (or *Stanwicks*) upon the cup, though that when built stood between *Aballaba* and *Axelodunum,* and is mentioned

In the *Notitia*, among the stations *per lineam valli*, looks as if the cup was more ancient than the *Notitia*, and prior to the building of the station at *Stanwicks*, near Carlisle. This, I think, is also more agreeable to the historical account of the Roman affairs in Britain; for I see no evidence of their having any garrisons or settlements in the west of England, so late as the *Notitia*, and it is more probable that this vase, of whatsoever kind it be, has been left at the place, where it was discovered, by the *Romans* themselves, rather than any other."

Dr. Bruce, *Roman Wall*, 2nd ed., p. 252, remarks :—

"The inscription manifestly contains a reference to five places in the neighbourhood [of the station of *Amboglanna*]. It has been read, A MAIS, ABALLAVA, VXELODVMO, AMBOGLANIS, DANNA. Except MAIS be the MAGNA of the *Notitia*, AMBOGLANNA is the only place named whose position can be said to have been ascertained with any tolerable degree of accuracy. As, however, ABALLABA and AXELODVNVM follow shortly after AMBOGLANNA in the *Notitia* list, though not continuously, all of these were no doubt camps situated on the western limit of the wall. DANNA is not mentioned in the *Notitia*; Hodgson hazards the conjecture that it was Newcastle."

Mr. MacLaughlan, *Memoir written during a Survey of the Roman Wall*, p. 74, expresses the opinion that *Stanwix* represents the *Axelodunum* of the *Notitia* :—

"The situation seems to agree, together with the nature of the ground, that it should have been so called [from *axel* or * achel*, *high*, *lofty*, and *dunum*, a *fortress*]; and equally so with the Rudge cup: for supposing the cup to have been consecrated to a party of hunters, no country could, in those days, have afforded more wild animals than the district between Stanwix and Burdoswald [*Axelodunum* and *Amboglanna*]."

To these observations he subjoins the note :—

"The words on the Rudge cup, in the Duke of Northumberland's possession, are: A. Mais Aballava Uxolodun Cambogians Danna. It will be observed that there is a stop placed on each side the letter *A*. which precedes the word *Mais*; hence we should be disposed to take *Mais*, Watchcross, first; *Aballava* Brampton, second; *Uxelodum*, Stanwix, third; *Cambogians*, *Petriana*, Walton House, fourth; and *Danna*, Burdoswald, fifth. The A. preceding *Mais* is doubtless the preposition as at the commencement of each iter of Antonine. The difficulty in identifying Danna has been stated. See page 54, note *ante*. It occurs in the Ravenna list, and on the altar to Silvanus, found at Burdoswald. Bruce, R. W., p. 805."

In the note, p. 54, Mr. M. remarks :—

"Amboglanna has been supposed by some to be the Banna of the Rudge cup; and there seems no reason why it should not be known by two equally descriptive denominations." * * * * * * Banna is mentioned as a station by Ravennas, in the description of Britain, written, as is supposed, about A.D. 650. The order in which the name there occurs would lead to the idea that it may be the same as Amboglanna or Petriana; whilst the former, being found on the Rudge cup, preceding Banna, seems to identify Banna with Petriana."

The first difficulty which presents itself, in treating this inscription, is as to the beginning. In my judgment, the commencement should be with Banna, as the words seem to have been intended for an Hexameter, scil.

Banna Camboglans Uxelodum Aballava Mais a.

As it seems doubtful whether it was intended that A should be taken into account, it may be that Mais should be read .Ma-is for *Mais*, the proper dative and ablative of *Maia, orum*. The doubt regarding A is suggested by the full point on either side of it, which may denote either that it is not to be connected with *Banna* or *Mais*, or that it may be joined with either.

There is no difficulty as to the metre, if A be regarded as the preposition governing *Banna*, or both *Banna* and *Mais*; nor even, without this, if we take *Banna* as the nominative, is the lengthening of the last syllable a sufficient reason for rejecting the intended Hexameter. Some of the verses found in epigraphy are very poor specimens of accuracy in syntax or prosody—*e. gr.*, Bruce, *Roman Wall*, p. 396.

> *Somnio præmonitus miles hanc ponere jussit*
> *Aram quæ Fabio nupta est nymphis venerandis.*

But with what object have the names of these places been inscribed on the cup ? The first thought, and that chiefly suggested by A regarded as a preposition, would be that the inscription recorded the route between two places, as in an Itinerary. This suspicion may be supported by the discovery noticed by Dr. Bruce, "of *three silver cups, bearing outside an inscription, containing the itinerary of the road from Rome to Cadiz." If this view be taken, and A be regarded as governing only *Mais*, the meaning will be that a person starting from *Maia* for *Banna* must pass through *Aballava*, *Uxelodum*, and *Camboglans*. If A be regarded as governing both *Banna* and *Mais*, the meaning will be—a person starting from *Banna* for *Aballava* must pass though *Camboglans* and *Uxelodum*, and a person starting from *Maia* for *Camboglans* must pass through *Aballava* and *Uxelodum*; or a person starting from *Banna* for *Uxelodum* must pass through *Camboglans*, and a person starting from *Mais* for *Uxelodum* must pass through *Aballava*. But what possible difficulty can there have been, such as to render it necessary or expedient to have any one of these routes recorded on a cup? Besides, a serious difficulty presents itself as to the order of these places, when compared with the statement in the *Notitia*. The latter authority—on the supposition that the stations *per lineam valli* are given in due order from east to west—would lead us to place *Aballava* between *Camboglans* (whether it stand for *Amboglanna* or *Petriana*) and *Axelodunum*, whilst on the cup *Uxelodum*, the presumed representative of *Axelodunum*, comes between *Camboglans* and *Aballava*. In support, however, of the arrangement on the cup it has been stated that the order on it is similar to that given in the chorography of the *Anonymus Ravennas*, viz., *Banna*, *Uxeludiano*, *Avalaria*, *Maia*. Here, although *Camboglans* is omitted, *Axelodunum* and *Aballava* may be regarded as represented respectively by *Uxeludianum* and *Avalaria*.

In my judgment, it is labour thrown away to endeavour to reconcile the order of the places on the cup with their geographical positions, as I believe that they are arranged as they stand, simply because this arrangement of them gives an hexameter, i. e.,

Banna | *Cambo* | *glans Ux* | *elodum A* | *ballava* | *Mais a.*

* See Marchi, La stipe tributata alle divinità delle Acque Apollinari, 1852; and Henzen, n. 5110, where the inscriptions are given. An examination of these inscriptions does not at all favour the suspicion.

The meaning of the two points, one before and the other after
A, may be to indicate that the hexameter may be formed with or
without it, and may begin with either *Mais* or *Banna*.

Of the various Hexameters, which thus result, I prefer either

    Banna Camboglans Uxelodum Aballava Mais a

or

    Banna Camboglans Uxelodum Aballava Ma-is ;

and regard A not as a preposition, but as °standing for *ami-
citiæ*, scil., *causâ*, or *amicitiam*, as we have commonly *salutem*,
with *Mais* in the dative.   In this I am influenced by the
conjecture that the cup was a token of the friendship sub-
sisting between the four towns and *Maia*, either presented by
them to the latter or made in commemoration of this amity
on some special occasion.   I prefer this conjecture, which
resembles that adopted by Horsley, to the suggestion that it
may have been a cup made for a party of hunters.   Horsley's idea
that it was "fixed on the top of an *hasta* or military ensign,"
seems to me highly improbable ; nor can I accept his view as to
its antiquity.   The shape of the letters and the style of the ornamental pattern seem to indicate a later date than any assigned to
the *Notitia*.

YORKSHIRE.

§ 100. In Horsley's *Britannia Romana*, n. 15, we have the following inscription :—

DMS
CADIEDI
·IAE FO·
TVNA·
PIA·V·AX·

He expands it thus : *Dis Manibus sacrum Cadiediniæ Fortuna Pia vixit annos decem.* Mr. Ward had previously read it: "*Cadillae Jeriae Piae Fortunata Pia,* all which names are in Gruter." It is obvious that Mr. Ward's reading should be at once rejected. According to the process which he adopted, almost any thing could be made out of any thing with the help of the Index to Gruter. I am not satisfied, however, with Horsley's expansion. The chief objection, which I have to it, arises from the singularity of the names *Cadiedinia,* and *Fortuna Pia.* There can, I think, be no doubt that *pia* is not a name, but an adjective expressing the character of the deceased female. There are many examples of this use of *pius* and *pia, e. gr.,* Renier's *Inscriptions de l' Algérie,* n. 2811 :—

D M S
SITTIA
MENOPHI
LA·PIA·VIX
ANXXV
Π S E

i. e., *Dis Manibus sacrum. Sittia Menophila. Pia vixit annis viginti quinque. Hic sita est.*

If this view be adopted, it follows that there are not two persons named in the inscription under consideration, but only

D 2

one, whose second name is FORTVNA or FORTVNATA. The question then is as to her first name. Adopting Horsley's conjecture, I would supply N. as the first letter of the third line, but would limit the name to the letters EDINIAE, which I regard as used for the more usual form AEDINIAE by the ordinary substitution of E for AE. The name AEDINIA frequently occurs, e. gr., in Renier's *Inscriptions de l'Algérie*, *Ædinia Julia* in n. 1924, *Ædinia Lurilla* in n. 2598, *Ædinia Rogata* in n. 3015, and *Edinia* in n. 2802. In n. 195, we have *Ædia Fortunata*. From what has been advanced, it may, I think, be reasonably inferred that the correct reading of the inscription, omitting CADI, is *Dis Manibus sacrum Ediniæ Fortunæ [or Fortunatæ]. Pia vixit annis X°*. But we have yet to examine CADI. I am inclined to suggest that it is a designation of the receptacle for the remains of the deceased. I am unable to cite an example from any other inscription, but Virgil, *Æn.* VI., v. 228, supplies the following authority :—

"Ossaque lecta cado texit Corynæus aheno."

It is well known that *cupa* and *cupula*, both signifying barrels, are used as designations of receptacles of the dead, and to these I think *culus* should be added, as denoting, perhaps, an earthen vessel of the form of a cask, used for the same purpose. Gutherius, *de jure Minium, Græc. Antiq.* xii., p. 1224, figures a *cupa* made of stone. As to the construction, *cadi* may be either in the nominative †plural or in the genitive singular. It is not easy to decide on the construction on the latter supposition; but there seems to be no doubt that it was used—*e. gr.*, Orelli, n. 4477 :—

D·M
LOCI IN QVO
CORPVS T·LV * *
SABINIAN LV
CIANI CREMA
TVM EST.

As it is not probable that the genitive is after *dis manibus*,

---

* Henzen thinks differently; see his *Index*, p. 106.

† It may also be the singular, if we read CAD·I., as we have OLL·I.

we must suppose the omission of some such word as *signum* or *titulus*, indicating that the stone was the mark of the place or receptacle.

P. S. In n. xvii. of the very interesting series of "Letters from Rome," by the Rev. J. W. Burgon, M.A., there is a copy of an inscription "scratched rather than engraved on a small tablet in the Museum Kircherianum."

```
" EGOSECUNDAFECICUPELLABONE
 MEMORIEFILIEMMEEMSECUN
 DINEM QEEFECESSIT·IN·FIDEM
 CCMFRATREMSCMLACERE
 TICMINPACERECESERUND
```

I Secunda have made a grave to the virtuous memory of my daughter Secundina, who departed in faith; with her brother Laurentius. They departed in peace.

Even De Rossi, the great patron of those who sleep in the Catacombs, will not approve of *cupella*, for the accusative; nor of *filiem meem*, in place of the genitive; though *cum fratrem sum* may admit of defence; and *recceserund* may only reflect the popular pronunciation. But in truth, look at the original of this inscription; and you understand the history of the inaccuracies at once. It belongs, in a word, to persons in humble life.

The chief point of interest, however in the preceding epitaph, is the word CUPELLA,—which (I humbly suspect) is new. At least it was unknown (in any such sense) to Du Cange. But he gives " cupa," and quotes for it a heathen inscription (to be seen in Gruter, p 815) which ends,—" In hâc cupâ mater et filius positi sunt." On this authority, Du Cange explains " cupa" to mean *urna*, *arca sepulchralis*. But he refers his reader to " Cuba," of which he says,—" forte pro *Cumba*, locus subterraneus;" and he quotes a monkish writer, who employs the word as follows:—" Ad pedes B. Sabini est altare S. Martini . . . . *in alia Cuba, juxta orientem, sepulchrum S. S. Victoria, Domnici*," &c.—" Cuba" and " cupa" are therefore probably one word, of which " cupella" will have been the diminutive. Whether allied to " cumba" or not, I have very serious doubts.

I suspect that " cupa," (the same word as " *cup*,") and its diminutive " cupella," originally meant a sepulchral vase which held the burnt bones of the dead. This kind of sense the word preserves to this hour,—" cupel" being, I am told, the established appellation of a little vessel used by refiners. But in early Christian times, the word will have readily sustained a change of signification, in connection with the remains of the departed. It will have indicated generally *the grave* where those remains were deposited. How closely connected from a very early period were places of sepulture and places of prayer,—what need to state before one learned in Christian Antiquities? Already then will you have anticipated the suggestion for the sake of which I am troubling you with this letter, namely, that we have here the etymology of the word CHAPEL, which has so long perplexed philologists,—yourself, I believe, among the rest. "Capella," (*Anglicè* "Chapel") is derived, I suspect, from "Cupella," which in the fourth or fifth century denoted a place of Christian burial,—as the humble inscription under consideration shows. Perhaps *l'oult* would be the nearest English equivalent for the word."

Mr. B. adds that "he is afraid to suggest further that 'Cupola' may be only another form of the same word."

There can be little doubt that *cupella* of this inscription is only another form of *cupula*, which I have above noticed. I have seen the word more than once in the African inscriptions, but am unable to recall any other example than that in Renier, *Inscrip. de l' Algérie*, n. 3939 :—

"OBMEMORIAM
MARITISVIVALSI
LVANITRIIRARCHI
CELIAMONNATA
CVPVLMASVPER
STIFENROGVSEIVS
VIXITANXLIMVDX

Ob memoriam mariti sui Val[erii] Silvani, tri[e]rarchi Celia Monnata *cupulma (*sic*) superstite[m] rogus ejus, vixit an[nis] quadraginta uno, m[ensibus] quinque, d[iebus] decem."

The proposed etymology for *chapel* seems doubtful, but I regard the suggestion relative to *cupola* as certain. *Cupula* is at present the Spanish form of our *cupola*.

§ 101. The following is the inscription, found at Ilkley, to which I referred in p. 59 :—

RVM CAES
AVG.
ANTONINI
ET VERI
IOVI DILECTI
CAECILIVS
LVCAN . S
PRAEF COII

* i. e., *cupulam*.

Horsley expands it thus : "*Pro salute* Imperatorum Caesarum Augustorum Antonini et Veri Jovi dilecti Caecilius Lucanus praefectus cohortis."

The point, which at once attracts attention, is the use of the unique phrase—*Jovi dilecti*—especially as applied to but one of the Emperors named on the stone. Horsley compares the Homeric διοτρεφέες βασιλῆες, but the illustration throws but little light on this remarkable compliment, so strangely limited to one of the emperors. It is possible that IOVI may refer to *Antoninus*, and the phrase is certainly classic, as the Horatian— *Dilectam penitus Jovi*, but I am persuaded that the reading is erroneous. There is a singular omission of the deity to whom the altar was erected. This should, in my judgment, be supplied from the fifth line ; and I venture to suggest that the true reading is IOVI· DOLIC·TI·, *i. e.*, IOVI DOLIC[HENO] TI[BERIVS], *Tiberius* being the praenomen of *Caecilius Lucanus*, or TI may be a misreading for H, *scil.*, DOLICH. The epithet appears in various forms, such as *Dolicenus, Dolcenus, Dolc,* and *D.*

§ 102. The following inscription is on a sarcophagus, or stone coffin, which was found at York several years ago, and is now preserved in the Museum of the Yorkshire Philosophical Society:—

MEI....AL·THEODORI
ANI..OMEN·VIXIT·ANN
XXX.V·M·VI·EMI·THEO
DO.A·MATER·E·C·

In removing it when found, it was unfortunately broken, and the inscription is consequently imperfect. The fracture extends between I and A in the first line, I and O in the second, X and V in the third, and O and A in the fourth.

Mr. Wellbeloved, *Eburacum*, p. 110, remarks :—

"The difficulty is confined to two words. The first word no doubt, when perfect, was MEMORIAL· for MEMORIALE, but the author has not met with that word in any other inscription. If L, which is undoubtedly the present reading, be an error for E, the difficulty is removed. EMI in the third line presents the next difficulty; it might, though unusual, be a contraction for EMERITI; but that would be very strangely introduced, after the mention of the age, and without any notice of the legion to which Theodorianus had belonged. OMEN was most probably NOMEN, and that the abridged form of NOMENTANI."

Dr. Thurnam, *Crania Britannica, Decade I.*, observes:—

"The principal difficulty is confined to two words; the first of the inscription, and the EMI in the third line. It seems most probable that both these are *prænomina*, the first that of Theodorianus, the other of Theodora; though what these names have been it is perhaps not possible to say." * * "The inscription is probably to be thus read: Diis Manibus [conjectured to have been on the *operculum* or lid, which has not been preserved] Mal...al. Theodoriani Nomentani vixit annis xxxiv., mensibus vi. Emi. Theodora mater efficiendum curavit." * * * "Altogether the external evidence is in favour of the remains found in this coffin being those of a Roman citizen and soldier, a native of Italy, and of the ancient Latin territory in the immediate neighbourhood of Rome itself."

There is no doubt that the only difficulties in the inscription are from M to L in the first line, and EMI in the third. Mr. Wellbeloved's conjecture of NOMENT· is confirmed, so far as the last letter is concerned, by *"an accurate rubbing," procured by Dr. Thurnam, "which shows distinctly the ligulate letter T in the word OMENT." It also seems to me evident that Mr. Wellbeloved's readings, MEMORIAL· and EMERITI, must be at once rejected, and for the reasons which he himself states. Nor can I concur with Dr. Thurnam in the view which he has taken of "the external evidence being in favour of the remains being those of a Roman citizen and soldier." The absence of the usual notice of the legion or cohort suggests the presumption, that Theodorianus had not been a soldier.

I am inclined to read from M to L thus: MEM· C·VAL·, i. e., Memoria Caii Valerii. MEM may stand for either MEMORIA or MEMORIÆ; if for the former, I regard it as meaning "The

---

* Since the publication of this article I have had the opportunity, through the kindness of Dr. Thurnam, of examining this rubbing, and now doubt the truth of my reading MEM, which I suggested in reliance on the accuracy of Mr. Wellbeloved's statement that the first word was "no doubt MEMORIAL" From this I inferred that he was certain as to the third letter being M.

monument;" if for the latter, "To the memory." I prefer the
first interpretation, which is confirmed by the words MEMO-
RIAM·POSSVIT (*sic*) on another stone coffin also found at
York. The abbreviation MEM· may be justified by the inscription given by Gruter, 894, 2, and the construction in the nominative by that given by Morcelli, cc.

As to EMI, I regard it as the perfect tense of the verb *emo*,
i. e., as meaning, "I Theodora his mother bought." It is scarcely
necessary to point out to any one familiar with Latin sepulchral
epigraphy the frequency of such a notice of the mode in which
the sepulchre was obtained. Fabretti, p. 153, gives many examples of such purchases. Nor is the use of the first person rare.
See Fabretti, pp. 236 and 252. The only doubt which remains
is as to the meaning of E·C. Various expansions may be
proposed, such as *ei carissimo*, *ejus carissimi*, *ejus causâ*, *ex
communi*, *scil.*, sumptu, or according to the received interpretation of these *notæ* on other stones, *erigendum* (*i. e.*, memoriam)
curavi, for such sarcophagi stood above ground.

According to my views, the whole inscription may be read
thus:—Memoria Caii Valerii Theodoriani Nomento. Vixit annos
(or annis) xxxiv., menses (or mensibus) vi. Emi Theodora mater
[et] erigendam curavi.

I have no grounds for the selection of *Caii* as the prænomen;
it is wholly conjectural. If there had been room for the *Nomen
gentilitium* and the *Nomen patris*, I should have supplied G or P
before AL, thus taking it for either GAL· or PAL·, the abbreviations of the Galerian or Palatine tribes. After *emi* I understand *locum* as is usual, (or *memorium*,) and supply *et*, the
omission of which is not rare, *e. gr.*, Fabretti, p. 307 :—

VALERIA·A·A·L·RVFA
EMIT·AEDIFICAVIT.

§ 103. In Wellbeloved's *Eburacum*, p. 90, we have an account
of an altar then (1842) recently found, "in excavating the ground
for the station [at York] of the York and North Midland Rail-
way." It was standing on a large brick and a square sheet of
lead, and bore the following inscription :—

DEAE
FORTVNAE
SOSIA
IVNCINA
Q·ANTONI
ISAVRICI
LEG·AVG

"It appears, from this inscription, to have been dedicated to the goddess Fortune by Sosia Juncina, the daughter of Quintus Antonius Isauricus, of the legion Augusta.   Three legions were distinguished by this appellation—the second, the third, and the eighth.   The third and the eighth are not known to have been ever in Britain.   The second came into Britain in the reign of Claudius, and from inscriptions on the wall of Hadrian, we learn that during his reign this legion was in the north.   In the time of Antoninus Pius it was employed in building the wall at the upper isthmus.   Afterwards it was at Isca Silurum (Caerleon, or perhaps Usk), which was probably from that period its chief quarters.   The form and character of the letters [?] concur with these circumstances to fix the date of this altar to the latter part of the reign of Antoninus, or the beginning of that of M. Aurelius, when the legion probably passed through Eburacum, and rested there on its way to the south."

Mr. Wright, *Celt, Roman, and Saxon,* p. 279 (p. 282, 2nd ed.), explains and reads it thus : —

"A lady whose father belonged to the second legion, dedicated an altar to Fortune at the head quarters of the sixth legion at Eboracum (York.) This monument, which may still be seen in the York museum, has the inscription :—

DEAE	To the goddess
FORTVNAE	Fortune,
SOSIA	Sosia
IVNCINA	Juncina,
F ANTONI	daughter of Antonius
ISAVRICI	Isauricus,
LEG AVG	of the Augustan legion.

If Mr. Wellbeloved's representation of the altar in pl. x., fig. 4, be correct, there is no authority for Mr. Wright's F before ANTONI in the fifth line.   Nor would I, with Mr. Wellbeloved, supply *filia:* I prefer *conjux,* which is sometimes omitted.

Where AVG· is applied to a legion in Britain, it is a just inference that the 2nd is intended: nor are we without examples of the omission of the rank of a member of a legion, whether he was an officer or a private, e. gr.,

FELICIVS·SIMPLEX·PATER·FECIT
LEG·VI·V .

I prefer, however, regarding LEG·AVG here as standing for *LEG·[ATI] AVG[VSTI]; and believe Q. Antonius Isauricus to have been legatus Augusti of the 6th legion.

§ 104. At the Mount, near York, there has been recently discovered "a slab, upwards of six feet long, with four incised figures in the upper part, and below them an inscription of six lines, of which nearly the whole is legible." The inscription, as far as it can be deciphered, reads as follows:

D·M· FLAVIAE·AVGVSTINAE
VIXIT·AN·XXXVIIII·M·VII·D·XI·FILIVS
NVS·AVGVSTINVS·VXT·AN·I·D.III
AN·I·M·VIIII·D·V·CAERESIVS
I·LEG·VI·VIC·CONIVGI·CARI
ET·SIBI·F·C."

[i.e., D[iis] M[anibus] Flaviae Augustinae;
  Vixit an[nis] xxxviiii, m[ensibus] vii, d[iebus] xi.]Filius
    nus Augustinus v[i] x[i]t an[no] i, d[iebus] iii,
      an[no] i, m[ensibus] viiii, d[iebus] v, Caeresius
        i leg[ionis] vi vic[tricis] conjugi cari-
        et sibi f[aciendum] c[uravit.]

The Rev. J. Kenrick lately read a paper on the subject before the Yorkshire Philosophical Society, from the report of which, in the Gentleman's Magazine for January, 1860, I have taken the foregoing particulars. On the interpretation of the inscription, Mr. Kenrick offered the following remarks:—

The monument appears to have been raised by Caeresius, a soldier of the sixth conquering legion, to the manes of his wife, Flavia Augustina, and two children, who died in their infancy, and prospectively for himself. Only the termination, NVS, of the son's name remains; there is room on

---

* He may have been governor of the province; but if he had, PR·PR· would most probably have followed LEG·AVG.

E 3

the stone for the letters necessary to form FLAVINVS, which is not unlikely to have been the name. But the space before the term of life, in the fourth line, is so small, that there is only room for a single name, and we must suppose an ellipsis of VIXIT to be supplied from the preceding clause. CAERESIVS is a name which, in the forms CAERETIVS and CAERECIVS, occurs in Gruter. The beginning of the fifth line may have contained the second name of Ceresius, which one might have expected to be followed by some designation of his military character or office, as CENT·, MIL. or TRID. MIL. It is difficult to find any word ending in I, which could grammatically have stood in this position. The number of the cohort is often prefixed to the names of auxiliaries, prætorians, &c., but not of legionaries; and though the number of *stipendia* and years of service is often noted in inscriptions to deceased soldiers, it could hardly be looked for on a monument which a soldier had prepared for himself. It is natural to conjecture that the I is a remnant of an L, in which case MIL may have preceded the title of the legion, but the appearance of the stone does not favour the conjecture. The space at the beginning of the sixth line is, no doubt, to be filled up with the remaining letters of CARISSIMAE."

The only difficulty in the inscription is, as Mr. Kenrick points out, in the I before LEG. He justly rejects the suppositions that the number either of the cohort or of the *stipendia* is denoted by I as a numeral. The natural conjecture is certainly that it should be read I, as the last letter of MIL.; but that is not favoured by the appearance of the stone. Under the circumstances, I am inclined to propose PRI·, as in §1, for PRI[NCEPS]. There is little use in speculating on the second name of *Ceresius*; but there seems to be sufficient space before PRI for one such as FVSCVS, the cognomen of the *Cæresius* mentioned in p. cclxxix, n. 6, of Gruter.

P. S.— In the *Gentleman's Magazine* for November, 1860, an account is given of the proceedings of the *Yorkshire Philosophical Society*, at their monthly meeting in October. Mr. Kenrick, Curator of Antiquities, "called the attention of the members to the inscription on the monument of Flavia Augustina, discovered at the Mount, near York," and to my suggestion that the letter I before LEG· was part of the abbreviation PRI. "This may have stood," the report proceeds, "either for Princeps or Primipilaris, examples of both occurring in inscriptions. The latter is perhaps the more probable. * * * * * * * * * * The monument in question, though coarse in execution, must have been costly, and we may conclude that Cæresius, who dedicated it to the memory of his wife and children,

was a person of higher military rank than a common soldier."
I have *already expressed a preference for *princeps* as the reading
of PRI·; and on reconsideration of the subject I see no
reason for altering my opinion. It seems to me very improbable
that the same contraction was used for the designations of two
high officers of different rank; and the enquiry as to the meaning
of PRI· appears to be no more than a search for a case in which
the abbreviation certainly denotes either of them. If such be
found, then it may, I think be reasonably concluded that it was
not used for the other. Now there is no example, so far as I am
aware, which proves that PRI was ever used for *primipilus*;
whilst PRI·PRI· in Orelli, n. 3451, (if that inscription be genuine) establishes the use of it for *princeps*. Moreover, in my notes
on the subject, I had no reference to *princeps*, as "a common
soldier," one of the *principes*, but to *princeps* as the designation of
the chief centurion of the *principes*, and the second in rank of
the centurions in a legion, for, as Vegetius, ii. 8, informs us,
*Vetus autem consuetudo tenuit, ut ex primo principe legionis
promoveretur centurio primi pili.* This use of *princeps*, as "the"
princeps, not "a" *princeps*, is not uncommon. Livy, xxv., 14,
calls the first centurion of the *principes* in one place, "*princeps
primus*," in another, "*princeps tertiæ legionis.*" See pp. 17,
121, of my notes, and Henzen, nn. 6717 and 6779.

The ordinary abbreviations for *primipilus* (otherwise *primo-
pilus*, or *primipilaris*, or *primipilariis*) are PRIM· and P. P.
There is no example of the former in the inscriptions found
in Britain, but there are, as I think, of the latter.

Horsley's *Cumberland*, n. xxxiv., is an inscription on a stone
found at Cambeck :—   †——

OMNIVM
GENTIVM
TEMPLVM
OLIMVETVS
TATECONIAD
SVMG·IVL·
PITANVS
P·P·RESITVIT

Horsley notices the expansions *propria pecunia*, *publica pecunia*, *præfectus prætorio*, *præfectus provinciæ*, but prefers *provinciæ præses*.

I regard the letters as standing for * *primipilus*. Again, we have the same *notæ* in an inscription on a slab found at Chesterholme, which is given by Bruce, *Roman Wall*, 2nd ed., p. 411 :—

D   M
CORN VICTOR·S·C
MIL·ANN·XXVI CIV
PANN·FIL SATVRNI
NI·PP·VIX·AN·LV·D·XI
CONIVX·PROCVRAVI

He expands and translates it thus :—

" DIIS MANIBVS
CORN[ELIVS] VICTOR S. C. (Sibi constituit.)
MIL[ES] ANN[OS] XXVI CIV[IS]
PANN[ONIAE] FIL[IVS] SATVRNI-
NI P. P. VIX[IT] ANN[OS] LV. D[IES] XI
CONIVX PROCVRAVI

To the Divine Manes; Cornelius Victor ordered this to be erected to himself. He was a soldier twenty-six years, a citizen of Pannonia, and very dutiful (P. P. *pientissime*) son of Saturninus. He lived fifty-five years and eleven days. I, his wife, saw his order executed."

This inscription has peculiarities, which are worthy of notice. It is not usual for the years of service to be stated before the birth-place or the years of life, or the parentage, nor for FIL. to precede the name of the father. Mr. Hodley, who first published this inscription, *Archæologia Æliana*, i., p. 211, expands it thus :—

DIS MANIBVS
CORNELIVS VICTOR, SIGNIFER COHORTIS
MILITAVIT ANNOS VIGINTI SEX, CIVIS
PANNON[I]CVS, FILIVS SATVRNI
NI PIENTISSIME VIXIT ANNOS QVINQVAGINTA
[QVINQVE DIES VNDECIM
CONIVX PROCVRAVI

---

* There are examples of the use of *primipilus* without mention of the legion.

I prefer Mr. Hedley's *militavit* and *Pannonicus* (or, rather, *Pannonius*) to Dr. Bruce's *miles* and *Pannonia*, but I do not approve of *signifer cohortis*, or *pientissime:* nor would I accept Dr. Bruce's *sibi constituit.* I am inclined to read S. C. *singularis consulis*, and would certainly take P. P. as standing for *primipili.* If the expansion *pientissime* be adopted, it should unquestionably be joined as an adverb to *vixit.*

§ 105. A block of lead, bearing the inscription,

IMP·CAES·DOMITIANO·AVG·COS. VII,

was found in this county about eight miles from Ripley. On this see § 16.

§ 106. In the year 1752, a small altar was found, in Micklegate, bearing a very perplexing inscription, which, so far as the letters are clearly legible, may be represented *thus :—

MAT·A†? ? IA ·? A
M ? I ? ? ? ? DE
MIL·LEG·VIVIC
GVBER·LEG·VI
V·S·L·LM

Mr. Wellbeloved figures it in his *Eburacum*, pl. x., and offers the following observations on it :—

"A writer in the *Gentleman's Magazine* of the year 1752, signing himself *Lancabiensis*, conjectured the age of the altar to be about the reign of Antoninus Pius, and read the inscription thus:—

MATribvs AFricis ITAlicis GALIicis
Marcvs MINVtivs MVDE
MILes LEGionis VI (sextæ) VICtricis
GVBERnatori LEGionis VI (sextæ)
Votum Solvit L L (libentissime) Merito

According to which, Marcus Miuutius Mudo, a soldier of the sixth legion victorious, in performance of a vow, dedicated the altar to the African,

---

* This reading is formed after a comparison of the sketches in Gough's edition of Camden and in Wellbeloved's *Eburacum* with a lithograph made from a rubbing of the stone, as given in the *Annual Report of the Yorkshire Philosophical Society for* 1841.

† The marks of interrogation indicate doubtful letters.

Italian, Gallican (Goddesses, the) Mothers, to the Gubernator of the
Sixth Legion. The writer confessed there was some inconsistency in the
dedications to the Matres, &c., and to the Gubernator; he did not presume
to think his interpretation tho true one; he wished only to excite the
attention of more able antiquaries. Mr. Pegge was not tardy in taking up
the subject; but in a communication to the *Gentleman's Magazine*, in the
following month, October, 1752, under his usual acrostic signature of Paul
Gemsege, agreeing with the preceding writer in the reading of the three
last lines, he differed from him in the interpretation of the two first; justly
observing, that 'Matribus' never occurs in inscriptions alone without
' Diis or Deabus.' Supposing the first letters of the first line to be not
MAT but MÆT, and the cognomen MVDE in the second line to be mutilated at the end, and the true reading of it to be MVRE ; he reads the two
first lines thus:—

> Marti ÆTolico AFro ITAlico GALlico
> Marcus MINVTius MVREns

Having settled the interpretation, he goes on to offer some explanatory
remarks. He observes that the altar was erected in consequence of a vow ;
that the votary had served in all the countries mentioned in his address, and
had been particularly preserved, as he thought, by the God of War. He
infers from this inscription, that the sixth legion was under the special protection of Mars; and understands Gubernator as put in apposition with
Marti in the first line. According to Gough, Drake sent a copy of the inscription to the Society of Antiquaries, reading the first line

> MATribus AILTA·GeNio,

in the second line, AVDE . . . and in the fourth line GVBERnator, supposing it in apposition with MILES; but he does not appear to give any
explanation of the address.

Other interpretations have been proposed, but so manifestly erroneous,
that it would be perfectly useless to record them. The author cannot presume to undertake what others, more skilful, have failed to accomplish.
Several letters of the first line, in which the greatest difficulty is found,
appear to have been originally so peculiarly formed, and now are so indistinct, that it is next to impossible to decipher them. The word GVBER in
the fourth is very perplexing, whether it be to read Gubernatori or Gubernator,—whether it be in apposition with MARti, supposed to be in the first
line, or with MILes in the line preceding. The proper word in connection
with MARti, would be Conservatori, and no such military legionary officer
as Gubernator is any other place ever mentioned. One remark only the
author would offer, and for that he is indebted to a learned friend, that the
last word in the second line is not MVDE, nor an erroneous reading for
MVRE, but ANDE, the abbreviation of Andegavanus or Andegavensis,
denoting that M. Minutius was of Andes or Andegavensis (Angers) in Gaul."

At a meeting of the Yorkshire Philosophical Society in January, 1862, the Rev. John Kenrick offered some observations on* it :—

"Mr. Kenrick remarked, that GVBER, in the fourth line, had created some difficulty, as GVBERNATOR, which the abbreviation must represent, was not the name of any legionary officer. He suggested, however, that as the sixth legion was so long settled at York, on the banks of a navigable river, the word might bear the ordinary sense of pilot or steersman; and that the dedicator of the tablet may have had the charge of the vessels, by means of which the legion communicated with places on the Ouse, or the rivers that fall into it."

Of the opinions, which are stated in the foregoing remarks, Mr. Pegge's and Mr. Drake's must be rejected, except the supposition of the latter that *gubernator* is in apposition with *miles*, which seems probable. The reading of the first line by Lasenbiensis is supported by another inscription to the *Deæ Matres* found in England, as given by Mr. Smith, *Collect. Antiq.*, iv., p. 41, who notices the similarity of the two inscriptions :—

MATRIB
ITALIS GER
MANIS
GAL · BRIT
.NTONIVS
CRETIANVS
.F·COS·REST.

i. e., as Mr. S. expands it :—Matrib[us] Italis Germanis Gal[licis] †Brit[annicis] [A]ntonius Cretianus [Bene]f[iciarius] co[n]s[ulis] rest[ituit.]

The idea of Lasenbiensis as to two dedications—to the Matres and to the Gubernator of the sixth legions—cannot for a moment be entertained. From what has been said it is plain that the difficulties in the inscription are in the first and second lines and in GVBER of the fourth. I am inclined to read the first :—

MAT · AFLIA · GAV

---

* It is now deposited in the Museum of the society by the Dean and Chapter.

† Brit[ish], as in Henzen's n. 5972, had occurred to me, but I prefer Brit[annicis].

and to expand it Mat[ribus] (or Mat[ronis]) Aflia[bus] Gar[a-diis.] See Henzen, nn. 5929, 5937.

This reading, so far as MAT · AFLIA ·, seems almost certain, and the appearance of the stone, as represented in the lithograph, favours GAV. There is certainly now no authority for GAL, and I suspect that there never was.

The feasible readings of the second line are M · MINV · MVDE, and M · MINV · ANDE; but I am not satisfied with either; and yet the only improvement, which I can suggest, is the reading NANDE instead of MVDE or ANDE. *Nande* was situated in that part of *Media*, called *Atropatene*. See Ptolemy, vi, 2, 10. Mr. Kenrick's explanation of GVBER· as *gubernator* taken in apposition with *miles*, is more satisfactory than any of which I am aware. See Muratori, mmxxxvi, 1. See also my notes, p. 84.

WALES.

CAERNARVONSHIRE.

---

§ 107. In Mr. Smith's *Collectanea Antiqua*, vol. iii., p. 201, we find the following notice of " an imperfect inscription found at *Caernarvon."

" It is on two pieces of stone, which, on comparison, appeared to have belonged to one and the same slab ;

```
 · · · EPT.SEVERVS.PIVS.PER · ·
 · · · VREL.ANTONINV · · · · ·
 · AQVAEDVCTIVM VETVS · · · ·
 · · · DS.COH.I.SVNC.RESIT · · · ·
       · · · VIPF · · ·
       · · · IVI. · · · ·
```

" The first two lines mention Severus and Caracalla ; the second and third [third and fourth] refer to an aqueduct or aqueducts, which, having become decayed through age, had been restored by the first cohort of the Tungri ; that is to say, presuming that SVNC of the engraving in the ' Archæologia Cambrensis' for April, 1853, should be TVNG. The remaining lines probably gave the name of the commander of the cohort, and that of the superintendent of the work of restitution."

It is plain that Mr. Smith correctly explains

[S]EPT[IMIVS] SEVERVS·PIVS·PER[TINAX]
[A]VREL[IVS] ANTONINV[S]

as standing for the Emperors Severus and Caracalla ; and

AQVAEDVCTIVM VETVS[TATE]
[COLLA]BS[VM] COH[ORS] I SVNC RESTIT[VIT]

as referring to an aqueduct, or aqueducts, which, having become

---

* The *Septentium* of Antoninus.

decayed through age, had been restored. Nor is his opinion as to
the contents of the fifth and sixth lines improbable; but I have no
doubt that the cohort named in the fourth line is not *cohors prima
Tungrorum*, but *cohors prima Sunuc[orum]*, the N and V being
ligulate. This cohort is mentioned in Hadrian's *tabula honestæ
missionis*, from which it appears that at the time (A. D. 124) it
was serving in Britain under the command of *Aulunius Claudianus*. This Caernarvon stone is valuable, as it and the *diploma*
are the only extant memorials of the cohort. The *Sunuci*, or
Sunici, were a Belgic people. They are mentioned by Tacitus
and Pliny, but their position has not been exactly defined. It is
probable, however, that they lived between Cologne and the Meuse
about the eastern part of the modern Belgic province of *Lim-
bourg*.

    Mr. *Foster*, *Archæologia Cambrensis*, iv., p. 72, remarks:

    " In reading the upper line, *Aqua luctium Vetus*, and comparing it with
the site of *Segontium*, it is difficult to conjecture how it can apply to any
military operations which have been erected on this spot, for nearly the
whole of the rising ground on which Segontium stood is at this day literally
springs of water."

    Aquæductus was applied not merely to an "aqueduct," but
also to a "drain." The form *aquæductium* is peculiar. It may
be for the genitive plural governed by some word on the lost
portion of the stone; or it may be the accusative of a word, not
met with elsewhere, *scil.*, *aquæductium*.

    § 108. In the *Archæologia Cambrensis*, ii., p. 51, we have the
following account of " a Roman inscription on a stone discovered
at Tycoch, in the parish of Bangor, about the year 1820 :—

    " It illustrates an historical fact recorded by Pausanias, the geographer,
in his Arcadia. This author, who lived at the time of the event which he
briefly relates, mentions that Antoninus Pius ordered an expedition to
demand satisfaction from the Brigantes, a powerful tribe in the north of
England, for having entered in a hostile manner into the neighbouring district, called Genounia, then in subjection to Rome. This expedition must
have been undertaken by Lollius Urbicus, Propraetor under Priscus Licinius,
about the year 140. The legions at this time employed in Britain had sig-
nallsed themselves a few years before under Hadrian, in his Judaic expedition, as may be proved by existing monuments; the title Arabicus
occurring on the imperial coins and other memorials of this period.

The only nations bordering on the Brigantes were the Otadiol on the north, and the Ordovices on the south and west ; and it may reasonably be supposed that the Greek geographer intended to express Gwynedd by the Greek term Genounia. This being premised and granted, it appears not improbable that the stone pillar at Tyooch was set up by the ninth or Arabic legion, as a record of the services performed in obedience to the imperial order, in ridding the country of the marauding Brigantes.

Gwynedd was so thoroughly reduced under the Roman yoke by the terrible example which Agricola had previously made of the inhabitants, that the remnant which he left, were glad to avail themselves of the imperial protection against the inroads of the Brigantes and other warlike tribes, such as the Picts and Belgæ; and hence in that emergency, which was of so important a character as to attract the attention of Paussnias, (probably when on his visit to Rome,) we may conclude that they solicited the aid of the emperor on their behalf. It may also be observed that the ninth legion had been employed in the reign of Claudius in garrisoning Britain ; having at that time Hispania engraven on their standard. The inscription alluded to is as follows :—

            NVMC . . . .
            IMP CAESAR. M . . .
            AVREL. ANTONINVS
            PIVS. TI. IX. AVG . ARAB.
                    IX. "

The author of this article has made some extraordinary mistakes: of these two or three, as being connected with the inscription, require notice. Lollius Urbicus was not proprætor under Priscus Licinius ; there is no evidence that the 9th or any other legion ever bore the title *Arabica*; and the emperor named in the inscription, as is obvious from the name *Aurelius*, was not the "Antoninus Pius," whose legate Lollius Urbicus was in Britain in A.D. 140. It is plain, too, that the emperor cannot be Marcus Aurelius Antoninus, the philosopher, for there is no evidence, except one inscription, that he was ever styled *pius* in his life time, and Commodus was the first emperor to whom *felix* was applied.

I have but little doubt that the emperor named in the inscription is Caracalla. I would read the second, third, and fourth lines thus :—

            IMP·CAESAR·MARCVS
            AVREL·ANTONINVS
            PIVS·FELIX·AVG·ARAB

i. e., Imp[erator] Cæsar Marcus Aurel[ius] Antoninus pius felix Aug[ustus] Arab[icus]. The letters read TI.IX· are doubtless FE IX, the I, between E and I, being obliterated.

From the statement of Spartian, which is confirmed by an inscription given by Gruter, cclxvii., 7, it appears that Caracalla used the titles of his father, *Arabicus* and *Adiabenicus*. Any doubt which I have relative to Caracalla being the emperor named in the inscription arises from a suspicion as to the reading ARAB[ICVS]. It seems very strange that of all Caracalla's titles this, which is so rare, should be the only one selected, and that it should occupy so extraordinary a position. Hence I should be inclined to conjecture that the true reading may be A·RAB, as we have on the Leicester *miliarium* A·RATIS, if I could find mention of any place in the neighbourhood beginning with *RAD.

The numerals in the fifth line (if we regard the stone as a mile stone, which "it was said to be by those who saw it") indicate the distance of nine miles.

If Tycoch, which is said to be "near Bangor," be between that town and Caernarvon, it is highly probable that the stone marked nine miles from *Segontium*, for the distance of Bangor from Caernarvon is about nine English miles.

As it may be assumed that both Severus and Geta were dead at the time of the inscription, its date will fall between A.D. 212 and 217.

On the NVMC in the first line I have no satisfactory explanation to offer. I have never seen any thing similar in a miliary inscription.

§ 109. Many years ago a cake of copper was found at Caerhên in this county. It bore the inscription SOCIO ROMAE, crossed obliquely by another—NAT·SOL. On this see "Additions, p. 54."

---

* Are these letters a mis-reading of BAB, i. e., BABIR for VARIS? If so, there must have been some numerals lost before the IX, and the miles must have been counted from *Deva* to *Segontium*, and v. v. as in the Itinerary.

SCOTLAND.

DUMBARTONSHIRE.

§ 110. Old Kilpatrick in this county was most probably the western *terminus* of the barrier of the upper isthmus known as *"the wall of Antoninus." Amongst the Roman relics, which have been found in its neighbourhood, are some legionary inscriptions of the class referred to in p. 116. Mr. Stuart, *Caledonia Romana*, ed. Prof. Thomson, pl. vii., figures three of them, bearing the following inscriptions :—

(1)	(2)
IMP·C	·MP·C·T·AE
T·AE·HADRIA	·ADRIANO
NO·ANTONINO·AVG·PIO·P·P	·NTONINO
VEX	·· G·PIO·P·P
LEG·XX	·EG·XXVV
VV·FE	··· DXI
PPITΠ CDXI	

* In the *Journal of the Archæological Institute*, 1858, there is an interesting and carefully prepared notice of the present condition of this work by John Buckman, Esq., to whom Archæologists are indebted for the preservation of many valuable relics. From his statements compared with those in Stuart's *Caledonia Romana*, it appears that the remains and traces of the northern barrier and its forts are much less perfect than those on the southern isthmus, as described by Dr. Bruce. This difference is mainly due to the less durable character of the work between the Forth and the Clyde, and to its position in the track of ancient violence and of modern improvement. The extant memorials, however, of its builders are more satisfactory than those of the southern wall. There is no doubt as to the emperor, by whose order it was constructed, nor as to the troops employed on the work, whilst it has long been a generic cause by whom the Southern barrier was built, and although the claims of Hadrian, put forward by Hodgson, have been zealously urged by Dr. Bruce, the able historian of the Roman wall, more recent enquirers have rejected this opinion, and probably there are now many who prefer Mr. McLauchlan's view, as stated in his Memoir, p. 59, whilst some, perhaps, may be disposed to accept the theory advanced by Mr. Merivale in the Quarterly Review, Jan., 1860.

(3)

IMP·C·T·AELIO
HADRIANO·ANTO
NINO·AVG·P·P·
VEX·LEG·VI·VIC
P·F·OPVS·VALLI
P.* ⊂⊃ ⊂⊃ ⊂⊃ ⊂⊃ CXLI

The following are Mr. Stuart's expansions:—

(1)

IMP[ERATORI] C[AESARI]
T[ITO] AE[LIO] HADRIANO
ANTONINO AVG[VSTO] PIO
P[ATRI] P[ATRIAE]
VEX[ILLATIO] LEG[IONIS]
VICESIMAE †V[ALENTIS]
V[ICTRICIS] FE[CIT]
P[ER] P[ASSVS] QUATUOR
MILLE QUADRINGENTOS
UNDECIM

(2)

[I]MP[ERATORI] C[AESARI] T[ITO] AE-
[LIO] [H]ADRIANO
[A]NTONINO
[AV]G[VSTO] PIO P[ATRI] P[ATRIAE]
Vexillatio LEG[IONIS] VICESIMAE †V[ALENTIS]
V[ICTRICIS]
per passus — — — DXI

(3)

IMP[ERATORI] C[AESARI] T[ITO] AELIO
HADRIANO ANTONINO
AVG[VSTO] P[ATRI] P[ATRIAE]
VEX[ILLATIO] LEG[IONIS] SEXTAE VIC[TRICIS]
P[ER]F[ECIT] OPVS VALLI [PER]
P[ASSVS] QUATUOR MILLE CENTUM
QUADRAGINTA UNUM

---

* Here and in pp. 13, 22, &c., I have been obliged to use an L laid on its side for the symbol of 1000. See fig. 4 of frontispiece. Horsley's idea that it was formed by connecting two D's—⊂I⊃, ⊂I⊃—is probable.

† Read VALERIAE. See note p. 3.

On examination of these expansions (which are almost exactly
the same as those by Horsley), there are some doubtful points
which require discussion. With a view to the elucidation of these,
and of the subject generally, let us consider similar memorials
found in other places :—

* (4)

LEG
II
AVG·F·
PIIIICXI

* (5)

IMP   ANTON
AVG   ·   PIO
P   P
     LEG
     II
     AVG
     FPIIIICCLXX

* (6)

IMP·C
T·AE·HADRIANO
ANTONINO
PIO·P·P·VEX·LEG
XX VV FEC
P·

* (7)

IMP·C·T·AELIO HADR
IANO ANTONINO·AVG
P·P·VEX·LEG·VI
VICTRICS·P· F·
OPVS·VALLI P·
∞ ∞ ∞ CCXL·P

† (8).

IMP C
T AELIO
HADRIANO
ANTONINO
AVG·PIO P·P
VEX·LEG·XXV
P·P   III

† (9)

IMP CAES TITO AELIO
HADRIANO ANTONINO
AVG·PIO PP LEG II
AVG·PERMP III DC
LXVI·8

---

* Stuart, plate viii.

† Stuart, pl. ix. In the 4th line of c. 9, it is given instead of III. See Cal. Rom. p.
864, and Brit. Rom., iii.

* (10)

IMP·CAESAR·T·AELIO
HADRIANO ANTONINO
AVG PIO PP·VEXILLATIO
LEG V̄I·VICTR·P·F
PER·M·P IIIDCLXVIS

* (11)

IMP·CAES·T
AELIO HADRI
ANTONIN·AVG
PIO P·P VEXILLA
LEG·VI·VIC·PF
PER·M P IIIDCL...

† (12)

IMP CAES TITO AELIO
HADRIANO ANTONINO
AVG PIO·P·P·LEG II AVG
PERMPIIIDCLXVIS

† (13)

LEG XX
V V FEC
MPIIIP
IIICCCIV

† (14)

IMP·CAESARI·T·
AELIO·HADRINO
ANTONINO·AVG
PIO·P·P·VEXILLA
LEG·VI·VIC·P·F·
PERM

‡ (15)

IMP CAES
TAE HADRI
ANTONINO
AVG PIO PP
VEXILATIOVS

§ (16)

VEXILLATIONS
LEG II AVG ET
LEGXXVVF

§ (17)

IMP·CAESARI
T·AELIO HADRI
ANO ANTONINO
AVG PIO PP
VEXILLATIO
LEGXXVALVICF
PER·MIL·P III

§ (18)

IMP·CAES·TÆLANT
AVG·PIO P·P·
COII I TVNGRO
RVM FECIT ∞

---

* Stuart, plate xvi.   Horsley and Stuart omit I between V & S.
† Stuart, plate 10.
‡ Stuart, plate xvii.
§ Stuart, plate xv.

From nn. (14) and (17) (if the reading of the first lines be correct) it appears that the Emperor's names were in the *dative case, in the sense " to" or " for." If it had been intended to define the time, we should have had the ablative, and the COS and TRIB·POT·, with their numbers, would have been stated.

In such records different constructions seem to have been used. Here we have the dative ; on the slab, p. 151, there is the nominative ; on another, p. 157, the ablative ; and in the inscription, given in p. 203 of Bruce's *Roman Wall*, we find the genitive. This variety of construction in epigraphy appears in other instances. In the numbers of consulships and of years of tribunitian power we have such forms as COS·TERTIO and TERTIVM, and TRIBVNITIAE POTESTATIS, or TRIBVNITIA POTESTATE followed by the numeral in O or VM. In both cases, however, VM is the usual form. In sepulchral inscriptions we find the name of the deceased in the nominative, the genitive, or the dative; and in the same class of inscriptions time " how long" is expressed by either accusative or ablative, and sometimes by both on the same stone, *e. gr.*, *vixit annos LVIV., M. uno, dies* XIV.

From ant inscription, given in *Caledonia Romana*, pl. xv., fig. 7, and *Britannia Romana*, xxv., we may infer that these works were executed in the 3rd Consulship of Antoninus, *i. e.*, A. D. 140–144, probably in the first of these years.

As he was styled *Imp.* ii. at the close of A.D. 139, it may be assumed that the victory of Lollius Urbicus was in the autumn of that year.

From nn. (10), (15), (16), and (17), it appers that VEX. in

---

* Morcelli, *de stilo*, II., p. 127, and Zell, *Delectus*, p. 413, give the ablative, in expanding v. (3).

† Horsley correctly reads the third line *cohors prima Cugernorum*. This corps is named in Trajan's diploma of A.D. 104. But if the stone is faithfully represented in the *Caledonia Romana*, his reading of the last line—TMOITI·MP—is certainly erroneous. There the letters resemble CIT, the ending of FECIT, followed by IMP. I suspect that I may be a relic of P. for *per*. It is certainly not a numeral: nor can Horsley's III be received, as the numerals should not precede, but follow M. P. I am also inclined to think that, as this stone was probably a mile-stone, the work recorded on it was done not on the *vallum*, but on the *via militaris*.

Q 2

nn. (1), (3), (6), (7), (8), and VEXILLA. in nn. (11), and (14), stand for VEXILLATIO, not for* VEXILLARII. It is also plain that there were three vexillations employed on the wall, scil., of the second, sixth, and twentieth legions; and I strongly suspect that these are the same which are mentioned in Henzen's n. 5456 : PRAEPOSITVS VEXILLATIONIBVS MILLIARIIS·TRIBVS EXPEDITIONE BRITANNICA. If this was the fact, they must have remained from the time of Hadrian, for the *expeditio Britannica* was probably his. It appears also that not only vexillations of the second and twentieth legions, but those †legions were employed ; there is no evidence, however, relative to more than a vexillation of the 6th legion.

In nn. (7), (10), (11), and (14), P·F· stand for PIAE FIDELIS, not ‡PERFECIT. The term for "executed" is FECIT, given in *extenso* in n. (18), abbreviated into FEC· in nn. (6), and (13), into FE in n. (1), and into F· in nn. (4),(5), (16), and (17), and understood (*i. e.*, to be supplied,) in nn. (2),(3), (7), (8), (9), (10), (11), (12), and (14). The phrase in *extenso* for executing a portion of the wall seems to have been—*opus valli fecit per mille passus*—but *opus valli* are seldom expressed. Where we find P·P·, as in the last lines of nn. (1) and (8), they stand for *per passus*, but where there is P alone, it is doubtful whether it stands for *per* or *passus*. I am inclined to prefer the preposition. The absence of either M·P· or P· before the number of paces is common on mile-stones. See p. 87.

In nn. (9),(10), (12), and (15), the last line ends with S, preceded

---

* Morcelli, *de stilo*, ii., p. 127, reads *Vexillarii*, in n. (3.)

† From the number of paces stated in these tablets it is improbable that their full force was engaged on the work.

‡ Morcelli, *de stilo*, ii., p. 127, gives *perseverant*, agreeing with *Vexillarii*. See my notes, p. 80, relative to *pia fidelis* as titles of the 6th legion. Mr. Stuart also expands P·F *perfecit*, and adds in a note on n. (3.) p. 256, the astonishing remark : " The word *perfecit* is translated by Gordon, (p. 62), ' carried on." Might we not rather say "perfected" or "finished?" Let this be granted, and no doubt will remain as to the Wall of Antonine having terminated about Kilpatrick. Independently of the objection that *perfecit* must, of course, apply only to the specified number of paces, Mr. Stuart's interpretation would place the termination of the wall at every place where an inscription was found giving P·F. Thus we should have the end of the wall at the points where nn. (9), (10), (11), and (14.) were found. See *Cal. Rom.*, index, pp. 301, 311.

in nn. (10) and (15) by V. Horsley supplies V in n. (12) before
S, and expands them all— V[otum] S[olvit.] I have no doubt that
this expansion is erroneous, and am persuaded that Mr. Stuart's
suggestion, that the S means "a half," i. e., stands for *Semis*, not
Semissis, as he erroneously states his own suggestion is the correct explanation. See my notes p. 118, and Orelli, nn. 817,
2844. As to (15) I am inclined to think that the last line
is a mis-reading of VEXILATIONS for *vexillationes*. See
n. (16).

The occurrence of the numbers 3666½ three times is very
remarkable. Nn. 10 and 11 were, probably, duplicates, for a
tablet seems to have been placed at each end of the work that
was executed. See *Cal. Rom.*, p. 310, where it is stated that a
pair set up by the 20th legion, have not only inscriptions almost
identical, but the boars, the cognizance of the corps, looking in
opposite directions towards each other. See also Prof. D. Wilson's *Prehist. Annals*, p. 376, where these facts were first noticed.
The number 3666 being so nearly a multiple of the number of
days in the year, and also of the number of days in some
months, might suggest the surmise that a certain quantity of
work was apportioned for each day ; but I am inclined rather
to conjecture that the work was laid out for the legions and
vexillations in sections, some of three miles, others of four, and
that the miles were subdivided into thirds, whence we have 3
and ⅔ miles.

There is a remarkable agreement, which I have not seen noticed
between the work done by the 2nd legion and the vexillation of
the 6th. In n. (4) read with Stuart, p. 299, 4111, and in
n. (5), with Gordon, 3270, and we have the same sum as 4111 in
n. (3) and 3240 in n. (7,) i. e., 7381. There will be a further
agreement in their work, if we read 3666½ in (n. 9,) as it is given
in the plate, instead of 4666½, and assume that nn. (9) and
(12), and nn. (10) and (11,) are duplicates.

As to the other odd numbers following 3000 and 4000, I
would suggest that they may indicate the difference between
the measured miles in a straight line and the actual distance
traversed by the *vallum* in consequence of curves. I was led to

form this conjecture by examining n. (13). The work executed is there stated to be MP*IIIP IIICCCIV—which I would interpret as indicating that they had finished their three miles, which in consequence of the curves extended over 3304 paces.

Horsley, *Britannia Romana*, p. 160, and Roy, †*Military Antiquities*, p. 165, have deduced from the number of paces on the tablets the length of the barrier, but such calculations seem very hazardous, and those which were made by them are not reliable. It may, however, I think, be inferred from the tablets, that we must either adopt the supposition that they were set up in pairs, or else have a large excess.

§ 111. An altar, bearing the following inscription, was found at Castle Hill, in, I believe, this county :—

" CAMPES
TRIBVSET
BRITTANNI
Q·PISENTIVS
IVSTVS PREF
COA IIII GAL
V·S·L·L·M "

Mr. Stuart, p. 309, expands and translates it thus :—

" CAMPESTRIBUS   *To the Eternal Field Deities*
AETERNIS BRITANNIAE   *of Britain,*
QUINTUS PISENTIUS   *Quintus Pisentius Justus,*
JUSTUS PRAEFECTUS   *Prefect of the Fourth Cohort*
COHORTIS QUARTAE   *of the Gaulish Auxiliaries*
GALLORUM   (dedicates this)
VOTUM SOLVIT   *His vow being most willingly performed.*
LIBENTISSIME MERITO

ET in the second line is plainly "and," i. e., *Campestribus et Britannicis, scil.*, Matribus. The *nomen gentilitium* of the Prefect was more probably PISENIVS; and for *libentissime* read *lætus libens.* See p. 247.

_____

* The III between P and P are doubtful. Mr. Stuart reads them as " three I's," but adds the note : " Could the doubtful marks be converted into an M, the sentence might, perhaps, be read—*Murum Perfecit*, (Per) *Mille Passus* (or *Millia Passuum*) Tria *Trecentos-Quatuor*." This suggested reading is highly improbable.

† In this work there is a well executed plan of the course of the wall and of the vestiges of the stations. An important addition to our knowledge of the southern wall has been made by the publication of of Mr. MacLauchlan's Surveys and Memoir, for which Archæologists are indebted to the munificence of the Duke of Northumberland.

---

§ 112. One of the most remarkable relics of the Roman period is a full length statue, found at *Birrens, in the year 1732: it is described by Mr. Stuart, *Caledonia Romana*, p. 124 :—

"This statue stands within a niche, is winged at the shoulders, and armed with a helmet encircled by a moral crown, over which is wreathed an olive branch. In her right hand she holds a spear and a shield, in her left a globe, and on her breast appears the representation of a Gorgon's head. The stone on which she stands is inscribed with the following words:—

> BRIGANTIAE. S. AMANDVS
> ARCHITECTVS EX IMPERIO IMP I.

According to the learned antiquary, Mr. Gale, the contractions ought to be understood thus:—

> BRIGANTIAE SACRUM AMANDUS
> ARCHITECTVS EX IMPERIO IMPERATORIS
> JULIANI.

To Brigantia, Amandus the architect, (erected this statue,) by order of the Emperor Julian.

From its general appearance, many were inclined to believe that this figure represented Minerva, others that it was meant either for a Victory, or a hybrid personification of several deities in one."

Horsley, *Britannia Romana*, p. 341, remarks :—

"As for the inscription beneath the figure, I cannot but agree with Mr. Gale supposing BRIGANTIA to be the name of the deity here represented; the S I would suppose to stand for *sacrum*; and AMANDVS is a proper name, not unfrequent in inscriptions. ARCHITECTVS may either be for *architectus*, as Baron Clerk supposes, observing that *architecti* are often mentioned in the *Codex*, as necessary persons in the provinces; or it may be to denote some other name or names of the same AMANDVS. If the last single stroke be an I, of which I find Baron Clerk cannot be certain, Mr. Gale's reading, *ex imperio imperatoris Juliani*, seems highly probable,

---

* This station, otherwise called Middleby, in the *Notum Belgium* of Antonious.

otherwise IMP. may perhaps stand for *impendii*, or some such word ; and
EX IMPERIO, that precede, signify the same as *ex jussu* or *jussus*, whether
this command was supposed to be received by a divine impulse, or might
be given by some superior."

The expansion IMP[ERATORIS] I[VLIANI] is, in my judgment, so highly improbable that it should at once be rejected. Henzen suggests the reading IMP·S and the expansion IMP[ENSA]
S[VA], *i. e.,* "at his own cost," but is not satisfied with it.
Mommsen also doubtfully proposes IMP·F, IMP[ERATVM
F[ECIT].   I prefer IMP[ERANTE] I[PSA] ; but perhaps the true reading is NIMP., *i. e.,* NIMP[HAE] I[PS-
IVS].   I strongly suspect that this Brigantia is the same
mentioned as DEAE NYMPAE BRIG, in the inscription
noticed by Selden, Pridaux, and Gale, if indeed that inscription be genuine. See Horsley, *Brit. Rom.,* pp. 179 and 315,
and Stuart's *Caledonia Romana,* p. 125. The use of I for
Y in this word is not rare. Thus we have in Orelli, nn.
1633, 1648, NIMPHIS SALVTIFERIS and NIMPHIS
AVFIDI. The meaning of *ex imperio nimphæ ipsius* is "by
command of the nymph herself," *scil.,* of Brigantia, a *Dea
Nympha.* The use of such phrases as *ex monitu, ex imperio,* or
jussu, indicating that the altar was executed in consequence of
some [supposed] order of the deity, to whom it was raised, is
common. See Orelli, nn. 1370, 1443, 1469, 1486, &c. Zell,
Delectus, nn. 279, 280, and 281, supplies examples of the use
of *ipse;* MATRONIS AFLIABVS * * * EX IMPERIO
IPSARVM, MATRONIS HAMAVEHIS * * * EX IM-
PERIO IPSARVM, MATRONIS VATRIABVS * * * EX
IMPERIO IP.

I also suspect that Brigantia, who, doubtless, was represented
by this statue believed by some to be an image of Victory, was a
native, or at least Celtic deity, probably specially worshipped
amongst the Brigantes. See p. 65. I identify her with the DVICI
BRIG of the inscription, given by Horsley, *Brit. Rom., Yorkshire,*
xviii, which he reads DVI CI[VITATIS] BRIG[ANTVM], *i. e.,*
"to *Dui*, the tutelar god *of the state of the Brigantes,*" but which
I would read D[EAE] VICT]ORIAE] BRIG[ANTIAE], and
interpret as denoting that the Romans identified their goddess

*VICTORIA with the British BRIGANTIA. It may be worth while to add that there are examples of *architectus*, or *arcitectus*, as a military office, *e. gr.*, Renler, *Inscriptions de l' Algérie*, n. 547.

```
            D  M  S
        MCORNELIVSFESTVS
        MILLEGIIIAVG
        ARCIIITECTVSVIC
        SITAN—NISXXX
```

§ 113. Fig. 1, plate ii, Stuart's *Caledonia Romana*, p. 128, is the representation of an altar, also found at Birrens. It bears the following inscription :—

```
            DEAE
        HARIMEL
        LAE·SACGA
        MIDIAHVS
        ARCXVSL
```

On this Mr. Smith, *Collect. Antiq.*, iii., p. 203, remarks :—

"This, with the exception of the first part, Mr. Stuart considers unintelligible. As it stands it would be 'sacred to the goddess Harimella; Gamidianus Arcx, &c.'; but it is doubtful if the dedicator's name was transcribed correctly. In another inscription found at Birrens, we find *Amandus Architectus* erecting a statue to *Brigantia*; and it is not improbable the above uncouth word may be a misreading for *Amandus* and *Arcx* an abbreviation of *Architectus*. The word *Harimella* seems also an importation from Germany, where dedications to *Hariasa* and *Malia* have been found, from which words *Harimella* may be compounded."

Mr. Smith's reading seems probable, except *arcx* as an abbreviation of *architectus*. It is better with Henzen, n. 5892, to regard X as standing for *ex*, *i. e.*, XV = *ex voto*, but his GAMIDIANVS is very doubtful. If Mr. S.'s conjecture as to the name be correct, and it is not improbable, it removes the objection to the expansion *architectus*, which may arise from having two *architecti* at the same place. It may be, however, that ARC· stands for ARCARIVS, an officer often mentioned in the African inscriptions. The deriva-

---

* Victoria is also identified with *Andraste*. See Dr. Thurnam, *Cran. Brit. &c.*, iv., p. 131; and p. 51, of my notes, on different identifications of barbarian deities.

tion which Mr. Smith suggests for the name of the goddess is not
probable. The only inscription, in which *Melus* is found, has
been proved to be a forgery. See Henzen, n. 5241.

§ 114. In p. 128 we have two inscriptions, also found at this
station, which present similar difficulties of interpretation :—

<table>
<tr><td>(1.)</td><td>(2.)</td></tr>
<tr><td>DEAE VIRADES</td><td>DEAE RICAGM</td></tr>
<tr><td>THI PAGVS CON</td><td>BEDAE PAGVS</td></tr>
<tr><td>DRVSTIS MILI</td><td>VELLAVS MILIT</td></tr>
<tr><td>IN COH II TVN</td><td>COH II TVNG</td></tr>
<tr><td>GR· SVB SIVO</td><td>V·S·L·M.</td></tr>
<tr><td>AVSPICE PR</td><td></td></tr>
<tr><td>AEFE.</td><td></td></tr>
</table>

Mr. Stuart's observations on No. (1) are :—

" With some few alterations—and considerable allowance made for the
errors that may occur in deciphering those time-worn legends—the [in-
scription] may be translated somewhat as follows :—" *To the goddess (or
deified)* - - - -, *Thisus Pagus Condrustus, a soldier of the second Cohort of
the Tungrian auxiliaries, commanded by Sirus Auspicius, Prefect, (dedicates
this altar.)* We are at a loss to discover the meaning of the word VIRA-
DES ; perhaps it has been erroneously copied [by Pennant,] and ought to
be read DRYADES or OREADES; in which case the difficulty vanishes,
and we have the German soldier offering up his vows to a particular and
perhaps tutelary class of the *Deæ Nymphæ*."

On the inscription No. (2) Prof. Thomson offers the following
note :—

" The altar appears to be dedicated to some provincial deity, possibly
Ricagmena Deda by name, by a soldier of the second cohort of Tungrians,
Pacus Vellaus, (vide Preb. Ann. p. 898,) or, to avoid imputing a serious
grammatical error to the sculptor, by two soldiers, Vellaus and Pagus."

Subjoined is the passage in the *Prehistoric Annals of Scotland*,
to which reference is made in the note :

" It appears to be dedicated by Pagus Vellaus to one of those obscure
local deities, apparently provincial names with Latin terminations, which
are more familiar than intelligible to the antiquary. It belongs to a class
of Romano-British relics which is peculiarly interesting, notwithstanding

the obscurity of their dedications, as the transition-link between the Roman and British mythology. These altars of the adopted native deities are generally rude and inferior in design, as if indicative of their having their origin in the piety of some provincial legionary embalters. In the obscure gods and goddesses, thus commemorated, we most probably recognise the names of favourite local divinities of the Romanised Britons, originating for the most part from the adoption into the tolerant Pantheon of Rome of the older objects of native superstitious reverence."

Henzen, n, 5921, gives the first inscription from the 1st ed. of Stuart's *Caledonia Romana*, and subjoins the brief notes :—

"Nomica barbara, fortasse etiam corrupta." "MILIt (avit)." "TVN-GROr." "Corr. PRAEF, cujus nomen male lectam est."

Mr. Wright, *Celt, Roman, and Saxon*, p. 296 (p. 299, 2nd ed.) translates (1) thus :—

> To the goddess Viradesthi,
> Pagus Condustris
> a soldier in
> the second Cohort of Tungrians
> under Sivus
> Auspex
> the Prefect.

PAGVS, in both inscriptions, seems to me to be not a proper name, but the ordinary term, used by Cæsar and Tacitus, for "a district." See Cæsar, *B.G.* i., 37; iv., 1 ; and Tacitus, *Germ.* 39. CONDRVSTIS (or perhaps CONDRVSTVS—a form used in the middle ages) and VELLAVS are, in my judgment, ethnic adjectives, the former derived from CONDRUSI, the latter from VELLAI. The *Condrusi* and *Vellai* are both mentioned by Cæsar, *B.G.* ii., 4, and vii., 75. The *Condrusi* were neighbours of the *Eburones*, who were succeeded by the *Tungri*. The *Vellai, Vellavi, Vellavii, *Vellauni,* or *Velauni* were a people of Gallia Celtica, or Aquitania, as the latter term was extended in signification under Augustus.

They are noticed by Strabo, iv., 2, and Pliny, iv., 19, and their name is found in inscriptions: e. gr.—

* See p. 172.

R 2

ETRVSCILLAE
AVG·CONIVGI
AVG.Ñ
CIVITAS VELLAVOR
LIBERA

The Etruscilla mentioned in this inscription is Herennia Cupressenia Etruscilla, the wife of the emperor Trajanus Decius, which fixes the date to the middle of the 3rd century after Christ.

Libera of course indicates the independence of the Vellavi. They were free, however, in the time of Strabo, although in that of Cæsar, *B.G.* vii., 75, they were in subjection to the Arverni.

For other inscriptions relative to this people, see *Mem. des antiquaries de France,* iv., pp. 87 and 528.

MILI (or MILT) and MILIT are abbreviations of *militans*— not of *militavit,* as Henzen states, for the verb is in the omitted final formula—and SIVO (or SIVOD, the ancient form of the dative and ablative, as given in the illustration), is an erroneous reading of SILVIO, as appears from the following inscription also found at Birrens :—

MARTI ET VICTO
RIAE·AVG·C·RAE
TI MILIT·IN COH
II TVNGR·CVI·
PRAEEST SILVIVS
AVSPEX PRAEF·
V S L M.

I regard the names of the goddesses, as they appear in the inscriptions, as VIRADESTHI (or VIRADETHI, as it is given in the lithographic representation in the *Caledonia Romana*,) and RICAGMBEDAE; or perhaps the latter is formed of two words. Nothing is known of these deities.   They may possibly have been connected with the towns Virodunum (*Verdun*) and Rigomagus (*Remagen*) ; and it appears to me more probable, that they were local deities of those who erected the altars, than that they were adopted from the Britons. See p. 63. If the reference to *Rigomagus* be correct, it may be inferred that the Vellavians, serving in a Tungrian cohort, adopted a Tungrian deity.

According to the views which I have stated above, I should translate the inscriptions thus :—

(1.) "To the goddess Viradesthi (or Viradethi) the Condrusian district, (*i. e.*, the men from that district) serving in the second Cohort of the Tungrians, under the command of Silvius Auspex Præfect."

(2.) "To the goddess Ricagmabeda the Vellavian district, (*i. e.*, the men from that district) serving in the second cohort of the Tungrians," &c., &c.

P.S.—Since the foregoing remarks were written, I have seen the 3rd vol., part iv., of the "Collectanea Antiqua" by Mr. C. Roach Smith, in which that able and ingenious antiquary offers his views relative to the two altars which have been under consideration. From these I find that he has anticipated me as to the interpretation of *pagus*, the reference to *Rigomagus*, and the emendation of the præfect's name. After a careful consideration, however, of his interpretations, I see no reason for changing the opinions which I had previously expressed.

Subjoined are his remarks :—

" I propose reading it [inscription 2,] thus : 'To the Goddess Ricamaga of the district (*Pagus*) of Beda, Vellaus, serving in the Second Cohort of the Tungri, in discharge of a vow, willingly dedicates.' The *Beda agus* was a tract on the line of the Roman road, from Treves to Cologne, some trace of the original name of which is retained in that of its modern representative Bitburg. In this region was a station or town, called *Rigomagus* or *Ricomagus*; and to this place, I suspect, may the goddess of the Birrens altar be referred ; especially as the dedicator was a Tungrian. The word *pagus* is not unfrequently found, in the sense in which it here appears, in similar inscriptions. Mr. Stuart gives one, copied by Pennant, and also found at Birrens, which was erected also by a Tungrian, to the goddess of the Viradethian (?) Pagus. * * * * Mr. Stuart's reading of the first part is evidently erroneous; and equally so *Sirus Auspicius*, as we may be assured by fig. 2 of our plate [giving the inscription already noticed,] where we have the same præfect in the nominative case, *Silvius Auspex*."

A decisive objection to Mr. Roach Smith's interpretations is that they are inconsistent with *pagus* in the nominative case. His reference to *Bedæ Pagus* seems to confirm the conjecture, that *Ricagmabedæ* was composed of two words, of which the latter *Bedæ* was the name of the goddess. Hence *Beda vicus*, (now Bitburg), in the route a *Treviris Agrippinam*, as given in the Itinerary of Antoninus, derived its appellation; and from it came *Pagus Bedensis*, which is noticed in Wesseling's note. *See Vet. Rom. Itiner. Amstel.*, 1735, p. 373.

§ 115. In the preceding article, I cited an inscription on an altar found at Birrens, with the object of establishing the correct reading of the *nomen* of a præfect of the second cohort of the Tungrians. As doubts, however, exist relative to the interpretation of parts of this inscription, I now propose directing special attention to it.

MARTI ET VICT°
RIAE · AVG.C.R**
TIMILIT · IN COH
II TVNGR · CVI ·
PRAEEST SILVIVS
AVSPEX · PRÆF ·
V S L M

Prof. D. Wilson (*Preh. Ann.*, p. 398) figures the altar, and renders the inscription thus :—"MARTI ET VICTORIÆ AUGUSTÆ CENTURIÆ TIRONUM MILITUM IN COHORTE SECUNDA TUNGRORUM, CUI PRÆEST SILVIUS AUSPEX, VOTUM SOLVERUNT LUOENTES MERITO."

In the *Caledonia Romana*, 2nd ed., by Prof. Thomson, p. 128, we have the following translation of this rendering :—

"To Mars and Victory, the Companies Augustæ of young soldiers in the second cohort of the Tungrians, commanded by Silvius Auspex, Præfect, most willingly have performed their vow."

As this interpretation is evidently unsatisfactory, Prof. Thomson suggests that "The letters C · RAETI probably refer to 100 Raeti, that is, soldiers drawn from the north of Italy and south east of Germany; if so, the term Augustæ must be taken as an epithet of the Goddess Victory."

Mr. C. Roach Smith, *Collect. Antiq.* iii. p. 203,—"suggests the following reading, emending that given by Dr. Wilson only as regards the name of the person who erected the altar :— *Marti et Victoriæ Augustæ C. Raetius militaris in cohorte secunda Tungrorum cui præest Silvius Auspex Præfectus votum solvit lubens merito.*"—but this reading of C·RAETI MILIT· seems very improbable.

AVG—for AVGVSTÆ—should unquestionably be joined with VICTORIÆ, as there are numerous similar examples ; C, as I think, stands for CIVES, as it is frequently used in inscriptions ; Prof. Thomson's suggestion, in my judgment, gives the true reading, RAETI, the ethnic adjective of RAETIA : and MILIT is the abbreviation of MILITANTES. From this and a preceding inscription relative to the Tungrians, we learn that in addition to their own countrymen, Vellavians and citizens of Raetia were serving in their ranks. This is as might be expected, and agrees with the inference which may be drawn from many sepulchral inscriptions, that the soldiers in the *alæ* or auxiliary cohorts were sometimes of nations different from that which gave name to the *ala* or cohort. See Henzen, *Annall. Inst. Arch.* 1850, and n. 5838.

§ 116. The following inscription, mentioning the same Præfect is on an altar, also found at Birrens : —

DEAE

MINERVAE

COH II TVN

GRORVM

MIL EQ CL

CVI PRAEEST CS L

AVSPEX PRAEF.

Prof. D. Wilson, *Preh. Ann.* p. 397, renders it thus :—DEÆ MINERVÆ, COHORTIS SECUNDÆ TUNGRORUM MILITIA EQUESTRIS CONSTANTINI LEGIONIS, CUI PRÆEST CAIUS LUCIUS AUSPEX PRÆFECTUS.

In the *Caledonia Romana,* 2nd ed., Prof. Thomson, p. 129, we find the following translation of this rendering :—" ' *To the Goddess Minerva, the Cavalry of the Second Cohort of Tun-*

grians of the Constantine legion, commanded by Caius Lucius
Auspex Prefect.' The cohort was the tenth part of a legion, and
hence the apparent *transposition* in this translation."

There are many obvious objections to this interpretation,
and it is plain that it cannot be received. COH II TVNG.
RORVM stand for COHORS SECVNDA TVNGRORVM
and indicate that the altar was erected by the cohort,
V·S·L·M· or the verb *posuit, dedicavit,* or some similar term
being omitted, as is of frequent occurrence. As to MIL EQ CL,
we have already, p. 15, met with these abbreviations applied to this
cohort in the sense, *Mil[iaria] eq[uitata] c[ivium] L[atinorum].*

The only other point, which deserves attention, is the name of
the Prefect, C·S·L·AVSPEX. Instead of the reading which has
been proposed, *Caius Lucius Auspex,* I would suggest that I
between S and L has been overlooked, that SIL is an abbreviation
of SILVIVS, and that the full names of the officer mentioned
in this and the other inscriptions, were *Caius Silvius Auspex.*

According to my views, the inscription may be translated
thus :—

" To the goddess Minerva, the second cohort of the Tungrians,
a thousand strong, furnished with cavalry, consisting of Latin
citizens, under the command of Caius Silvius Auspex, Prefect,"—
have erected this altar.

§ 117. There was also found here a pedestal of a small statue
of Fortune, bearing an inscription : Mr. Stuart, p. 129, expands
and translates it thus :—

FORTVNAE R	FORTVNAE REDVCI PRO
SALVTE P. CAM.	SALVTE P·CAMMII
ITALICI PRAEF CO	ITALICI, PRAEFECTI COHORTIS—
TVN CELER LIBER	TVNGRORVM, CELER
LLM	LIBERTVS, VOTVM SOLVIT
	LIBENTISSIM*O MERITO

Which may be translated: *To returned Fortune, in gratitude for the restored health of Cammius Italicus, Prefect of the . . . cohort of the Tungrians
Celer the freedman [dedicates this,] most willingly performing his vow.*

---

* Read R.

To these observations is subjoined the note :

The number of the cohort is illegible. This *Celer* was, we may suppose a former slave of *Commius*, and had most probably erected the altar to Fortune as a grateful expression of his feeling for benefits conferred. [A learned friend has favoured me with a different version of this inscription, taken from a copy in the hand-writing of the well known antiquary, Dr. Robert Clapperton of Lochmaben, whose name repeatedly occurs in the early transactions of the Society of Antiquaries of Scotland.

FORTVNAE RECVPERATA	To Fortune, on the recovery of his health,
SALVTE P.CAMPANVS	P. Campanus, Prefect of the First Italic
ITALICAE 'P.PÆ COH.I	Cohort of Tungrians . . . willingly per-
TVNG FLER. LIBERTVS	his vow.—Ed.] [formed
V. I. L. M.	

To Mr. Stuart's expansion I see no objection except the use of *libentissime* for *libens' lotus*. The note L· L· were read by Scaliger and by many since his time, as, *libentissime*, but Orelli, n. 2101, points out that the words *votum solvit latus libens*, being *in extenso* in that inscription, determine the correct reading. See also Henzen, n. 5875. His translation, also, requires emendation. *Fortuna relux* does not mean *returned fortune*, but *fortune causing the return, bringing home*. See p. 18. Celer's master was most probably absent when he erected the altar. *Pro salute*, also, does not mean *for the restored health*. If that had been the meaning we should have had *ob salutem*. The version of the inscription, noticed by Professor Thomson in the note, has not the semblance of probability to recommend it. It is both unprecedented and unintelligible.

§ 118. "Another stone," Mr. Stuart continues, on the same page, "is said to have been found at or near Birrens, which refers to the same "Tungri;" it bears an epitaph to the memory of Ordinatus, most likely one of their tribunes, who was probably interred at this station, and had been erected by his widow, as we learn from the inscription :—

"DIIS MANIBVS AFVTIANO BASSI ORDINATO
Tribuno COHortis II
TVNG*rorum* FLAVIA BAETICA CONIVNX FACiendum
CVRAVIT"

The name of this tribune was certainly not *Ordinatus*. It was contained in the words, which have been misread as AFVTIANO BASSI. ORDINATO is used in the same sense as ORDINATVS > IN LEG. IIII in Henzen's, n. 6773, i. e., *ordinatus centurio in legione quarta*. Lange, p. 46, thinks that *ordinatus* is there used in the sense of *ordinarius*. I question it, but I have not been able to satisfy myself as to the distinction. A similar doubt exists as to ORD. in the inscription given by Bruce, p. 196.

§ 119. In the *Caledonia Romana*, p. 202, we find the following note by Professor Thomson :—

"A Roman inscription found on the right bank of the Rhine, has already been referred to, which is the work of one of the Horasti stationed there as a body of Roman Auxiliaries. Another inscription from the same locality, which supplies the date, (consulship of Presens and Albinus, A.D., 239,) is as follows :—

> I N Π D D BAIOLI
> ET VEXILLARI COL
> LEGIO VICTORIEN
> SIVM SIGNIFER
> ORVM GENIVM D
> E SVO FECERVNT
> VIII KAL OCTOBR
> PRESENTE ET ALBINO
> COS
> II.XIII.D.S.R.

"This inscription, for which we are indebted to Mr. C. R. Smith,(" *Collect. Antiq.*, vol. ii., p. 135,) has been thus extended by him :—' In honorem domus divinæ, Bajoli et Vexillarii collegio Victoriensium signiferorum, genium de suo fecerunt, VIII Kal. Octobris, Presente et Albino Consulibus, Heredes† XIII de suo restituerunt.' That is, so far as correct translation is possible :—' In honor of the abode or temple of the gods, the carriers and standard-bearers of the guild of the Victorian standard-bearers, erected this to their tutelary deity at their own expense, on the eighth Kalends of October, Presens and Albinus being consuls. Their thirteen heirs restored it at their own expense.' D D may perhaps more probably be an abbrevia-

---

* Mr. Smith, in the passage referred to by Prof. Thomson, observes :—" This inscription commemorates the restoration of the monument (by the persons whose names appear on the sides,) which originally had been erected by the porters, (bajuli,) the *vexillarii*, and the standard-bearers (and the *vexillarii* in the guild of the standard bearers) of the Victoriana, in honour of the divine house, during the consulship of Presens and Albinus, (A. D. 239."

tion for Deorum [Deorum]. The Victorienses mentioned in the inscription
are supposed by local antiquaries to have been natives of the locality; but
Mr. Smith, with greater consistency, refers it to the VICTORIA of North
Britain, which Ptolemy names as one of the towns of the Damnii. The
Notitia furnishes abundant evidence of the care with which the barbarian
auxiliaries were removed to a distance from their native provinces, and
enables us to trace those drafted from Britain to Gaul, Spain, and even to the
East, as well as, from the evidence furnished by such inscriptions, to the
banks of the Rhine."—ED.

There are serious errors in this note, some of which it may
be useful to point out. The consulship of Præsens and Albinus
was not in A.D. 239, but in A.D. 246. D D do not mean
" the abode or temple of the gods," nor are they an abbreviation
for *Deorum*. They signify the " imperial family," for which they
are very commonly used. See p. 126. The words *genium de
suo fecerunt* do not mean " erected this to their tutelary deity at
their own expense," but " erected this Genius at their own expense," viz., the figure, which stood on the base bearing the inscription. In the expansion of H·*XIII·D·S·R—*heredes *XIII
de suo restituerunt*—Prof. Thomson follows Mr. Smith, who
seems to have derived this strange reading from Steiner, *Inscript.
Rom. Rhen.*, n. 759.

There cannot, I think, be a reasonable doubt that the expansion of H, adopted by Orelli, n. 988, is preferable, scil., *hi*, referring
to the persons named on two other sides of the base. I also much
prefer the opinion that *Victoria* was the ancient name of *Nieder-
baber*, where the inscription was found.

Mr. Smith, *Collect. Antiq.*, ii., p. 134, gives another inscrip-

---

* This is given by both Mr. Smith and Prof. Thomson in mistake for XIII., as there are
14 names on the sides, scil.,

PATERNVS	SATVLLVS
PRVDENS	SATTARA
MARIANVS	MACRINVS
DAGOVASSVS	LAETVS
CERIALIS	APOLLINARIS
ATVRO	SECVNDANVS
VICTOR	VASVS

In the date also they both give VIII.KAL.OCTOBR. instead of VIIII.KAL.OCTOBR. It is
worthy of remark that the day is the same as that mentioned, p. 126, in the inauguration of
a building at Caerleon. Was there the same reason for the selection of the day? And was
it because it was the birthday of the first Augustus?

I 3

tion found at the same place, in which, following Steiner, n. 756, he finds mention of the Horesti, a tribe of North Britons. Prof. Thomson, *Caledonia Romana*, p. 102, adopts Mr. Smith's views. The inscription is variously read, and is very difficult to interpret. Neither the reading nor the interpretation, given by Steiner and adopted by Mr. Smith and Prof. Thomson, appears to me to be satisfactory. I prefer the reading given by Lersch, C. M., iii, 101, and subsequently adopted by Steiner in *Inscript. Dan. et Rhen.*, n. 919, scil. :—

IDVS OCTOB GHNIO
HOR N BRITTONVM
A · IBKIOMARIVS · OPPI
VS POSITTVM QVINTA
NIISIS POSIT VII

I also prefer the interpretation suggested by Borghesi, *Ann.*, 1839, p. 138, *scil.*, GENIO HOR[REORVM] N[VMERI] BRITTONVM. There is no ground for the supposition that "the Quintanenses were probably a people of the locality." Henzen's conjecture—*quintanensis*—a soldier of the fifth legion—is much more plausible. See Henzen, n. 5781.

§ 120. In Horsley's *Britannia Romana*, Scotland, n. xxix., we have a copy of the inscription on an altar found at *Cramond :—

MATRIBALA
TERVIS. ET
MATRIBCAM
PESTRIBCOIII
TVNGRINS
VERSCARM
OI²· SXXVV

"The altar was erected to the DEAE MATRES, here called ALA-TERVAE, (probably from the ancient name of the place,) as also CAM-PESTRES, by the *cohors prima* TUNGRORUM. So far I think all the copies agree. Indeed the numeral I does not appear distinctly; but since it is the first cohort of the Tungrians that occurs in other inscriptions, 'tis probable that it has been the same also in this. But what to make of the rest of the inscription I know not. I sometimes imagine the next words might have been *instituerunt sacram aram*. This appears not disagreeable to the remains of the letters; and then the last line may possibly have been thus: CONL·RES·XX·V·V : *conlapsam restituit (legio) ricerima valens victrix.*"

Gough, *Camden's Britannia*, iv., p. 55, observes : "Dr. Stukeley read the last lines

VIP·COMIM
Q·LEG·XXV."

Stuart, *Caledonia Romana*, ed. Prof. Thomson, p. 167, adopts Horsley's suggestions as to the interpretation, but, following Gordon, gives as the reading of the last two lines

VEP·SNM
OIRS XXVV.

Of the origin of the epithet ALATERVIS I have already

---

* See p. 144.

expressed an opinion in p. 146; I shall therefore limit my present remarks to the difficulty which exists relative to the last two lines. They are so defective, and the differences of the proposed readings are so great that it is, I fear, hopeless to attempt to restore them. I entertain but little doubt, however, that they contained the name and rank of some officer, probably a centurion or tribune, of the 20th *Valeria Victrix*, and that INS at the end of the 5th line stands for INSTANTE, denoting that the altar was raised by the Tungrian Cohort, under the superintendence of that officer. See p. 16.

This opinion is supported by the inscription on an altar, found at Rough Castle in 1843, and figured in *plate* xv., Stuart's *Caledonia Romana*. The inscription is read and expanded by him thus :—

VICTORIAE	VICTORIAE
COH VI NER	COHORS SEXTA NERVIORVM C — —
VIORVM C — —	A · BEL - O CENTVRIO
A · BEI - - x) LEG.	LEGIONIS VICESIMAE
XX VV	VALENTIS VICTRICIS
V·S·L·L·M	VOTUM SOLVIT LIBENTISSIME ME.
	[RITO.

Stuart regarded the inscription as " a dedication to victory by the Sixth Cohort of the Nervian auxiliaries, who were commanded, as far as we can ascertain the name, by A · BELIO, a Centurion in the Twentieth Legion *Valens Victrix*" To his remarks he subjoins the note: " We cannot be certain of the letters which ought to be inserted here, they are so indistinct upon the stone; but they are most probably the initials of the words CVI PRAEFST, 'commanded by.'" I have but little doubt that the* indistinct letters (as represented in the plate) in the third line after VIORVM are INS· standing for INSTANTE and that the symbol before LEG in the fourth line is the ordinary > for centurion. It is not easy to form an opinion relative to the name of the individual. Stuart's A · BELIO would suggest *Aulus Belius*, which I disapprove : perhaps the *cognomen* was BELLICVS or BELICVS.

* Mr. Stuart reads the first letter C : if this be true, the letters are CVR· for CVRANTE.

These altars furnish additional illustrations of the usage of placing legionary centurions, detached from their legions, over auxiliary bodies. See Henzen, nn. 6740, 6787. This usage explains the meaning of *suo* in the inscription, given in p. 147. In Horsley's *Yorkshire*, n. 1, we have the very rare case of one auxiliary body executing a work under the direction of the commanding officer of another :—

COH·I·THR
ACVM·REST
ITVIT·CVRAN
TE·VAL·FRON
TONE PRAEF
EQ·ALAE VETTO

i. e., cohors prima Thracum restituit curante Valerio Frontone praefecto equitum alae Vettonum.

§ 121. In Stuart's *Caledonia Romana*, p. 159, ed. Prof. Thomson, we find the following explanation of an inscription on an altar found at Inveresk :—

" APOLLINI
GRANNO
Q LVSIVS
SABINIA
NVS
PROC
AVG
V·SS·L·V·M

Apollini Grannico Quintus Lusius Sabinianus Proconsul Augusti ; votam susceptum solvit lubens volens merito.

To Apollo Granicus, Quintus Lusius Sabinianus the Proconsul of Augustus [dedicates this] a self-imposed vow, cheerfully performed."

To this is subjoined the following note :—"The *pronomen Lusius* is frequently given in Gruter. *Lucius* or *Luscius* is, however, more common."

GRANNO and PROC. are the only parts of the inscrip-

tion which present any doubt worth considering. Stuart
seems to have adopted the opinion expressed by Camden, that
" *Apollo Grannus* among the Romans was the same with the Grecian
'Απόλλων ἀκερσεκόμης, that is, *long-locked ;* for Isidore calls
the long hair of the Goths *granni.*" Dr. Thurnam, *Hist. Eth-
nol. Cran. Brit. Dec.* iv., more probably traces the name to
grian, the Gaelic name of the sun, and observes that the old
name of Aix la Chapelle, *Aquis granum*, shows the same derivation. He also refers to Orelli, nn. 1997–2000, where we
have the same 'Apollini Granno.'

As to LVSIVS, it is plain from Stuart's remarks that he mistook the meaning of *prænomen.* Accordingly he makes statements which are erroneous and suggests doubts, where there is
no room for one. Horsley, in his expansion, unaccountably reads
LVCIVS, for which there is no reason. The LVSIA is a well-
known *gens*, members of which are named in several inscriptions.
The expansion of PROC. into *proconsul* is erroneous : it probably stands for *procurator.*

§ 122. A funereal tablet, which was found many years ago in the Roman station at Ardoch, is figured in Stuart's *Caledonia Romana*, ed. Prof. Thomson, pl. v., fig. 5, and the following explanation is given of the inscription :—

DIS MANIBVS
AMMONIVS DA
MIONIS * COH
I HISPANORVM
STIPENDIORVM
XXVII HEREDES
F C

"To the shade of Ammonius Damion, Centurion of the First Cohort of the Spanish Stipendiaries, who served for 27 years, his heirs have erected this monument."

To this translation are subjoined notes to the effect, that others have regarded *Damionis* as governed by *filius* or *servus* understood; and that it would perhaps be more correct to join xxvii to *heredes,*— i. e., his twenty-seven heirs.

Horsley, *Britannia Romana*, p. 205, expresses his preference for considering *Damionis* as the nominative case, and compares such names as *Petilius Cerealis.*

It is not easy to discover where Stuart found any authority for the word *Stipendiaries*, which he introduces into his translation, for on the supposition that he mistook the meaning of *Stipendiorum*, we are then at a loss for the Latin denoting "who served for." Nor is it possible to reconcile *Ammmius* in the nominative with his translation—"of Ammonius Damion." Professor Thomson's suggestion to connect xxvii with *heredes* is so obviously unwarrantable, that it is surprising that any one could for a moment have entertained the idea. There is no doubt that the words—COH I HISPANORVM STIPENDIORVM XXVII HEREDES F·C·—mean "of the first cohort of Spaniards, of twenty-seven years' service, his heirs have caused [this memorial] to be erected;" and the only questionable point is as to *Damionis*. I am inclined to take it as the genitive case, F either being omitted as is not rare, or perhaps obliterated by the fracture of the stone between S and C, where there seems to be sufficient space both for it and for >, the symbol of *centurio*.

§ 123. An altar, probably found at or near Eildon, is figured in Stuart's *Caledonia Romana*, ed. Prof. Thomson, pl. vi., fig. 2. Prof. Thomson reads and translates the inscription thus :—

"CAMPESTR	Campestribus
SACRVM AEL	Sacrum Ælius
MARCVS	Marcus
DEC° ALAE AVG	Decurio Alæ Augustæ
VOCONTIO	Vocontio
V·S·L·L·M	Votum solvit libentissime meritis

Dedicated to the field-deities by Aelius Marcus Decurion of the Augustan Wing, a Vocontian[d] (who) performs his vow most cheerfully.

"*d.* The Vocontii inhabited the S. E. of Gaul. We have rendered the above as if it had been *Vocontius*."

I would read the inscription thus :—

CAMPESTR[IBVS]

SACRVM AEL[IVS]

MARCVS

DEC[VRIO] ALAE AVG[VSTAE]

VOCONTIO[RVM]

V[OTVM] S[OLVIT]·L[AETVS] L[IDENS] M[ERITO]

The deities, to whom the altar was erected, were the *matres campestres*. *Marcus* is a rare *cognomen*, but in Mommsen's *Inscript. Neap.*, n. 3836, we have another example of it as borne by an individual also a member of the *Ælia gens*. The *ala Augusta Vocontiorum* is also mentioned in an inscription, given in *Monum. Hist. Brit.*, n. 112 a., as a part *exercitus Britannici*.

Mr. Wright's reading, in the *Celt, Roman, and Saxon*, p. 253 (p. 257, 2nd ed.), of the name of the dedicator as "Marcus Decius Voconticus" is singularly erroneous.

x 2

§ 124. In the year 1830 an altar, in perfect preservation, was found not far from the village of Fildon. It is figured in Stuart's *Caledonia Romana*, p. 152, ed. Prof. Thomson, and bears the following inscription :—

DEO SILVA
NO PROSA
LVTE·SVA·ET
SVORVM CAR
RIVS DOMITI
ANVS > LEGXX
VV·VS·LL·M

Stuart expands it thus : " Deo Silvano, pro salute sua et suorum *Carrius Domitianus centurio legionis vicesimæ valentia victricis votum solvit libentissime merito."

I would emend this expansion by reading *C. Arrius* (*Caius Arrius*) for *Carrius, Valeria* for *valentis,* and *latus libens* for *libentissime.* See pp. 3, 247.

§ 125. Many years ago there was found at *Kilsyth*, near the wall of Antoninus, a grave-stone bearing the following inscription, as given in Gough's Camden, iv., p. 95 :—

D·M
C·IVLII
MARCELLINI
PRAEF
COH·I·HAMIOR

i, e., Diis Manibus Caii Julii Marcellini præfecti cohortis primæ Hamiorum.

Reinesius (*Syntag.* p. 520) suggests THAMIOR, instead of MAMIOR, which was the reading in his copy, and traces the name to *Tamia*, a town in Britain mentioned by Ptolemy. Stuart, *Caledonia Romana*, ed. Prof. Thomson, p. 338, regards the *Hamii* of the inscription, as "auxiliaries, it is probable, from the neighbourhood of the Elbe." Böcking, *Notitia*, ii., p. 932, is disposed to regard the reading HAMIOR as a mistake for NERVIOR, i e., Nerviorum. The name of this people also appears on an altar, found, as Horsley believed, at *Little Chesters* in Northumberland.

DEAE SVRI
AESVBCALP
VRNIO AOR
ICOLALEG·AVG
PR·PR·A·LICINIVS
CLEMENS PRAEF
III·A·IOR

i. e., Deæ Suriæ, sub Calpurnio Agricola legato Augusti pro prætore, Aulus Licinius Clemens præfectus, * *

Horsley states that some had read the last line I HAMIOR,

i. e., primæ Hamiorum, but that he preferred IV GALLOR, *i.e.,*
quartæ Gallorum. In 1831 another altar was found at *Carr-*
corran in Northumberland, which gives further information as to
this people, *Archæologia*, xxiv., 352 :—

> FORTVNAE·AVG·
> PRO·SALVTE·L·AELI
> CAESARIS·EX·VISV
> T·FLA·SECVNDVS
> PRAEF·COH·I·HAM
> IORVM·SAGITTAR
> V·S·L·M

i. e., Fortunæ Augustæ pro Saluto Lucii Ælii Cæsaris ex visu
Titus Flavius Secundus præfectus cohortis primæ Hamiorum
sagittariorum votum solvit libens merito.

From what has been stated, there can, I think, be no doubt
that the first cohort of a people called *Hamii* served in Britain during
the Roman occupation ; but it has not been ascertained who they
were. The conjectures of Reinesius and Stuart are so improbable,
that we must look elsewhere for a solution of the difficulty. Mr.
Wright, *Celt, Roman and Saxon*, p. 295, remarks :—

> "An altar was found at Thirwall, on the wall of Hadrian, dedicated to a
> *dea Hammia*, who is supposed by Hodgson to have been named from *Hamah*
> on the Orontes. Perhaps, however, this goddess may have been named from
> the Hamii, a tribe on the banks of the Elbe, who are found stationed in this
> part of Britain."

Mr. Wright's suggestion that *Dea Hammia*, Bruce's *Roman
Wall*, p. 400, was a local goddess of the *Hamii* seems probable,
but Mr. Hodgson, has, in my judgment, pointed out the native
place of both the deity and the people, when he refers us to
Hamah on the Orontes. The inscription *Deæ Suriæ* supports
this reference, and it is not improbable, that it is the place mentioned in the *Notitia*, *Dux Syriæ*, p. 88, ed. *Böcking*, as *Amatt-*
ha. It was otherwise called by the Syrians, *Hemmath, Hamath,*
and *Chamath*, and is commonly known by its Greek designation,
Epiphania.

§ 126. In Stuart's *Caledonia Romana*, ed. Prof. Thomson, p. 330, we have the following account of one of the altars found at Auchindavy :—

"The second is inscribed, as copied below, to a whole list of the Immortals—Mars, Minerva, the Field Deities, and Victory—besides, apparently, two others, called HERO and EPONA, regarding whom there is much field for conjecture. Professor Anderson imagined the former to be some particular Hero whom Firmus worshipped, and the latter to be the name of a German goddess :—c

"MARTI	MARTI
MINERVAE	MINERVAE
CAMPESTRI	CAMPESTRIBUS
BVS HERO···	HEROI EPONAE
EPONA	VICTORIAE
VICTORIAE	MARCUS COCCEIUS
M· COCCEI	FIRMUS
FIRMUS	CENTURIO LEGIONIS
OLEG·II· AVG.	SECUNDAE AUGUSTAE"

"c He also gives another reading, in which the word CAMPESTRI is coupled with MINERVAE—making the dedication to the Rural Minerva—and for the word HEROI he supplies BVSHERIO—In his opinion another deity of the Germans. It seems, however, to be HEROI in the original."

There can be no doubt that Stuart's reading is correct, except as to* HERO···, which, I am persuaded, should have been read HERO, i. e., HERCVLI or HERCLI. His remark, however, that there is much field for conjecture regarding EPONA is inaccurate. *Epona* is well known to classical scholars from Juvenal, *Sat.* viii., 157, and Apuleius, *Metam.* iii., (cited by Prof. Thomson in a note,) and to epigraphists from some altars on which she is named. See Bruce, *Roman Wall*, p. 398. P. S. Orelli, p. 1555, has anticipated me in conjecturing *Herculi*.

§ 127. Mr. Stuart, *Caledonia Romana*, ed. Prof. Thomson, pl. x., fig. 3, figures the fragment of a tablet, which bears the following imperfect inscription :—

P·LEG· II A
Q·LOLLIO VR
LEG AVG·PR·PR

*Mr. Wright, *Celt, Roman and Saxon*, p. 292, (p. 266, 2nd Ed.) adopts this reading and translates—"to Hero."

Caledonia Romana. In No. 1 of plate VI. of that work,[*] a stone, preserved in the Museum of the Society of Antiquaries of Scotland, is figured, in which the name Lysimachus occurs; but the stone was found, not in Scotland, but in Africa, and Prof. Thomson, in his preface, points out Mr. Stuart's mistake, and acknowledges his own oversight.

[*] The stone is a sepulchral memorial of Antiochis, the daughter of Lysimachus. It is not easy to tell, from the faint copy which I have before me, what the letters are which Mr. Wright read "Caius;" but they unquestionably do not stand for that name. The first letter seems to be L, from which I infer that they most probably are sigla for the year of the Emperor, as is common in the Greek inscriptions of Egypt and Cyrene.

P. S.—Mr. Burgon, *Letters from Rome*, p. 166, strangely remarks, relative to the use of this letter on a grave-stone, bearing a Greek inscription, in the Museum Kircherianum:—

"Would the use of the initials of Αυεδδος, instead of the common word ἔτος, indicate some connection of the persons commemorated with Egypt? It is only on Egyptian coins, I think, that dates are indicated by the initial of that very unusual word for year?" Has he forgotten the numerous examples on stones found, as I have stated above, in Egypt and Cyrene? See Boeckh, *Corp. Inscr. Grœc.*, vol. IX. The L was formerly regarded as standing for Α the first letter of Αυεδδος, an ancient Greek term for a year. See Homer, *Od.*, xiv., 161, xix., 306. This opinion is rejected by Franz, *Elem. Epig. Grœc.*, p. 372.

INDEX.

ADDITIONS AND CORRECTIONS.

P. ix., note. In addition to the authorities stated in the notes, I have also in some cases had the advantage of inspecting photographs, rubbings, and drawings. I have not, however, admitted conjectural readings into the text, even where I had no doubt of their correctness, as my object was to give as correct a representation as I could of what may be regarded as the received text.

P. 3, note †. Mr. Roach Smith, *Collect. Antiq.*, vi., p. 37, prefers tracing this name to *Tanarus*, the river in the north of Italy. The other derivation seems more probable.

P. 3, note ‡. In the *Archæologia Cambrensis*, 3rd series, iv., p. 464, it is stated that "fragments of Roman tiles with the stamp of the Twentieth Legion, VALERIA VICTRIX," were exhibited in the museum at Rhyl. Does this mean that the titles were given in extenso?

P. 4. The *legitimus ordo nominum* is—(1) *prænomen*, (2) *nomen gentilitium*, (3) *nomen patris*, (4) *tribus*, (5) *cognomen*, (6) *patria; e. gr.*, P·SALLIENIVS·P·F·MAECIA·THALA-MVS·HADRIA, in which P·, *Publius*, is the *prænomen*, *Sallienius* the *nomen gentilitium*, P·F·, *Publii filius*, the *nomen patris*, *Maecia* the *tribus*, *Thalamus* the *cognomen*, and *Hadria* the *patria*.

P. 8. For "again," read "†† again."

P. 10. Mr. Roach Smith, *Collect. Antiq.*, vi. p. 30 observes:

"Furius Fortunatus, who set up the altar to Minerva, appears to have held the office of *Magister*, a title of very wide significance; but which, in this instance, may be taken to mean the *Magister* either of some temple dedicated to Minerva, or the consecrated place upon which the statue, yet extant, stood. Thus, in continental inscriptions we find *Magister Fani Dianæ*, *Magister Fani Jenonis*, etc."

I see no reason for changing the opinion, which I have expressed as to the meaning of MAG.

From Mr. Smith's drawing of the altar it seems as if I at the end of the first line, E at the end of the second, and VS at the end of the third, had been lost by fracture of the stone.

P. 13. In Gruter, p. 1085, n. 10, we also have GORDIANO-COS·III ; Clinton, *Fasti Romani*, ii., p. 48, suggests II as a correction.

P. 20. Horsley expands Cumberland, n. lii., thus : " Jovi Optimo Maximo cohortis secundæ Gallorum equitum Titus Domitius Heron de Nicomedia præfectus." We should read *equitata* for *equitum*, as suggested in note p. 59, and I prefer *cohors secunda* for *cohortis secundæ*, supplying *cui præest* before the name of the præfect.

P. 20. Horsley expands n. lv. thus : "Jovi Optimo Maximo pro salute imperatoris Marci Antonii Gordiani pii felicis invicti Augusti et Sabiniæ Furiæ Tranquillæ conjugis ejus totaque domu divina eorum ala Aug. Gordiana ob virtutem appellata posuit cui præest Aemilius Crispinus præfectus equitum natus in provincia Africa de Tusdro sub cura Nonnii Philippi legati Augustalis propraetoris Attico et Praetextato consulibus."

P. 20. Horsley expands Cumberland, n. lvii, thus : " Jovi Optimo Maximo ala Augusta ob virtutem appellata cui præest Publius Ælius Publii filius Sergia [*tribu*] Magnus de Mursa ex Pannonia inferiore præfectus Aproniano et Bradua consulibus."

P. 20, note. For " aro" read " is."

P. 24. For "*cui, præest*," read " *cui præest*."

P. 26. For " *casedesiero*," read " *case desiero*."

P. 27, note. For " third.," read " third ?"

P. 30. Add the note—" Carlisle is regarded as the *Luguvallium* of Antoninus."

P. 30. Add as an example of the use of *civitas*, Henzen, n. 6833: NATVS IN · PROV·THRACIA · CIVIT · PHILIP POL.

P. 32. After " BRITANNIC·· AVG" add II. See p. 48.

P. 46. For " having" read " have."

P. 51. We have here, as I think, an example of the production of lead by a "firm," who leased a mine, *scil.*, "the Roscii brothers ;" and in Orelli, n. 426, we find mention of "a company" for this manufacture. The inscription is SOCIETAT on a block of lead, "in massa plumbea." In n. 427, we have on another block of the same metal S.LVC.RETI, which is explained by Druck-ner as standing for *Societatis Lucii Reti.* I would accept *Socie-tatis* in both, but rather suspect that LVC·RETI stand for LVCRETIORVM or LVCRETIANAE. Perhaps there was a *pagus Lucretius* in Switzerland. From this use of *societas*, we may, perhaps, explain a perplexing inscription on a cake of copper, found at Caer-hen in Caernarvonshire. It is figured in Gough's ed. of Camden, iii., pl. 9, fig. 13, and thus described : "On an oblong square, sunk in the middle," are the letters—

SOCIO
ROMAE

and obliquely across these in smaller characters, NATSOL. Mr. Lluyd supposed the inscription to be "a merchant's stamp or direction to his correspondent at Rome." Mr. Pennant, *Tour in Wales*, i., p. 63, thought that "the mass was consigned by a mer-chant here to his partner at Rome." "The other inscription may be *natio solvit* or *natale solum.*"

There can be but little doubt that neither of these interpreta-tions can be accepted. Does any one suppose that there ever was a time when a consignment, addressed "to my partner at Rome" would have reached its destination ? And what has *natio solvit* or *natale solum* to do with such an article as this ? And yet it is extremely difficult to suggest a feasible explanation of either of the inscriptions. Can it be that SOCIO stands for SOCIORVM, and that NAT·SOL· are abbreviations of the names of the partners ? The meaning of the stamp will thus be that the cake was the manufacture or property of NAT·SOL partners at Rome. I am disposed to prefer this to a conjecture, which at one time occurred to me, that this object had been an offering. The letters SOL SOCIO suggested SOLI SOCIO, often found on altars to Mithras ; and NAT· seemed to be either a misreading of MIT for MITHRAS or N·AT·, N[VMINI] AT[TINOS], *i. e.*, *Numini Attinos, Soli Socio, Romæ.*

P. 59, note. Horsley expands Cumberland, n. lxi., thus:
" Jovi optimo Maximo Lucius Cammius Maximus prefectus
cohortis primæ Hispanorum equitum votum solvit libens merito ;"
and Northumberland, n. lxxxviii., thus : " Numinibus Augustorum cohors quarta Gallorum equitum fecit."

P. 59, note. For " Cumberland, liii.," read " Cumberland, lii."

P. 61. The *duplicarius* received double rations, the *sesquiplicarius* one and a half, and the *derurio* was *triplicarius*. See
Lange, p. 58, not 38, as erroneously given in the note.

P. 62. The designation *Petriana* applied to an *ala* that
served in Britain, as is known from the *Notitia* and several
inscriptions, may be suggested as an exception to this mode of
derivation. Some have traced the name to *Petra*, an Arabian
town ; Pauciroli regards it as derived from the name of its quar.
ters, *scil., Petriana ;* Brotier suggests that it was called *ab equiti-
bus illustribus, quibus Petra nomen ;* whilst Henzen asserts that
it was formed from the name of some man. Böcking questions
this opinion of Henzen, on the ground that the man's name
should have been *Petrius*, of which there is no example, although
there is authority for *Petreius*, which would give *Petreiana.* I
am inclined to agree with Henzen, and also believe it to be more
probable that the place derived its name from the *ala* than the
ala from the place.

P. 69. Omit "(Arab)."

P. 70, note. In Avellino, " Osservazioni sopra alcune iscriz-
ioni e disegni graffiti," p. 20, we have the following inscription,
in which II are used for both E and I :

HIIC VIINATIO PVGNABIIT
V K SIIPTIIMBRIIS
T FIILIX AD VRSOS PVGNABIIT

P. 65, note. Mr. Roach Smith, *Collect. Antiq.*, iv., p. 131,
has anticipated me in the reading "*ex cohorte.*"

P. 71. For "supposition. [Originally, &c.]" read "supposition,
[originally, &c."]

P. 76. For " *vigintiduorum* and " *fuciendum,*" read " *viginti
duorum,*" and " *faciendum.*"

P. 78. Add the note: "Lincoln is the *Lindum* of Antoninus and Ravennas."

P. 80, note. For "MAPONA," read "MAPONO."

P. 83. For " APO[L]INI," read " APOL[L]INI."

P. 87. This stone may have been erected at any time between August 11., 120, and August 11., 121.

P. 92, note. For "BRVSCFIL," read BRVSCF. F may stand for FILIVS, but more probably for FECIT.

P. 93. For "observations" read " observation."

P. 99. For " I " the first letter in the third line of the inscription, read " A." See p. xxxiv., n. cxxvi. In the note, and here, I have not counted D·M· and hence have used third for what is really the fourth line.

P. 104, note. For "evasion" read " resort," which more nearly expresses the meaning of the German word.

P. 107. For "opinion," read "opinions."

P. 107. For " ETThONO" read ETDONO.

P. 111. For "*praefectus*," and " *secundæ*," read "*praefectus* and *secundæ*." There are, I fear, other instances in which the italic *æ* and *œ* have been confused.

P. 114, note. For "MAXSV" read "AXSV."

P. 123. For " 207," read " 208."

P. 134. In the *Gentleman's Magazine*, December, 1862, there is a report of the proceedings of the Society of Antiquaries of Newcastle-upon-Tyne, at their meeting on November 5. The Rev. Dr. Bruce gave the following account of a recent discovery of two altars at the station of *Condercum*:

"On Saturday last (Nov. 1) when the workmen, who are putting in order the ornamental ground adjoining the recently-erected edifice of O. W Rendel, Esq., at Benwell Little Park, were proceeding with their labours, they hit upon something that seemed to be unusual. By Mr. Rendel's directions, they proceeded with caution, and thoroughly excavated the spot which had attracted their attention. The portion of the ground which has been examined lies just outside the east rampart of Condercum, near its south-east angle. There are here, as well as on the south of the station, numerous remains of suburban dwellings, which seem to be straggling to

N 2

free themselves from the sod which envelopes them. A square building, measuring about 15 ft. (inside measurement) each way, was laid bare; four or five courses of wall were standing. Near the south wall two altars were found, lying obliquely, with their inscribed faces downwards (as is usually the case); and in various positions near the spot were several large stones, portions of a statue, and the fragment of an inscribed slab, which may be afterwards alluded to. At the same spot some burials seem to have taken place. Both the altars contain much that is new to the students of lapidary literature: in attempting to make any remarks upon them therefore, after only a few hours' consideration, we may justly claim the liberty of altering or amending at a future time any opinion we may now give.

"The first altar which I shall describe is 4 ft. 4 in. high, and 16 in. wide in the body. It is formed of a sandstone of the district, and is in some places reddened by fire. The decorations upon it are of a highly ornate character, tastefully designed and skilfully executed. The face of the capital has been broken off; but a portion of the face was found close at hand, and it enables us to ascertain what the whole was when complete. The altar is carved on all four sides; this is an unusual, though not quite singular circumstance; an altar now at Castle Nook, near Alston, being also ornamented on the back as well as the sides. The altar is provided with a focus; and the volutes on each side of it seem to have had for their model a bundle of leaves of Indian corn. An altar which I saw in Florence last autumn, impressed me with the idea that the rolls on the top of the capitals of the Roman altar were symbolical of the fagots which were to consume the offering; this altar confirmed me in the opinion. On the sides of the capital we have vine-branches shaded with leaves, and laden with bunches of grapes. The mouldings of the base are graceful; two of them are of the kind called the cable pattern, so often used in Norman architecture, and thought to be peculiar to the Gothic style. One side of the altar has, in basso relievo, the sacrificing knife, the other the pitcher for holding the wine used in the sacrifice; and on the back is a circular garland. The inscription on the face of the altar is well cut, and the letters are of most tasteful form, but several of them are tied together after the manner of our modern diphthongs. These tied letters are generally understood to indicate a somewhat advanced period of the empire. The inscription, deprived of its complications, is—

DEO
ANTENOCITICO
ET NVMINIB.
AVGVSTOR.
AEL. VIBIVS
⊃ LEG. XX. V. V.
V. S. L. M.

which may be read in English,—'To the god Antenociticus and the deities of the Emperors, Ælius Vibius, a centurion of the Twentieth Legion, styled the Valerian and the Victorious, freely dedicated this altar, in the discharge of a vow to objects most worthy of it.' The god *Antenociticus* is quite new to us. Prior to this discovery, we had no idea that any such demon as he graced the calendar of heathen Rome. Beside the greater and lesser deities of Greece and Rome, there is a crowd of local deities that are only known to the 'painful students' of stony mythology. Among the district gods of Roman Britain we have Vitres, Hamia, Setlocenia, Mounus, Mogon, Belatucader, and Cocidius; and an altar recently found near Petriana (Walton-house) seems to reveal to us another strange god of the name of Venauntii. This altar, so far as I can understand it, makes known to us still another. Whether the name is derived from the district where the deity was supposed to exercise his sway, or whether it is descriptive of his qualities, I am at present unable to give any opinion. The genius or godship of the emperors was often worshipped, and that seems to have been the case here. It will be observed that the emperors are spoken of in the plural number,—AVGVSTORVM. The other altar also which we have to consider, speaks of a plurality of emperors. Who can have been intended? We have a plurality of emperors in the time of Antoninus the Philosopher, when he shared the purple with Lucius Verus; in the time of Severus, when he associated his two sons with himself; and at the close of the short reign of Elagabalus, when he called Severus Alexander to divide with him obloquy and danger. We need scarcely go farther in this enumeration, for the style of this altar does not belong to a later age. Possibly it was carved when Septimius Severus, and his sons Caracalla and Geta, were the lords of this lower creation.

"The other altar is not nearly so ornate as the first. Neither its design nor its execution is good. The letters of the inscription are rudely formed. It has probably been committed to unskilful hands, for circumstances seem to warrant the opinion that it must have been nearly contemporaneous with the other. It has no focus. The inscription reads thus :—

DEO ANOCITICO
IVDICIIS OPTIMO-
RVM MAXIMORVM
QVM IMPP. N. SVB TID: (VLP.?)
MARCELLO COS. TINE-
IVS LONGVS IN PRAE-
FECTVRA EQVITV. .
LATO CLAVO EXORN. .
TVS ET Q. D.

which may be translated,—'Tineius Longus, holding office in the Praefect-ship of knights, adorned with the broad stripe, and a quaestor, dedicated this altar to Anociticus (gg. Antenociticus), in consequence of the decisions of our most excellent and most mighty emperors given under Tibius Marcellus, a man of consular rank.' The first thing that perplexes us in this inscription is the similarity of the name of this god with that on the other, and yet they are different. Probably the same god is meant, and most likely the first A on this altar is intended to stand for ARX on the other, though there is nothing to indicate it. At the end of the first line there is a character resembling a q; close examination induces me to suppose that it is only the leaf-shaped stop so often introduced in inscriptions. I was in hope when I saw the epithets *optimorum maximorum* that I should have been able by them to have ascertained the emperors to whom they were applied; but I have not succeeded. These terms (*optimus* and *maximus*) are frequently applied to Trajan, both on coins and sculptures, and occasionally to Antoninus Pius, but I can find no instance of their being applied to any of the conjoint emperors. The nearest approach to it that I have yet observed is on the Arch of Severus at Rome. Originally the names of the two sons of Severus were appended to his own, but when Caracalla murdered Geta, he had his brother's name struck out from the inscription, and the gap filled up with the words OPTIMIS FORTISSIMISQVE PRINCIPIBVS. It may be that this altar belongs to the time of Severus. The flattery implied in the use of the words *optimus maximus* will be noticed when it is remembered that these are the epithets almost universally applied upon altars to Jupiter, the king of gods and men. The last letter on the fourth line is indistinct; it looks like an N, but it is possibly a B, the rounded parts of the letters having been worn off with the angle of the altar. *Tincius* is a somewhat peculiar name, but several examples of it occur in Gruter. The expression *Lato clavo exornatus* is now in the altars of the north of England. It no doubt indicates that the person possessed senatorial rank. In Rich's 'Illustrated Latin Dictionary' we have the following explanations of *Clavus Latus*:—'The broad stripe; an ornamental band of purple colour, running down the front of a tunic, in a perpendicular direction, immediately over the front of the chest, the right of wearing which formed one of the exclusive privileges of the Roman senator, though at a late period it appears to have been sometimes granted as a favour to individuals of the equestrian order.' There is a passage in Suetonius's Life of Augustus Cæsar which seems to throw some light upon this subject. He says, 'That the sons of senators might become early acquainted with the administration of affairs, he permitted them, at the age when they took the garb of manhood (*toga virilis*), to assume also the distinction of the senatorian robe, with its broad border (*latum clavum induere*), and to be present at the debates in the senate-house. When they entered the military service, he not only gave them the rank of military tribunes in his legions, but likewise the command of the auxiliary horse. And that all might have an opportunity of acquiring military experience, he commonly joined two sons of senators in command of each troop of horse.' Although Suetonius refers to a state of things more than a century earlier than the erection of this altar, it almost seems as if he had written this sentence by way of explaining to us this inscription. Tincius Longus, though probably not having a seat in the senate-house, was a man of senatorial rank, and was sent to flesh his sword in the flanks of

Caledonians worthy of his steel. The last two letters in the inscription may admit of some question. Probably in addition to his other orders, he held the rank of quæstor, which is indicated by the initial letter of the word. Most likely D stands for *dicavit*, 'he dedicated.' It will be observed that Tineius Longus, while doing honour to his god, does not neglect his own dignities. These he blazons forth in considerable detail. Is he the only person who has made religion a stalking-horse to personal applause? For many a century the name of Tineius Longus was buried in oblivion; now at length the altar, once more brought to the light of day, is true to its trust, and the blushing honours of its dedicator will gain greater celebrity than ever. All who are familiar with the inscriptions found in the north of England will be prepared to admit the fact, which this stone presses upon us, that Rome sent some of her greatest men to Britain. A leaf fills up a blank at the close of the last line. The letters on this altar have been coated with red paint. The remains of this are clearly to be discerned. I think that the other altar has been similarly treated, though the marks of it are not distinct. Most of the inscriptions found in the catacombs of Rome are painted red, but this is the first time I have known any of our local inscriptions to be coloured."

The report then gives a conversation relative to the building and skeletons, in which Mr. Reudel, Mr. Clayton, and Dr. Bruce took part.

"Mr. Clayton then said that he had that morning inspected these altars, and sketched out a reading of the inscriptions, which he had the satisfaction now to find was substantially the same as that of Dr. Bruce. The altars are dedicated to a god hitherto unknown, probably a British god. One of them is very beautiful in design and execution, and (with the exception, perhaps, of the fine altar preserved by Lord Lonsdale in Whitehaven Castle) is superior to any thing yet found in Britain; this altar is probably of the date of Hadrian, it is dedicated by a centurion of the 20th Legion, which was stationed in this part of the country in the reign of Hadrian, and was soon afterwards moved southwards. The other altar is of ruder workmanship, and would seem to belong to a lower period of the Empire. If he (Mr. Clayton) rendered correctly the words SUB ULPIO MARCELLO, the date would be fixed in the reign of Commodus. Dr. Bruce had justly observed that Tineius Longus, the dedicator of this altar, appeared to have been a vain man. Not so Ulpius Marcellus, the general of Commodus, who retrieved the Roman affairs in Britain, then in a desperate state, and yet no traces of his name have been found any where on the Roman Wall, except on a fragment of a stone at Cilurnum. It was the practice of the Roman soldier, in dedicating to a god of the country in which he was placed, to join one of his own divinities. The combination with the British god of the 'deities of the emperors,' on the first altar, is not unusual. The combination on the second altar of the 'judicial decrees of the best and greatest of our emperors' was, he believed, unique.

"Dr. Bruce said that as soon as he had seen the altars he wrote to Mr. Roach Smith, one of their best Roman antiquaries, asking for his opinion upon it. He had received a reply to that letter on his way to the meeting. The Rev. Dr. then read the letter alluded to, in which Mr. Smith, after the usual acknowledgments, went on to say, 'I am quite delighted to see such discoveries. I hope we shall be puzzled with them much more. Who the god Antenociticus was, I expect will, after all our researches, be a question. It may be a topical name; or it may be an epithet applied to Apollo, or the Sun. . . . I never before met with the *lotus clavus* in an inscription.'

"Dr. Bruce said he thought Mr. Clayton's suggestion, that the praenomen of MARCELLUS was ULPIUS and not VICTOR, was very valuable, and most likely correct. The only letter about which there could be a question was the L, and as the three letters VLP, were crowded together at the end of the line, it would be nothing wonderful if the bottom stroke of that letter should be shorn of its due proportions. The last letter, the R, L, or P, was confessedly imperfect, in consequence of the angle of the stone. Profiting by Mr. Clayton's suggestion, he would again examine the altar."

In the number for January, 1863, there is a notice of the December meeting of the Society of Antiquaries, Newcastle-upon-Tyne, in which further information is given relative to this discovery.

"Dr. Bruce produced rubbings of the two altars recently found at Benwell, shewing clearly that V L P, as suggested by Mr. Clayton, was the correct reading. If, however, the general Ulpius Marcellus had been meant, he would have been designated as legate; and the stone also speaks of a plurality of emperors. But there was a jurist of the name, the legal adviser of Antoninus Pius; he flourished during the period of Aurelius and Verus, who were both Augusti in the years 161—169. There may be some connexion between the jurist and the judleis of the inscription. The jurist seems distinct from the soldier of the reign of Commodus."

The difficulty common to the two inscriptions is the name of the deity. It is not improbable that *Antenociticus* and *Anociticus* represent the same god, but I have never before met with either designation, and am unable to offer any probable suggestion on the subject. The other portions of the first inscription are so plain that it is unnecessary to offer any remark on them; but the second is by no means clear. Dr. Bruce's translation and interpretation appear to me very unsatisfactory; nor can I at all understand on what ground he states, with reference to the passage that he cites from Suetonius, *Augustus*, 38,—"it almost seems as if he had written this sentence by way of explaining to us this inscription." To me it seems to render the interpretation more difficult, for on the stone we find Tineius Longus, whilst he was *præfectus equitum*—for this is clearly the meaning of *in præfectura equitum*—adorned with the laticlave. There is a passage, however, in Suetonius, *Claudius*, 25, which when compared with Vegetius, ii., 7, seems to me to throw much light on the inscription. The first is—*equestres militias ita ordinavit, ut post cohortem, alam; post alam, tribunatum legionis daret;* the second—*tribunus major per epistolam sacram Imperatoris judicio destinatur. Minor tribunus provenit ex labore.* From these passages we learn that Claudius made the tribuneship of a legion a higher grade of service than the præfecture of an *ala, i. e.,* that the promotion should be from *præfectura equitum* to *tribunatus legionis.* We also learn that there were two classes of tribunes—the greater and the less. The higher office was conferred by order or division of the emperor—the other, the lower, was obtained by service. There can, I think, be no doubt that these two classes are the same otherwise called—*tribuni laticlavii,* and *tribuni angusticlavii.* Compare Suetonius, *Domitian,* 10, *Otho,* 10, and Horace, *Sat.* i., 6, 25-28. Accordingly I regard the words—*in præfectura equitum lato clavo exornatus*—as denoting that Tineius Longus was promoted to the office of *tribunus laticlavius* whilst he held the office of *præfectus equitum.* And in precisely the same sense I understand the verse, in the inscription found at Caervoran, given by Dr. Bruce, *Roman Wall,* p. 393 :

> *Tribunus in præfecto dono principis.*

Henzen, n. 5863, remarks :—" *Tribunus in præfecto* quid sit nescio, nisi forte ita se appellavit tribunus cohortis auxiliaris, quippe qui, re præfectus, honore tribunus esset."

The meaning I believe to be that Marcus Cæcilius Donatianus was, by the gift of the emperor, promoted to the office of *tribunus laticlavius* whilst he was *præfectus equitum,* or in the words of the Benwell inscription, *in præfectura equitum lato clavo exornabatur.*

Although I have used the word "promoted," I am inclined to think that the *tribunatus legionis* was merely a brevet rank—*titulo tenus*—held along with the *præfectura equitum.*

It is proper that I should add that Lange, *Hist. mut. rei milit.*

Rom., p. 58, asserts that the regulation of Claudius was not continued, and that in the time of Hadrian the *præfectus equitum* was of equal rank with the *tribunus legionis.*

As to Q·D·, I am inclined to take them as standing for *quæstor designatus*, as in Horsley's *Westmoreland*, viii.

But we have to take up the preceding lines, *scil. judiciis optimorum maximorumque imperatorum nostrorum sub Vilio* (or *Ulpio*) *Marcello consulari.* The term *judiciis* is plainly not to be regarded as a deity, as Mr. Clayton strangely understood it ; nor yet is there any ground for Dr. Bruce's supposition that "there may be some connexion between it and the jurist, Ulpius Marcellus." It is evidently used in the same sense as *judicio* in the passage cited from Vegetius, and the reason of its being in the plural seems to be, that by one *judicium* the appointment of *tribunus laticlavius* was conferred, by another that of *quæstor designatus.* Hence it appears that there is no necessity for looking for conjoint emperors in explanation of IMPP·N·, nor for an example of *optimi maximique* applied to such. These *judicia* may have been by different emperors at different times ; and, in my judgment, it is not improbable that the two emperors referred to are Trajan and Hadrian, each of whom was styled *optimus maximus, e. gr.*, Orelli, nn. 795, 3742; or, it may be, Nerva and Trajan. The Marcellus, under whom Tineius Longus served when he was promoted, was, as seems to me, neither Ulpius Marcellus, the general under Commodus, nor Ulpius Marcellus, the legal adviser of Antoninus Pius, but L. Neratius Marcellus, who is named in Trajan's diploma of A.D. 104. See p. 6 of my notes. He was *consularis*, for he had been consul in A.D. 103, and there are examples of the omission of both *legatus* and *propærtore.* But how can this opinion be reconciled with the statement that Dr. Bruce's rubbings "shewed clearly that VLP. as suggested by Mr. Clayton, was correct !" Can it be that Marcellus had two *nomina gentilitia—Ulpius* and *Neratius ?* Or may I venture still to question the reading and to suggest a re-examination of the stone, with the view of ascertaining whether the letters may not be NER. or L·NE, or NE !

P. 140.   For "Horsley, n. xcvi," read "Horsley's n. xcvi."
P. 144.   For "ENDOVELICO," read "ENDOVELLICO."

P. 157. For "IMPERATORES" read "IMPERATORI." For this error Dr. Bruce is in no way responsible: it is a typographical mistake of my printer.

P. 181. The suggestion, noticed in §87, is based on the suspicion that Horsley's drawing does not correctly represent the figures as they were originally cut on the stone, or perhaps even as they appeared in his time, for he may not himself have examined the original. It is certain that his figures differ in some important particulars from those given by Dr. Stukely, in his *Itinerarium Curiosum*, p. 196. The authority of the former, however, is much to be preferred to that of the latter. My suggestion had been so favourably received by those to whom I mentioned it, that it seemed worthy of notice, but I must confess that I regard its correctness as very doubtful.

P. 151. For "AVG." in the sixth line of the restoration, read "AVGG," for on comparing the representations of this slab, in the *Archæologia Æliana*, iv., and i. (new series), and Dr. Surridge's *Observations, &c.*, I am of opinion that the abbreviation is not AVG. applied to Caracalla alone but AVGG· applied to both him and his father. We should, of course, remove, the AVG· in the third line of the restoration. Dr. Hübner's strictures, *Rheinische Museum*, 1856, p. 44, on this inscription as read by Dr. Bruce and Mr. Hodgson, especially his suspicions as to the names *Alfeni Senecionis* and *Advento*, are unjust.

P. 151, note.* For "P F and P." read "P. F. and F."

P. 155. For "TRIB·POTEST XVIII.," read "TRIB·POTEST XVIIII."

P. 182. For "V3·PO," read V3·O.

P. 206. I find that I have inadvertently omitted two points, which I intended noticing relative to this inscription. One of these is the strangeness of the collocation, whereby we have to read from left to right of the circle. The only example, which I remember of this, is in the verses denominated ἀντιστρέφοντα, but this is certainly not one of them. The other peculiarity is that A may be introduced after each of the names, and yet the appearance of an Hexameter will be preserved. I say *appearance*, for it will not be metrically correct.

P 217. "LEG·AVG for LEGATI AVGVSTI." The Rev.

o 2

J. B. Deane in the same way explains the same abbreviations in an inscription found at Chester, referring them to the commanding officer of the 20th legion. See Mr. R. Smith's *Collect. Antiq.*, vi., p. 41.

P. 220. *Senator consulis* may also be suggested as an expansion, fig. 2, of S. C. See Mr. C. R. Smith's *Collect. Antiq.*, iv., pl. xiv.

P. 236. For " COA." read " COH." This inscription has unaccountably been omitted in p. xx.

P. 238. For " NYMPAE" read " NYMPHAE."

P. 260. I have not seen Mr. Hodgson's statement relative to the *Dea Hammia* as noticed by Mr. Wright. Mr. Roach Smith, *Collect. Antiq.*, vi., p. 39, remarks :—" The first cohort of the *Hamii*, mentioned in several inscriptions found at Magna, and in one found in Scotland, Hodgson considered, with his usual sagacity, as coming from Apamea on the Orontes. The conclusion indeed seems obvious ; and it may be added, that while the inscriptions naming the Hamii appear to be not much later than the time of Severus, and one or more, earlier, this cohort is not named as being in Britain when the *Notitia* was compiled ; but the *cohors prima Apamenorum*, no doubt the same, was then stationed in the Thebaid, having been recalled, as we may infer, from Britain. The *Dea Hamia*, whose name is found in the footsteps of the Hamii, is, of course, the goddess of Apamea or Hamea, or, in the convertible nomenclature of the Pagan mythology, the *Dea Syria* herself."

In the absence of Mr. Hodgson's work, I am at a loss to understand the meaning of Mr. Smith's remarks, nor can I reconcile them with the statement of Mr. Hodgson's views as given by Mr. Wright. According to the latter, the *Dea Hamia* was " named from Hamah on the Orontes," and to the same place I supposed that the first cohort of Hamii was traced, until I saw Mr. Smith's observations, from which it appears that Mr. Hodgson considered this corps " as coming from Apamea on the Orontes." It seems very probable that both the goddess and the corps derived their name from one and the same place : and yet it is certain that the town on the Orontes, called Hamah, viz., Epiphania, was not the same as Apamea. Nor is there the slightest ground, so far as I am aware, for identifying the *cohors prima Hamiarum* of inscriptions with the *cohors prima Apamenorum* of the *Notitia*.

www.ingramcontent.com/pod-product-compliance
Lightning Source LLC
Chambersburg PA
CBHW020943030726
47496CB00005B/1334